Cold War Fighters

Studies in Canadian Military History
Series editor: Dean F. Oliver, Canadian War Museum

The Canadian War Museum, Canada's national museum of military history, has a threefold mandate: to remember, to preserve, and to educate. Studies in Canadian Military History, published by UBC Press in association with the Museum, extends this mandate by presenting the best of contemporary scholarship to provide new insights into all aspects of Canadian military history, from earliest times to recent events. The work of a new generation of scholars is especially encouraged, and the books employ a variety of approaches – cultural, social, intellectual, economic, political, and comparative – to investigate gaps in the existing historiography. The books in the series feed immediately into future exhibitions, programs, and outreach efforts by the Canadian War Museum. A list of the titles in the series appears at the end of the book.

Canadian War Museum
Musée canadien de la guerre

Cold War Fighters

Canadian Aircraft Procurement, 1945-54

Randall Wakelam

UBCPress · Vancouver · Toronto

20 19 18 17 16 15 14 13 12 11   5 4 3 2 1

Printed in Canada on FSC-certified ancient-forest-free paper (100% post-consumer recycled) that is processed chlorine- and acid-free.

Library and Archives Canada Cataloguing in Publication

Wakelam, Randall T. (Randall Thomas),
Cold war fighters : Canadian aircraft procurement, 1945-54 / Randall Wakelam.

(Studies in Canadian military history, ISSN 1499-6251)
Includes bibliographical references and index.
ISBN 978-0-7748-2148-3

1. Canada. Royal Canadian Air Force – Procurement – History. 2. Airplanes, Military – Canada – Procurement – History. 3. Aerospace industries – Military aspects – Canada – History. I. Title. II. Series: Studies in Canadian military history

UG1125.C3W35 2011   358.4'162120971   C2011-903969-9

Canada

UBC Press gratefully acknowledges the financial support for our publishing program of the Government of Canada (through the Canada Book Fund), the Canada Council for the Arts, and the British Columbia Arts Council.

Publication of this book has been financially supported by the Canadian War Museum.

This book has been published with the help of a grant from the Canadian Federation for the Humanities and Social Sciences, through the Aid to Scholarly Publications Program, using funds provided by the Social Sciences and Humanities Research Council of Canada.

UBC Press
The University of British Columbia
2029 West Mall
Vancouver, BC V6T 1Z2
www.ubcpress.ca

Contents

Illustrations

Figures

Tables

Preface

Before I turn to the history of Cold War fighters, it is appropriate to present a number of factors that have helped me frame the story and to discuss one or two matters of terminology. As well, there are many people who deserve special thanks.

Being an Air Force officer and one with some practical experience with aircraft procurement in the late 1980s (among other things, I was part of the initial staff processes that ultimately resulted in the sale of Canada's first Chinook helicopters to the Dutch), I was intrigued by the prospect of exploring how Canada had gone about defining and filling aircraft requirements in the early days of the Cold War. My research for a graduate course paper that looked at the military aviation sector up to 1945 had suggested that Canada had not been particularly effective in terms of strategic planning, in either establishing an aviation industrial base or defining a coherent defence strategy leading to the acquisition of specific aircraft types. What, then, occurred in the decade after the Second World War to enable Canada to surge ahead, for a while at least, in a range of aircraft types, from fighters to Short Takeoff and Landing aircraft? What role had government played, the Air Force, industry, our allies?

My review of the literature turned up little that touched on the decisions and actions that converted the policies into flying units, or about the roles the Royal Canadian Air Force (RCAF) needed to undertake, with what aircraft, and in what numbers. And there was little that described the individuals who had made these decisions.

With these questions in mind, I set out to examine the primary sources of the government, the Air Force, and industry. Although a number of different paths could have provided answers to these questions, I was drawn for a variety of reasons to the issues surrounding the procurement of fighter aircraft in the decade between 1945 and 1954. For one thing, this period predated the still-volatile story of the Avro Arrow; by looking at fighter aircraft and the activities of the A.V. Roe company, I hoped I might be able to shed some light on government and RCAF thinking behind the genesis of the Arrow and on the ability of Avro (as A.V. Roe Canada is more commonly known) to produce such an advanced design.[1]

Ultimately, this book is a case study that examines the decisions that led to the procurement and introduction into service of two fighter aircraft that still hold much attention in Canadian aviation history. From the evidence, we begin to understand the complexity of the procurement cycle and how decision makers across government, the military, and industry are often forced to work with incomplete information and conflicting priorities.

In order to delimit the breadth of discussion for a book of this size, it was necessary to look at only a very select part of the RCAF's postwar requirements in both time and function. Availability of material, as described below, also forced some decisions about what to look at and how to analyze the material. In the years between 1945 and 1968, the RCAF raised requirements and bought aircraft not just to equip fighter squadrons, in both Canada and Europe, but also to train Canadian and NATO aviators, to conduct anti-submarine patrols over the Atlantic, and to transport materiel and personnel anywhere in the world. Canadian builders produced aircraft ranging from the F-86 and the maritime patrol Argus to the ill-fated Arrow and the diminutive but extremely successful Chipmunks and Beavers, for both Canadian and allied air forces and armies. To conduct an adequate study of the full range of aircraft needs and production, even if limited to those types built specifically for the RCAF, would have been a task of substantial proportions.

Thus, though more work still needs to be done, be it for a fourth volume of the official history of the RCAF or other publication, what follows in this book has been restricted in time and function to looking at Canadian fighter requirements in the decade following the end of the Second World War. From the perspectives of both the Air Force and the aircraft industry, this was a busy and complex period. The RCAF had no sooner demobilized than it began to plan and re-equip to face a new and unparalleled threat. An industry that had been given to seeking any work possible to keep its doors open was soon building aircraft as good as or better than its American and British counterparts. This postwar phase reached its denouement in 1954 with the completion of the build-up of NATO's Integrated Force and at about the same time as the realization that the threat did not warrant the resources being expended either by Canada or its NATO partners. This story, therefore, ends in the summer of 1954.

Readers may have noticed by this point that I have used both "air force" and "Air Force." In this book, I employ the former as a common noun, whereas I use the latter interchangeably with Royal Canadian Air Force and RCAF. Similarly, the two forms "service" and "Service" are common and proper nouns referring to air force and Air Force matters, respectively. I also use the term "Air Staff" to refer to those senior officers and their subordinates who worked the problems within Air Force Headquarters in Ottawa. I would like to define two other terms: "force structure" and "formation." This is a story about how the RCAF "structured" itself – in other words, a story about the roles and missions it organized itself to accomplish, and with what equipment and units. As a result, much of the discussion of organizational plans centres on the concept of the structure of the force. Also, although I have just used the term "units," Air Force leaders and staff would have frequently thought in terms of "formations" – these being groups of units. Thus, the four wings (each consisting of three squadrons) deployed to Europe as part of 1 Air Division would have been formations (as would the Air Division) in an organizational or force structure context. To be sure, "formation" in air force parlance also refers to a group of aircraft flying together on some particular mission, but that sense of the word is not used in these pages.

Finally, although technology is at the centre of this story, this is not a story uniquely about technology but about how the Air Force defined its needs for that technology and how industry responded to those needs. Thus, though some technical aspects of the aircraft and engines will be included where essential to the narrative, I have done my best to render the meanings of "rates of climb," "Unit Establishment," "Mach numbers," and other air force terminology as clear as possible. And for the pilots who pick up this volume, there are some airplane pictures.

The abundance of apparently unexamined material available in government archives coupled with the relative paucity of industry documents also helped steer this study. In particular, material, or rather the lack of it, from Avro (long defunct), Canadair, and de Havilland Canada, the latter declining access to its archives, precluded a detailed exploration of the companies' strategies. In this respect, one must be satisfied with secondary sources, which, with few exceptions, lack any analysis of the firms' decisions. The secondary and primary materials that were used in the writing of this book are listed in the Bibliography.

Chapter 1 provides two distinct historical contexts. First, it looks at Canada's aspirations in the immediate postwar years, as well as Ottawa's preoccupations in the interrelated domains of foreign policy, economic policy, and security and defence policy. A second discussion touches on Canada's experience with designing and building aircraft for both civil and military needs before 1945 and examines briefly the unique national conception of air power that had framed Canadian thinking from 1919 to 1939. The remaining chapters tell the story of Air Force actions to shape postwar procurement and force structure from 1943 onward. The discussion flows chronologically for the most part, although, in deference to the realities of government policy, defence procurement, and aircraft manufacture, I deal with certain issues in their entirety and then return to the original time period to continue looking at contemporary matters. As mentioned, this is a short story that ends in the months leading up to the 1954 target for positioning credible NATO forces in Europe.

The process of producing a book that hopes to make a worthy contribution to the story of Canadian aviation has been a long one, and there are many people who have contributed along the way. I would like to thank not just those who have helped me with this project but also those who have made the War Studies graduate program at the Royal Military College of Canada, which I entered in 1993, possible for hundreds of members of the Canadian Forces as well as a growing number of civilian students. My first appreciation must go to Dr. Ron Haycock, Dean of Arts at RMC and for years the doyen of the program. Without his persistence, this valuable educational opportunity would, I am convinced, not be available with the same breadth or richness that it has. I must also thank those who guided me during my research. Dr. Barry Gough, Dr. Jack English, and Dr. Al English all challenged me to seek newer levels of appreciation and to express my views with ever-greater precision. I am very much indebted for the guidance and patience of Dr. Mike Hennessy, who endured my errant attempts and patiently refocused me when I wandered off course. Most importantly, he showed me that history is much like detective work, where one needs to establish not just the facts but also motive.

A number of other people helped me directly with my research. Dr. Steve Harris and Dr. Carl Christie of the Directorate of History and Heritage (formerly the Directorate of History) at National Defence Headquarters in Ottawa were great supporters and gave me some important leads. Dr. Harris was also present at the birth of the project, opining that someone with a background in aircraft procurement might surely want to take a crack at telling part of the story. Dr. Isabel Campbell, also of DHH, was unreserved in helping me find the best, and often uncatalogued, material to help make this story as complete as possible. The staff of Library and Archives Canada were always professional, patient, and friendly. I must also acknowledge the assistance of Ms. Cathy Murphy and the Information Resource Centre at the Canadian Forces College – the big room with all the books – not just with this project but with many endeavours over the years. Dr. Tom Dececchi, Academic Director at the Canadian Forces College while I completed the original research, offered encouragement in the workplace, particularly when the day job could easily have absorbed all my time and energy.

Recent help has come from Dr. Dean Oliver, Director, Research and Exhibitions at the Canadian War Museum, whose institution partners with UBC Press in this very important military series. The value of the works published by UBC Press under the editorship of Emily Andrew is hard to overstate. Under her direction, military history spans many disciplines and interpretations, showing that the field is about much more than great men and great battles. Last and certainly not least, I wish to thank Megan Brand and her editorial team for helping transform the manuscript into the book in your hands.

All of these people have helped me gain new insights into the story that this book presents. I can only hope that my interpretation does credit to their support and to the events.

Finally, and most importantly, I must thank my wife, Norma, and my children, Christian, Karen, and Kevin. There is little doubt in my mind that without their understanding and support, without the countless hours when they amused themselves on so-called family holidays, this work would have remained unfinished. I dedicate this volume to them, with all my love.

Abbreviations and Acronyms

AAFCE	Allied Air Forces in Central Europe
A/C	Air Commodore
A/C/M	Air Chief Marshal
AFHQ	Royal Canadian Air Force Headquarters
A/M	Air Marshal
AMAE	Air Member for Aeronautical Engineering
AMAP	Air Member for Air Plans
AMAS	Air Member for Air Staff
AMOT	Air Member for Operations and Training
AMP	Air Member for Personnel
AMRD	Air Member for Research and Development
AMSO	Air Member for Supply and Organization
AMTS	Air Member for Technical Services
AOC	Air Officer Commanding (the commander of a group of units, e.g., AOC Western Air Command)
A/V/M	Air Vice-Marshal
CAS	Chief of the Air Staff
CDC	Cabinet Defence Committee (replaced the Cabinet War Committee in the fall of 1945)
CEPE	Central Experimental and Proving Establishment
CGS	Chief of the General Staff (Army)
CNS	Chief of the Naval Staff
CSC	Chiefs of Staff Committee
CWC	Cabinet War Committee
D/AMAP/O	Deputy Air Member for Air Plans (Organization)
D/AMAP/P	Deputy Air Member for Air Plans (Plans)
DAO	Director of Air Operations
DDP	Department of Defence Production
DEA	Department of External Affairs

DM	Deputy Minister
DMS	Department of Munitions and Supply
DOR	Director of Operational Requirements
DPR	Director of Public Relations
G/C	Group Captain
GFP	Government Furnished Property (components of limited quantity for which distribution is controlled by an oversight organization in order to ensure maximum efficiency)
IDB	Industrial Defence Board
MCC	Military Cooperation Committee (planning component of the PJBD)
MDAA	Mutual Defense Assistance Act
MND	Minister of National Defence
MND(A)	Minister of National Defence for Air (created during the Second World War and maintained until early 1946)
NATO	North Atlantic Treaty Organization
PJBD	Permanent Joint Board on Defence (cooperative board formed between Canada and the US during the Second World War and continued after the war)
PM	Prime Minister
RAF	Royal Air Force
RNAS	Royal Naval Air Service
SCS	Screening and Costing Staff of NATO
S/L	Squadron Leader
SSEA	Secretary of State for External Affairs
TCC	Temporary Council Committee (NATO force structure review organization)
UE	Unit establishment (the number of aircraft allocated to a flying squadron)
UNO	United Nations Organization
VCAS	Vice Chief of the Air Staff
W/C	Wing Commander

Cold War Fighters

1
An Air-Minded Middle Power

THE YEAR 1950 WAS a monumental one for the Royal Canadian Air Force (RCAF) and for the Canadian aircraft industry. Forty-one years after the flight of the Silver Dart, Canadian aircraft were again on the world stage.[1] In January, the Canadian-designed and manufactured Avro CF-100 all-weather interceptor took off on its maiden flight from Malton, Ontario, and just eight months later Montreal's Canadair Limited produced the first of thousands of Canadian-manufactured F-86 day fighters. Both aircraft were unquestionably state-of-the-art machines in 1950, and Canadians – in the Air Force, in government, and in industry – were justifiably proud of the nation's achievements.

Indeed, at a time when both the United States and the United Kingdom, Canada's senior partners in aircraft production during the Second World War, were working on designs that were not as capable as the CF-100, it seemed clear that Canada had made significant strides in the capability and quality of its aerospace industry. By harsh comparison, although sixteen thousand aircraft had been turned out in Canada during the war, not one engine had been built in the Dominion; Canada had been a manufacturer of airframes but an assembler of aircraft.[2] Even there Canada lagged behind, for not one of the aircraft produced was of Canadian design; every type built in Canadian factories was of American or British origin.

What had changed in just five short years? How had Canada come to have the impetus and the resources to produce, and in one case design, not one but two world-class jet fighters, not to mention a wide range of other military aircraft? As we shall see, at the end of 1945 there had been only the most remote possibility that Canada would ever have an Air Force equipped with such highly capable machines. Yet by the time these two flights occurred, plans were in place for an air arm that would make the formidable wartime Air Force seem unremarkable.

The context within which the RCAF was reconstituted is not new to the student of Canadian history who is familiar with both the postwar demobilization of Canada's armed services and the equally rapid build-up that occurred beginning at the end of the 1940s in the face of the Communist threat. What is less well known is the association between Canada's air requirements and the explosive growth of the nation's air industry. Indeed, Canadians tend to see the Avro Arrow as Canada's major initiative in the field of military aircraft, but this venture was possible only as a result of the work that had begun in the latter part of the war and continued, initially with little fanfare, through the second half of the 1940s. This book examines the parallel developments of Canada's fighter aircraft requirements and its industry's attempts to satisfy those needs while integrating two other critical aspects of the nation's journey in the postwar world: statecraft and finances. The interconnections between all of these issues – security and defence, economy and industry, international affairs and politics – are not new, but this book examines them from the perspective of the Air Force leaders who both advised government and dealt with business while preparing their Service for the possibilities of either a cold or a very hot war.

To set the stage properly, this chapter is divided into three parts. The first examines the central issues of foreign affairs, economy, and defence that confronted Ottawa immediately after the war. The second briefly discusses Canada's air power experience, including questions of manufacturing and defence requirements up to 1945. In the third part, I will lay out the hypothesis with which my investigation began.

Three interconnected themes captured the attention of Canada's leaders as the prospect of an allied victory emerged in 1943. First, the nation and the world would need to look again at an international association that would effectively promote goodwill between member states and permit the peaceful resolution of conflict. This in turn would allow for the re-establishment of economic prosperity. Spending on security might contribute to peace but certainly not to prosperity and might not be all that necessary if the nations could ensure a peace dividend. Whatever the calculus of interaction, however, decisions on these issues would have to wait for the end of hostilities.

For Canada, these questions came with both old baggage and hopes for a clean start. The baggage was Canada's colonial past; only recently had the nation broken completely free from mother Britain. The independence won with the signing of the Statute of Westminster in 1931 had been exercised with some difficulty in the years since, although there had been a number of clear demonstrations of that independence. In the years leading up to 1939, the Canadian government had been adamant about making its own defence policy decisions. Possibly the most prominent of these had been Canada's own declaration of war against Germany on 10 September 1939, a full week after Britain had entered the conflict.

Canada had gone on to be a full and significant partner in the conduct of the war, contributing far more than the country's population, economy, and wealth might have suggested. By the end of the conflict, and even during the fighting, Canadians, particularly statesmen and bureaucrats, had come to see the nation as a "middle power." But what was a middle power? Ottawa viewed it as a nation that merited consultation in areas of relative strength, but this Canadian self-definition was not necessarily recognized or respected by the superpowers.[3] Certainly, Canada's status during the war had been one of a partner but a very junior one who was not always asked to the important meetings.[4]

Nonetheless, Canadian leaders were well aware that they had been present at the birth of the Pax Americana and, as close neighbours and relatives, wanted to play a role in that paradigm. Although the nation was not a big power, politicians in Ottawa wanted to benefit from Canada's comparative strength at the end of the war and did not "intend to become mere pawns" in international affairs. Figuring out what Canada could do was the challenge.[5] The answer appeared to lie in part in the intersection between Canada's political and economic aims for the postwar world and the heightening tensions between the US and the Soviet Union. Rather than be followers, as had been the case before and during the war, Canadian leaders were determined to get out in front of the issues and use what influence they had to shape the solutions. They recognized clearly that the power base in the Atlantic had shifted to the United States and that, as its nearest neighbour, Canada would always be affected by American decisions. At the same time, they understood that only the US could counter the spread of Communism should it become a serious threat, as appeared to be the case. If Canada could influence US decision making in the direction of international alliances that were good for both security and economic prosperity, it would have achieved about the best that it could, and a not insignificant achievement at that.[6]

This approach was a significant departure from the isolationism of the Mackenzie King governments of the 1920s and 1930s. By 1945, King's hold on power was starting to slip, and although he remained Prime Minister and Liberal Party leader until 1948, younger, more internationalist ministers were starting to shift the focus. Louis St-Laurent, who replaced King first as Minister of External Affairs and then as Prime Minister, and his colleagues were firmly committed to an engaged outlook. And whereas King had had little trust in his Cabinet, St-Laurent took the completely opposite approach, giving Lester Pearson, who replaced him at External Affairs, Brooke Claxton at National Defence, and C.D. Howe, with his various economic portfolios, his confidence and the freedom to operate their ministries as they saw best.[7]

This new vision was placed before the Canadian people in early 1947. Presenting the Gray Lecture at the University of Toronto in January, St-Laurent tied the threads together:

> We are aware ... that economic revival is a matter of great importance to us. We are dependent on markets abroad for the large quantities of staple products we produce and cannot consume, and we are dependent on supplies from abroad of commodities which are essential to our well being. It seems to me axiomatic, therefore, that we should give our support to every international organization which contributes to the economic and political stability of the world.[8]

St-Laurent's speech set the framework for Canada's foreign posture (and by extension, security and defence policies) for the next decade.[9] Although there were obvious links between the three issues, St-Laurent was Minister of External Affairs and so it is to international matters that we turn first.

The Department of External Affairs (DEA) had begun consultations on postwar issues with Canada's allies in 1943. The department's Post-Hostilities Planning Committee focused its efforts not only on international cooperation and organizations but also on Canadian representation. Thus, in discussions with allies, diplomats firmly opposed the notion of regional associations where there would be a risk of Canada's being represented by the Commonwealth or by Britain. King, for all his isolationist tendencies, still wanted Canada to have an independent voice when there was occasion to participate internationally.[10]

By the end of the year, Canadian leaders had established three principles that they deemed to be of fundamental importance in setting up any postwar international structure. First was the need for a system of collective security to protect international society. In Canada's view, collective, or common, security was not a series of regional arrangements where only those nations in a region affected by a crisis might be expected to resolve it. Unlike Britain, Canada wanted a true world body. Second, Canada held that the decisions of any such international body should not be made only by the great powers, but that all member states should have some voice. As King would say, "we cannot accept the idea that our destinies can be entrusted to the four larger powers." The third principle was the "functional idea" – in essence, having lesser nations join in the decision making where their own expertise in the matter in question was significant. This was hotly contested and eventually dismissed by Britain and the US – to allow Canada to join in any decision making would set a precedent for other nations. Although Canada might well have legitimate expertise in many areas, this was not to be considered a rationale for giving the Dominion any decision-making authority.[11]

These discussions were taking place during a trying political period in Canada – the question of conscription for overseas service was being hotly debated nationwide, and the government was keenly aware of the importance of national unity. Views about whether Canada should contribute to a collective Commonwealth foreign policy or have its own voice were about evenly split nationally. In Quebec, however, 70 percent of the population favoured an independent Canadian policy, compared with 21 percent who would accept a Commonwealth approach. For a government that had just weathered the rigours of the war and the Conscription Crisis of 1944, there was little doubt that a policy that was largely acceptable to Quebec was the preferred option.[12]

There was also a bilateral aspect to Canada's insistence on independence on the world stage, for although the US treated Canada as a more or less equal economic and industrial partner, the same was not true in matters of foreign and defence policies or military decisions. And so Canada was fundamentally supportive of a new world organization that, at least in theory, would advantage it in its dealings with the US. The United Nations structure would allow Canada a degree of independence that some American interests would not otherwise favour. The UN link "might help to balance a hemispheric connection that had raced ahead in the realms of economics and military planning."[13]

Part of the counterargument to Canada's desire for functional recognition had to do with the overriding requirement to keep the Soviet Union engaged in discussion: to do this meant not challenging the privileged positions of the great powers.[14] It had been apparent to DEA personnel well versed with the Soviets that problems could arise, but both Canadian and allied leaders were unprepared for the revelations resulting from the defection of an Ottawa-based Soviet embassy staffer, Igor Gouzenko, which exposed espionage activities throughout government offices in Canada, the US, and Britain. These revelations and the associated tension would ultimately lead Churchill to make his 1946 declaration on the existence of an Iron Curtain.[15]

It is important to remember that Churchill made his pronouncement in the United States. It was clear to Britain and to Canada that keeping the US engaged in international dialogue was every bit as important as keeping the Soviets talking. After the war, Canada was keen to have the US actively involved in the transatlantic process as a means of ensuring and preserving at least European regional security. Above all, Canada did not want the US to revert to isolationism. At the same time, however, it did not want to be the junior – or worse, silent – partner in either a partnership between Britain and the US or between Europe and North America. Canadian officials and politicians were even prepared to promote a union that went beyond military and economic cooperation towards a North Atlantic political union.[16] The union could be seen from another angle, too. It would enable Canada to be a partner with the United States, its large and potentially overwhelming neighbour and ally.[17]

The notion of a commonality of purpose, with the New World making secure the Old – a concept that would come to be called "Atlanticism" – had originated in the collaboration between the US and Britain during the war. Its postwar manifestation would eventually be the North Atlantic Treaty Organization (NATO). Although the great powers would be given credit for the concept, Canada, too, had long seen the usefulness of a transatlantic linkage on a variety of political, economic, and cultural planes.[18] Two new US programs would demonstrate that the Americans had not abandoned the principle and practice of collaboration but rather were prepared to extend and broaden it.

On 12 March 1947, President Harry Truman introduced a new bill calling for economic and military aid. These measures, comprising the Truman Doctrine, would "support free people who are resisting attempted subjugation by armed minorities or outside pressures." The bill was in part a response to Britain's inability to assist the Greek government in its fight against Communist factions, due, ironically, to an earlier US decision to cut financial support to Britain.[19] Only weeks later, George Marshall, Truman's Secretary of State, announced the European Economic Recovery Program, which soon became known as the Marshall Plan. (The Marshall Plan had several names, including the "European Recovery Program" and the "European Cooperation Act" or "European Cooperation Administration Act.") Intriguingly, Canada quickly sought to access funds through the plan, not because the Dominion was at risk of Communist influences but because it agreed with the notion of stemming the spread of Communism through economic stability and because it was itself under considerable stress from balance-of-payments disparities.[20]

St-Laurent and his colleagues applauded the commitments of Truman and Marshall to international stability, but the soon-to-be Prime Minister would say, "there is little point in a country of our stature recommending international action, if those who must carry the major burden of whatever action is taken are not in sympathy." And though there remained concerns about developments outside Canada's borders, there were also many issues of nationhood to be settled at home. Matters such as the entry of Newfoundland into the Dominion, the creation of a fully independent Canadian citizenship, the adoption of a Canadian flag, and a federal election all contributed to the complex political terrain.[21]

Not to be dismissed was the economy, in terms of both domestic prosperity and Canada's trade balances in the North Atlantic markets. Like the US, Canada had come out of the war prosperous, whereas Europe and much of the rest of the world had been beggared both physically and economically. Ottawa realized the need to rebuild its traditional trading networks and made loans to Britain totalling $1.25 billion and grants to European nations of approximately $1 billion. Together these added up to close to 20 percent of Canadian gross domestic product (GDP). This was not economic altruism but a way to sell Canadian products and resources abroad in order to keep Canada's economy healthy.[22]

Although there was an economic bottom line, Canada agreed with the US and Britain that long-term security and the related success of the United Nations would be best served by the rapid re-establishment of a worldwide capitalist economy. In August 1945, President Truman advanced the concept of an "open door" for trade in both goods and capital. Truman said that "a durable peace cannot be built on an economic foundation of exclusive blocks, discriminatory policies, prohibitive barriers, autarchy, and economic warfare."[23] Canada's foreign economic strategy was enunciated in the 1945 White Paper on Employment and Income: "International security and freedom from threat of war are the first objects of collaboration and are essential prerequisites of international prosperity."[24] The two philosophies displayed considerable concordance.

Speaking in the House of Commons in April 1947, Minister of Finance Douglas Abbott described a situation that appeared enviable in all respects. Canada had almost full employment, demand exceeded supply, and, thanks to the loan and grants made to European nations that continued to rebuild, Canada was again trading with its traditional partners. The loans were of course, temporary expedients but did ensure the trade. The problem, if there was one, was that although currency was flowing in from Europe, it was flowing out to the US, whose industries had the capacity to satisfy growing Canadian consumer desires, particularly when Canadian firms were selling so much of their products to Europe. What Abbott said privately was that the situation with regard to the balance of trade and payments with the US gave him significant concern.[25]

Of particular worry to the government was the loan of $1.25 billion to Britain, without which that country would not be able to finance purchases of Canadian goods. The actual terms of the loan included the writing off of war debts from both nations as well as the actual transfer of money to Britain. It had been agreed that the funds would be made available not in one lump sum but over a three-year period. Abbott explained his concerns to Canadian newspaper mogul Grant Dexter: "This was essential and was agreed to because we must find US dollars in substantial amounts to buy materials which enter into our exports to the United Kingdom."[26] Canada could simply have spent the money in Canada and gotten the economy going quite nicely, but the whole point of the loan was to reinvigorate the world economy, and both sides of the House of Commons had agreed with that logic.[27]

The economic problem boiled down to a significant deficit with the US. This was not a new phenomenon and had in the past been offset by a surplus in exports to Britain and the rest of Europe. Now, however, there was no surplus from overseas trading; the only trading going on was bankrolled with Canadian loans and grants, which actually made the imbalance greater.[28] When Britain bought Canadian products, it did so in sterling, which it could no longer allow to be converted into dollars. As a result, in 1946 Canada had a $500 million surplus with Britain and at the same time a parallel deficit with the US, from which Canadians were buying a range of consumer goods. To make matters worse, Britain and other European nations were reluctant to buy anything from Canada with any funds other than those loaned by Canada. By the fall of 1947, Canada held reserves of just US$460 million, prompting the government to place an embarrassing tariff on US imports. Only in 1948, after considerable lobbying by Ottawa, did the US Congress finally allow Canada to qualify as a venue in which to spend Marshall Plan dollars.[29]

Indeed, one of the potential correctives for the trade imbalance would involve the United States buying more from Canada. Through the spring of 1947, the Canadian government applied what leverage it could. The Canadian ambassador to Washington, Hume Wrong, recommended, without much hope, that the US purchase Canadian foods for its relief programs, strategic materials for stockpiling, and finally Canadian military goods for use by US forces overseas. The root of Canadian discouragement was the realization that although the Truman administration understood that only the US could resolve the problem, it was Congress that controlled the purse, and the members of that body were not prepared to spend in an internationalist fashion.

What might save the day was the Marshall Plan. Presenting the idea in a speech at Harvard University on 5 June 1947, the general-turned-statesman called on European nations to put their needs on the table so that the US could provide coordinated assistance. The problem with the grand scheme, from a Canadian perspective, was that it seemed likely that only US goods would qualify for purchase, since, after all, it would be US dollars that the Europeans received. Until that large detail was worked out, the Marshall Plan appeared good only in principle. Indeed, by the closing days of the year, and despite much negotiation, Canada had not secured any special status vis-à-vis the plan.

To shore up the exchange rate, it was now necessary for Canada to secure a standby credit line of $300 million from the Export-Import Bank, investigate options for $200 million in loans from the New York money markets, and put in place a number of trade restrictions. These did not sit well with Ottawa or Washington, but at least they stopped the immediate crisis and enabled Canada to continue trading effectively with its major trade partner.[30]

Throughout the fall, as American officials drew up the detailed Marshall document, they wrestled with the concept of foreign purchase using US dollars. They were not blind to Canada's specific issues and to the formal and informal collaboration in economy, security, and defence between the two neighbours that had been growing since the 1930s. In the end, Marshall's presentation to Congress recommended buying from foreign markets when the needed commodities were not readily available in the US; the real benefit, it was noted, was that such purchases would strengthen the supplier's economy, which would then have an overall positive effect on the world economy. By the time the formal proposal moved forward, the US was actually facing a shortage of wheat, petroleum, and fertilizer, so these commodities were identified as being suitable for foreign supply.[31]

Much as Lend-Lease had stabilized matters in 1941, this postwar infusion of American funds would help again. Indeed, with the limitation on foreign sources removed, and once British wheat contracts were factored in, Canada garnered some 22 percent of all Marshall Plan expenditures and continued to benefit. Before the Marshall Plan had run its course, Canada turned out, unintentionally, to be arguably among its greatest beneficiaries.[32]

Before leaving the question of economic circumstances, we should briefly mention their linkage with defence procurement. It became increasingly evident, as had been the case during the war, that the health of the economy and defence procurement could not be considered in isolation from each other. The Ogdensburg Declaration of 18 August 1940 led to the establishment of a Permanent Joint Board on Defence (PJBD), which was mandated to coordinate the defence of the North American continent, including questions of personnel and materiel. The PJBD agreement was followed by the Hyde Park Agreement of 20 April 1941, which was intended, among other things, to address the imbalance in defence spending. It was noted at the time that although Canada was spending extensively in the US, there were no offsetting US purchases of Canadian materiel. One of the key concepts of Hyde Park was that each nation should concentrate production efforts on what it could build best, with the subsequent coordinated exchange of products as military needs demanded. The modalities of Hyde Park were continued after the war and reaffirmed with the establishment of the Joint Industrial Mobilization Planning Committee on 9 April 1949, which provided a link between the US National Security Resources Board (NSRB) and Munitions Board and the Canadian Industrial Defence

Board, which was set up in April 1948.[33] Before that, the Joint Statement Regarding Defence Cooperation, signed on 12 February 1947, called for such practices as "common design and standards in arms, equipment, organization, methods of training and new developments."[34] The renewal of the main agreement was followed in October 1950 with a Statement of Principles for Economic Cooperation that highlighted the need for coordinated defence production, including "a coordinated program of requirements, production and procurement ... [and] the removal of barriers that impeded the bilateral flow of goods essential for the common defence effort."[35]

From an economic perspective, this was good news for Ottawa and did much to address frustrations resulting from closed doors in Washington. As with the larger case of European rebuilding and US balance of payments, Canada wanted to be able to sell military goods to the US or at least have the Europeans buy Canadian goods with their Marshall Plan dollars. It was simply a matter of economic stability, which, by 1949, was apparently recognized by US officials:

> As for US military procurement in Canada, which amounted to something on the order of $1.25 billion during World War II, there is practically none at present in the sense of manufactured products. Raw materials are of course being imported in volume, but Canada wishes to be able to maintain its industrial war potential at a fair level as well as to balance off the US dollar purchases it contemplates making here by equivalent US purchase there.[36]

If defence procurement could be structured in the same fashion as the Marshall Plan, there would be an opportunity for Canada to buy and sell to the US, to have European nations buy Canadian goods with US dollars, and to work towards common equipment, structures, and doctrine, all of which were much desired by military planners. Canadian politicians and bureaucrats continued to press the matter, reminding US officials that Hyde Park had provided an opportunity for each nation to produce what it was best able to build and to sell it to the other. Nothing more was asked now, but to achieve this level playing field, the Buy American Act of 1933 would somehow have to be circumvented. In April 1950, a solution was found in a previously unused clause of the act that permitted exemptions should buying in the US be "inconsistent with public interest." Some $15-25 million could now be spent in Canada, and with the outbreak of the Korean War just weeks later, a foot was firmly in the door.[37]

The realpolitik of these industrial circumstances, like those encountered in the building of international organizations and the brokering of economic well-being, was evident. The end sought was a stable, prosperous world. The ways and means included not just international governance and healthy international commerce but also a coherent security philosophy and the associated defence capabilities. In this regard, there were two predominant scenarios based on which defence planners were obliged to produce force structure needs for the immediate postwar period. The first scenario saw a great-power-dominated collective commonwealth in which any nation or nations that did not meet the expectations of the collective would be dealt with promptly, but not necessarily with violence. Complementing this collaborative setting would be a number of mutually beneficial social programs. Taken together, these policies and programs would lead to a safe and prosperous community of nations. The alternative scenario was one of conflict, where the spirit of the United Nations would not be respected and where nations would soon return to the use of war and violence to achieve their ends.

For a defence planner, the two had little in common; indeed, there were considerable differences in the sorts of forces that a nation would require if it followed one path or the other. In the first case, a capable constabulary might suffice. In the second, a robust military would be needed both to defend national sovereignty and for possible overseas actions. The need for overseas action would be dictated by the nature of the threat and the identity of the threatening nation, as well as by a government's desire to become engaged; the latter factor brought to bear all the issues of national unity that were so unique to Canada. This was the theory and those appeared to be the options, but the defence budget for 1946 was in no way tied to the funding of military structures, or to a recognition of the strategic situation, or even to the two scenarios. Rather, the budget was based on the premise that it was too soon to know where the world's security was headed and on the government's overriding emphasis on finances and the economy.[38]

Intriguingly, when pressed to define the purpose of the military during the parliamentary debate over the 1946-47 estimates, Douglas Abbott, who by 1947 would find himself in charge of the finance portfolio, stated that "Canada's post-war defence forces are designed to provide, first, a representative group of all arms of the services. We need them now as a permanent professional trained army. In addition they are to provide a force to train a civilian army ... which has been the basis of Canada's fighting force in two wars and would be the basis of any war we fight in the future, assuming we fight the war with an army which I take it we would." When questioned further, Abbott admitted that this small professional force was a cadre for possible expansion should that become necessary.[39] One might conclude from this that the government was prepared to fight the last two wars and not the one that was coming quickly to the fore.

Canada was slow to move into formal defence relationships with the United States because of King's posture on defence generally but also because, as we have seen, Ottawa did not want to enter into an unequal arrangement. Although discussions about defence plans and cooperation did occur, a regional multimember arrangement, philosophically not unlike the United Nations, was perceived as much less threatening to Canada's sovereignty. Moreover, Canada was initially more interested in economic than in defence partnerships with the US. Changes to defence relationships came on the heels of a change in US defence spending in 1947. The opportunity to make money and balance the foreign exchange ledgers through defence was not lost on Ottawa.[40] International voice, economic stability, and security and defence – the three arms of the triangle came together well.

On the heels of the Gouzenko revelations, circumstances in Europe and elsewhere pointed to a creeping Soviet domination and influence that had been recognized by Churchill in 1946. The need for a counterbalance was apparent, and though the Truman Doctrine provided a philosophical riposte, across the Atlantic five nations allied themselves in March 1948 through the Treaty of Brussels. The United Kingdom, France, and the three Low Countries – Belgium, the Netherlands, and Luxembourg – agreed to a defensive strategy and at the same time to closer political, economic, and cultural ties to push back any Communist infiltration.

Additional talks followed almost immediately. These were tripartite discussions between the UK, the US, and Canada but with a view to having the North American nations join the European league. The value of being an equal partner among a small group of closely aligned nations was not lost on Canadian officials. Norman Robertson, the Canadian High Commissioner in London, cabled Ottawa: "Ever since we have been in a position to shape our own policy abroad, we have had to wrestle with the antinomies created as a North American country and as a member of the Commonwealth, by our special relationship with the United Kingdom and at the same time ... with other nations in western Europe." In short, Canada appeared to find itself at the confluence of several regional concerns and could be a broker in bringing these concerns and the nations involved into some sort of association. This was not a new concept to Canadians. In July the previous year, Escott Reid, Pearson's senior advisor at External Affairs, had proposed a new regional security arrangement. It would go beyond Churchill's Iron Curtain vision to involve more than the three English-speaking nations and would foster economic and cultural links. The realization of this vision would have to wait, however, until the spread of Communism and the British call for assistance against the looming menace in

1948 spurred the US to act. From that point, it was not long until the drafting of the NATO charter, which was ratified by the member nations in April 1949. A number of related issues were more important to the North American partners: nuclear weapons policy, North American air defence, and industrial mobilization took centre stage. Less important were questions of land or maritime defence. The US took the lead on these matters, but Canadian officials were quick to take the necessary steps to ensure the integration of Canadian views, policies, and capabilities.[41]

There was no question that as the Canadian government and its senior officials, both civilian and military, wrestled with these issues, a complex series of cross-cutting questions and decisions arose. Although these factors would have important impacts on Air Force structures and acquisition decisions, they would also reverberate across both the nation and the alliance. It is to gain an understanding of the RCAF perspective that we now turn to these issues.

Compared with the period that is the focus of this book, the first thirty-five years of air activity in Canada had not been propitious for either the air service or Canadian aircraft builders. Despite Sir Alexander Graham Bell's successful first flight at Baddeck, Nova Scotia, in 1909 – a first for the entire British Empire – the fledgling Canadian Aerodrome Company had been unable to convince the Department of Militia to purchase any of its airplanes. When the Great War began, Minister of Militia Sam Hughes rather precipitously decided to form a Canadian Aviation Corps but elected to equip it with just one flying machine, an American Burgess-Dunne.[42] Subsequently, as would happen again in the Second World War, it was decided to set up aircrew training in Canada through an extension of Britain's Royal Flying Corps, which provided the impetus to expand aircraft production. The government created Canadian Aeroplanes Limited (CAL), which bought out a small manufacturing operation previously set up in Toronto by American aviation pioneer Glen Curtiss and began manufacturing a modified Curtiss design that became known as the JN-4 Canuck. Over a twenty-one-month period, CAL built some twenty-nine hundred Canuck airframes in addition to a number of other smaller projects, including thirty F-5L flying boats for the US Navy.[43]

After the Great War, there was no perceived need for a Canadian military flying service. This, coupled with a gift of some 114 surplus war machines, led to a rapid tapering off of manufacturing in the Dominion.[44] By 1922, however, Canadian Air Board officials had realized that there was a definite need for new types, better suited to the paramilitary work being undertaken by government fliers. The stopgap solution was to buy surplus flying boat hulls from the US Navy, but thc Air Board was after a Canadian manufacturing capability.

A definition of air power for Canada had been developed in the closing days of 1918 by John Wilson, a naval bureaucrat who was to become the first secretary of the Air Board, and Major-General Willoughby Gwatkin, at that time the Canadian Chief of the General Staff, an army appointment, and soon to be the first Inspector General of the Canadian Air Force. In their view, air power included not just an air force but also the domestic ability to supply the fighting service with up-to-date equipment. The third component of their air power equation was an air transport industry.[45] The deliberate connection between the air force and aircraft manufacturers became a key, if not always effective, aspect of Canada's aviation experience and remains so to the present. It is this interplay between the RCAF and the major postwar builders that this book focuses on.

By the close of the 1920s, the aviation manufacturing situation in Canada was a relatively rosy one. Two British parent firms had opened Canadian operations. Canadian Vickers was producing a range of Canadian and overseas types in Montreal, and de Havilland had opened a factory in Toronto in 1928, selling 130 aircraft the following year.[46] By comparison, the situation for the RCAF was not so good. Tight money and lack of coordinated government support generally meant that the Air Force was obliged to buy what it could, when it could. The aviators were thus unable to offer the industry any sort of long-term requirements on which to base production plans. More often than not, the RCAF would end up purchasing aircraft in ones and twos at the end of a fiscal year. The Depression only made the dilemma worse, although the industry was able to continue making sales to commercial operators.

The second half of the 1930s saw a change of orientation on the part of the Canadian government. Given the deteriorating world scene, it was apparent that Canada would have to increase its defence establishment and at the same time spend more on defence equipment and activities. In terms of political expediency and public acceptability, Prime Minister Mackenzie King seized on the idea of concentrating efforts on building an air force that could be presented to Canadians as a potent home defence force. Moreover, air operations carried with them much more positive memories than the naval debate that had preceded the Great War, or the horrors of trench warfare experienced by the Canadian Corps.[47]

Increased budgets did not immediately translate into new aircraft, however. Britain's industries, Canada's source of military aircraft from the beginning, were fully occupied in rearming the Royal Air Force.[48] And the British doubted, with some justification, that Canadian firms were even capable of producing the complex combat aircraft then being manufactured by the more experienced British factories. A 1939 British Air Ministry Mission concluded that there was almost no existing capacity in the Dominion: engines and instruments would have to come from Britain (it would be impracticable, the study noted, to establish an aero engine production capability in Canada); there was no research and development (R and D) capability; and the trained workforce numbered only about fifteen hundred. On this evidence, the mission estimated that if Canada were given an order for 200 Wellington bombers, it would take two years from the time any orders were placed to get production started and another two years to complete deliveries.[49]

That Canada could not turn to its own aircraft industry meant that, on the eve of war, its Air Force would have to make do with those few British types that it did have and hope that modest production, finally underway by 1939, would eventually be enough to equip its war structure of twenty-three squadrons.[50]

Even when Canada went on a war footing in the fall of 1939, there was no overnight change in the aircraft procurement situation. Although the RCAF budget for the first year of the war exceeded $77 million, and the Air Force was able to field fourteen operational squadrons, new problems arose in the form of the British Commonwealth Air Training Plan (BCATP), a massive and ambitious program to train tens of thousands of aircrew from across the Commonwealth on airfields scattered throughout the country.[51] In 1939, there were neither the airfields, nor the instructional and support personnel, nor the aircraft. Measured from the perspective of the British Air Ministry's earlier judgment of Canadian capabilities, the requirements being made of the Dominion's aircraft builders looked daunting indeed. By the end of September, Britain was looking to Canada for production of 275 aircraft monthly: 200 trainers for the BCATP, 20 Stirling heavy bombers, 20 Hurricane single-seat fighters, and 35 Lysander army cooperation aircraft.[52] This could only be considered a staggering demand on an industry that just a year earlier had produced a total of 282 aircraft.[53] What made the request all the more onerous was the great technical leap that Canadian factories would have to make in shifting production from small bush planes to large and complex fighters and bombers.

The political and fiscal situations were also far from clear for the first year of the war. King did not want to become too committed or spend too much, and British builders did not want too many orders placed in the Dominion, which could lead to lost profits or the creation of a potential postwar aviation industry rival.[54] All these factors combined to make the successful manufacture of large numbers of aircraft in Canada problematic during the first two years of the war.

With the fall of France in 1940 and the dramatic and very real escalation in the threat to Britain, Canada increased its defence spending from $125 million to $681 million for fiscal year 1940-41. At the same time, a Department of Munitions and Supply (DMS) was set up under Clarence Decatur Howe, a successful industrialist turned politician. Howe and DMS were given the mandate to get defence production moving, and they worked tirelessly during 1940 to do just that. Once involved with aircraft manufacturing, Howe became one of its key proponents, and it was not long before he was seeking to maximize the potential of the aviation sector. Where King was reluctant to take on the production of four-engine bombers, Howe was not; he was of the opinion that manufacturing aircraft of this type would "complete the industry" in Canada.[55]

Howe had come to Canada from the United States in 1908. Educated and qualified as an engineer, he taught at Dalhousie University and formed his own company to build grain elevators before entering politics and winning a Liberal seat for Fort William–Port Arthur (what is today Thunder Bay, Ontario) in the 1935 general election. King appointed him Minister of Munitions and Supply in 1940, with the mandate to coordinate Canadian and allied defence production requirements and manufacturing within the Dominion.[56]

The entry of the US into the war at the end of 1941 changed the practices of building and distributing aircraft. Although the situation could be considered more confusing than before, with a three-way exchange of requirements, parts, and deliveries, it also meant that a large "common pool" had been created that would allow "all to draw from in accordance with their need." By extension, particularly in the case of aircraft, "supply arrangements became so fluid, transfers and diversions so frequent, that it was not possible to isolate with any high degree of precision the contributions made in the matter of aircraft and air supplies by one Commonwealth country to another, or between the United States and their allies."[57]

To the air marshals who understood the need to put scarce resources in the hands of those with the greatest operational need, a system with this sort of flexibility should have seemed ideal, and if all participants in the process had had equal access to the resources, it would have been just that. In the first days of 1942, however, Canadian aviators would find that despite their country's significant contributions to allied aircraft production, their own needs were not being fairly considered. For Howe, on the other hand, the business case was clear. Production was up and deliveries were being made. That Canadian aircraft did not always make it to the RCAF seemed less important. Thus, there were documented cases where the RCAF could not get its hands on aircraft being produced in Canada. One such example occurred during the panic after Pearl Harbor caused by the largely imaginary threat to the West Coast. The RCAF requested some of the Hurricanes then being built for the RAF by Canadian

Car and Foundry at Fort William, ironically in Howe's own riding. The request was refused by the allied munitions coordinating body – the Munitions Advisory Board – and the aircraft were sent overseas.[58]

Problems and differences of opinion aside, by the end of the war Canada had produced over sixteen thousand aircraft for the allied effort. Strikingly, however, no engines were produced in Canada, a circumstance not lost on the senior Air Force and industrial leaders. Even before wartime production had reached its peak, and not many months after the Hurricane incident, senior RCAF officers were looking at the question of postwar aircraft needs and production. The aviators, perhaps even more than Howe, had long recognized the value and potential of the aircraft industry.

The chapters that follow describe the successes and failures of fighter aircraft procurement in Canada between 1945 and 1954. Unlike the decade following the First World War, this was a period when the military potential of air power was both well understood and generally accepted by politicians and the military. It was also a time when the world could not presume that there would be no more war.

Before turning to the details of that story, it is necessary to set out my argument. Armed with the context just presented, I began to look at both secondary and primary sources touching on the first postwar decade. After an initial review of the material, it seemed that the primary sources were offering me a different interpretation of events than those that I was seeing in the secondary material. Quite simply, I came away with the hypothesis that RCAF leaders had played a significant, often crucial, role in the formulation of defence policy and subsequent equipment decisions. In contrast, none of the secondary sources that I consulted had given me useful clues to the part played by these leaders and their staffs. Many months later, a review of my findings led me to formulate the following conclusions.

First, the shape of the RCAF by 1954 was not that envisaged by the air marshals or politicians in 1945. That said, Air Force leaders had not sat mutely waiting for the politicians to design defence policies and force structures before going off to form the squadrons and fly the associated aircraft. Instead, they had developed a coherent concept of what the RCAF could and should be, which, though properly subordinate to the direction of the country's political leadership and frequently influenced by international developments, was founded on sound analysis. This is not to say that all recommendations and internal decisions were right and that time and energy were not occasionally wasted pursuing poor ideas, but, by and large, the leaders of the RCAF maintained both their direction and their reason throughout a challenging decade.

Second, support for a domestic defence aviation industrial base proved problematic and costly. One of the RCAF's most basic beliefs was in the need for a national capability to produce combat aircraft. Air Force leaders had convinced the politicians of the importance of this capability even before the end of the Second World War, and although the decision to build and buy in Canada was ultimately made by Cabinet, the logic and impetus had come from the Air Staff. Once embarked on this program, the air marshals displayed a fundamental sense of accountability. Their central purpose was to produce the best possible aircraft but to do so within the limits of the available funds: pragmatism and fiscal probity were the basis for decisions. Where resources were constrained, interim solutions were found. When one source of aircraft or parts failed, other suppliers or alternative designs were used. In short, the air marshals sought fast, inexpensive yet effective solutions to their operational problems. They were not beyond cutting a fully domestic program if it could not satisfy overriding needs, no matter how politically and philosophically attractive the made-at-home alternative might have originally appeared.

Third, Avro, the manufacturer of the CF-100, was incapable, at the time, of meeting the demands for increased production resulting from the Korean War. In 1945, the RCAF had set out to develop, build, and operate a Canadian jet fighter of impressive standards. When that aircraft, the CF-100, did not get off the drawing board in time to meet either expected or unexpected needs, the Chief of the Air Staff and his deputies were not slow to seek and employ another aircraft, the F-86. At the same time, senior politicians were more than ready to prod Avro towards meeting its obligations.

Overall, the crash program of 1950-54 fundamentally changed the force structure, roles, and deployments of the RCAF, disrupting the moderate plans for organizing and equipping a fighter force with the CF-100 as its centrepiece. Then, in the same way that a unique combination of events had permitted the Air Force to believe it could realize its dreams, a change in circumstances led to a rearticulation of national priorities. In 1954, with the end of NATO's scramble to build up field forces to stabilize the Communist threat, Canada, like its alliance partners, was able to reduce the emphasis on defence spending. By that year, the RCAF had deployed its postwar indigenous fighter capability – not as originally planned but to its satisfaction and credit nonetheless.

2
Planning for Peace

Nearly three years before the end of the Second World War, the Royal Canadian Air Force began to think about functions, organizations, and aircraft needs for the coming peace. Regardless of which question the air marshals and their political leaders addressed, the overriding element always seemed to be finances. Despite budget limitations, a small group of Air Force leaders succeeded in gaining support for a domestic capability to design and build warplanes. Then, in the closing months of 1945, the air marshals presented a plan for a small but balanced air arm that accepted the inevitability of using obsolescent wartime fighters.

Throughout the following year, as the federal government and the services re-established peacetime relations with the allies and began to see the potential seriousness of the Soviet menace, much attention centred on the RCAF. Although the senior services did not like the notion, it became apparent that the Air Force now formed Canada's primary line of defence. This was all the more reason to take the first tentative steps in adapting the philosophy of a domestic aircraft capability into viable fighter production. Throughout all of this, the leaders of the Air Force were at the centre of both the decisions and the action.

The first discussions of postwar RCAF requirements were based on the need to have a product that a postwar aircraft industry could manufacture and that would at the same time assure the Air Force of a domestic source of combat aircraft. On 6 November 1942, Air Vice-Marshal (A/V/M) E.W. Stedman, the RCAF's Director General of Air Research, initiated discussion of a postwar aircraft industry based on the design and production of service (combat) aircraft. The proposal was supported by the Air Staff and the Chief of the Air Staff, although the requirement was shifted away from a combat aircraft to a commercial transport type.[1] By 12 February 1943, Ralph Bell, Director General of the Aircraft Production Branch of the Department of Munitions and Supply (DMS), the federal department charged with all defence production, was able to report that his minister, C.D. Howe, had been briefed and supported the idea completely. Bell asked the RCAF to develop requirements for "at least two post-war commercial types, one of which will be a four-engined transport."[2]

Interest remained focused on the transport requirement, and during the first half of 1943 considerable work to define the requirement was done by both the RCAF and DMS.[3]

On 20 May of that year, Stedman reminded the Chief of the Air Staff (CAS) that in his initial suggestion he had talked about combat aircraft. He held that there would be no need for large numbers of transports and that if it did not build combat aircraft, Canada would find itself once again obliged to go to its allies for warplanes.[4] Despite his urgings, at the first meeting of the Committee on Post-War Manufacture of Aircraft, held on 7 June 1943, A/V/M Alan Ferrier, the Air Member for Aeronautical Engineering (AMAE) (the RCAF's senior aeronautical engineering officer), stated that the Air Council, chaired by the minister, C.G. "Chubby" Power, was "of the opinion that Canada should not attempt to embark upon the design and development of combat aircraft in competition with other major powers."[5] (It should be noted that when the minister was present, the senior decision-making body was known as the Air Council; when the minister was absent, the group was identified as the Air Members.)

Several months passed before additional high-level attention was paid to the issue. Then, at the beginning of March 1944, Ferrier, in a precis to the Air Council, reminded the members that in early 1943 they had been of the opinion that "a sound Aircraft Industry capable of producing its own designs was an absolutely essential foundation for future Canadian air power." If the Council's premise had been correct, said Ferrier, the time had come to place actual orders for aircraft so that the industry could survive in the coming years.[6] Ferrier returned to the Council on 18 April and gained general support for approaching DMS with a proposal to conduct a competition for a two-engine general utility crew trainer, not unlike the existing and successful Avro Anson. The value of this competition was estimated at $1 million and would allow for two bidders to build three trial aircraft each.[7] This was not a large sum of money, yet when the proposal was presented to the Treasury Board in early May, it was set aside for three months based on an earlier Cabinet War Committee (CWC) decision to temporarily defer all postwar projects.[8]

It was not until the fall that the money was approved for the trainer. At the CWC meeting of 27 September 1944, the issue of the postwar aviation industry was again tabled. Development money for the trainer was not the only air issue on the agenda; Aircraft Lodge Number 712 of the International Association of Machinists, a union local in Montreal, had written to the Prime Minister expressing concern over possible employment opportunities. Where the RCAF had failed to get Cabinet's attention, the voters succeeded: the CWC "approved, in principle, the recommendation ... for the expenditure of up to $1,000,000 for design and construction of prototypes" for the trainer.[9] Postwar national stability and economic health would become increasingly important, as Howe's April 1945 White Paper on Employment and Income, offering policies aimed at ensuring full employment, would show, but the driving force for postwar activity in military aircraft design and manufacture came from the RCAF.[10]

Although this decision represented a move towards designing an aircraft for the Air Force, it was not by any stretch of the imagination a combat aircraft. Still concerned, Stedman did not let the matter rest and prepared a memo that was reviewed by the CWC on 3 May 1944. The document laid out the problems that the RCAF had experienced up to that point in the war as a result of not having domestic aircraft design or manufacturing capability to meet Air Force needs. He argued that this could not be allowed to persist but cautioned that government's commitment would be considerable and long-term. He went on to add that Canada was losing talented aeronautical personnel to other countries where they could find opportunities to work on advanced aircraft. If the government was going to support the aeronautical manufacturers, it should do so in a way that would keep these people at home. He pointed to the new field of jet propulsion and recommended that research be started with a view towards developing a propulsion unit for service requirements. The CWC noted these points and agreed to re-examine the matter in three months.[11]

The whole question of aircraft engines was a touchy one, for there had been a highly visible debate in 1940, resulting in a decision by Cabinet not to build engines in Canada during the war.[12] By November 1943, it appeared that sufficient time had passed to reconsider the question. Discussion among members of the Air Council suggested that C.D. Howe's only concern was that no effort should be expended on setting up manufacture of any engine already in production. Might it not, the minutes of the 10 November Air Council meeting recorded, be appropriate for Canada "to prepare the specifications for an experimental type of aircraft, such as a fighter or small bomber, to use the [jet] engines being developed"?[13] Ralph Bell was very much in favour of the jet propulsion initiative, and although he disagreed with Stedman's combat orientation for the postwar industry, he believed that Canada should go "all out," not just in research but also in design and manufacture.[14] Even Howe was keen on the idea. In an address to the Canadian Manufacturers' Association on 14 June 1944, under the general theme of using wartime industrial initiatives as the basis for postwar growth, he pointed to jet propulsion as a prime example. He explained that the government was already starting research in the field, and stated, "the gas turbine promises to become a prime mover, ranking in importance with the steam engine and the present day combustion engine."[15]

Howe's first exposure to jet engines had come some eighteen months earlier. In October 1942, he and Bell had visited England and had been briefed on jet engine developments.[16] Returning to Canada, they had immediately set about exploring the technology. The prospect of researching a new means of aircraft propulsion apparently caught on quickly both in DMS and the RCAF, and over the next three years Canada sent many young engineers to Britain for training, while at the same time helping the British with cold-weather trials in Canada. The newly trained Canadians set up a domestic R and D operation known as Turbo Research Limited, which in early 1945 was awarded a government contract to design a 4,200-pound-thrust research engine that was given the designator TR-3.[17]

It was fine to do research in jet propulsion, given that the field was so new, but at the 6 September 1944 Air Council meeting, the AMAE recommended that since Turbo Research was not necessarily working towards a flying capability, the RCAF should go forward with a firm requirement for twenty engines (of 3,400 pounds static thrust) and "not less than three samples of [a] long range jet propelled fighter." Just over $2 million would be earmarked, $1.34 million for the engines and $720,000 for the aircraft, with these funds to be spent over fiscal years 1945-46 and 1946-47.[18] This was approved by the Air Council and the matter was tabled in Cabinet on 13 December. Both Howe and the Minister of National Defence, General Andy McNaughton (who had an extensive engineering background), "felt that this proposal was of considerable importance and that approval should be given, at least for the preliminary work involved." The CWC approved the design, reserving the question of manufacture for later.[19]

On 14 March 1945, Stedman provided Turbo Research with the specifications for both a Single-Seat Jet Fighter and an associated Gas Turbine Jet Propulsion Engine.[20] He appeared to have won his initial argument for a domestic capability to design and build combat aircraft. His persistence and the eventual support from the RCAF high command had been the catalysts for the government's decisions.

These were bold plans for a nation that was still having trouble even constructing contemporary aircraft designs of British and American firms. De Havilland's difficulties in producing the Mosquito fighter-bomber at its Toronto factory demonstrate the challenge; although the firm would produce close to a thousand aircraft of this type, the early stages of the project were plagued with trouble. Indeed, even after the decision to manufacture the aircraft in Canada was made in 1941, major problems persisted for the better part of two years. The difficulties illustrate the range of critical challenges that were involved in producing sophisticated foreign aircraft in Canada in wartime. Manufacturing data and drawings, and various subassemblies such as hydraulic components, had to come from England. Two sets of the former were lost at sea, and although Canadian firms were supposed to be capable of manufacturing these various components from the engineering plans, they proved unable to meet deadlines, thus necessitating the supply line from England.[21] The irony of British plants providing the wherewithal for Canada to support Royal Air Force needs was hard to miss, and yet the de Havilland experience was not unique: difficulties of similar nature and complexity were commonplace throughout the industry. Whether or not things would be better when the new fighter was produced from scratch in Canada would become apparent in just a few years.

Possible production challenges aside, even if the postwar types could be designed and manufactured in Canada, there was not, by the end of the war, a definitive military need for such advanced aircraft. Even as discussions of postwar supply issues continued, 1943 also witnessed work on the design of a peacetime air force. In December, Air Commodore (A/C) K.M. Guthrie prepared a "Brief on Post-War Planning for the Royal Canadian Air Force" that called for an air force capable of offensive and defensive actions and of swift conversion from peace to war. The RCAF, he proposed, would maintain a balanced force of sixteen to seventeen squadrons capable of all major combat functions. It was assumed that initially the RCAF would operate modern wartime aircraft, and that there would thus be no need for new procurement for about five years.[22] Guthrie's report was just the first step. The Post War Organization Committee – RCAF was formed on 12 February 1944 at AFHQ, with a mandate "to develop and prepare proposals for the organization, operation and administration of the Post War RCAF, including Regular, Auxiliary, and Reserve."[23]

Part of the remit called for a review, among other issues, of "organizational structure, employment and operational requirements, including services for other Government Departments." In order to conduct this organizational review over the summer, the committee sought the views of senior fliers and staff officers. Submissions to the committee covered the full range of concerns, but few of them proposed aircraft requirements in any detail – that is, by type and quantity. Those officers who did make such proposals stuck firmly to existing service models. Wing Commander (W/C) E.W. Beardmore of RCAF Station Coal Harbour wrote, for example, that the aircraft employed should be of contemporary standards, but "the numbers of the most modern aircraft [should] be limited, however, as they become obsolete very quickly." Group Captain (G/C) A.A. Rabnett of Vancouver replied that "aircraft should be of Canadian manufacture and American standards." Both of these sentiments would return to council tables over the next decade. The committee itself recommended forty-three squadrons operating over a dozen types of operational and training aircraft, with a total complement of close to nine hundred machines. Chubby Power took a version of this plan to the CWC on 27 September: operating forty-four squadrons, the RCAF would employ 45,000 Regular and Auxiliary personnel and have an annual budget of some $60 million. The CWC noted the proposal.[24]

By early January 1945, Air Force planners were able to state what the flying units would need in terms of aircraft, at least in a global sense. A memo was circulated by the Assistant Chief of the Air Staff on 16 January 1945, advising the Air Member for Supply and Organization (AMSO) of the estimated aircraft numbers after the end of the war. The total was 2,132, of which only 290 were for Regular operational squadrons. Another 696 were for the Auxiliary squadrons, and the balance were for all types of flying training. As anticipated, no postwar designs were included in the estimates.[25]

Perhaps it was these seemingly grandiose plans on the part of the RCAF and similar schemes from the other services that caused the CWC to revisit the issue of the postwar defence establishment. On 29 March 1945, Cabinet directed the Advisory Committee on Post Hostilities Problems to "initiate a preliminary study of the nature and extent of the Permanent Forces which Canada should establish and maintain in the period following the cessation of hostilities."[26]

The services' plans were transmitted to Cabinet in June. The total bill, estimated at $290 million, did not compare favourably with the 1939 budget of $35 million.[27] Some weeks later, following a new round of considerations, Colin Gibson, the new Minister of National Defence for Air, was able to table a revised RCAF proposal at the first postwar meeting of the Cabinet Defence Committee (CDC) (as the CWC was renamed after the end of hostilities) on 13 August 1945. The revised model called for 30,000 personnel and a budget of some $79 million. As for new aircraft, the proposal stated, "estimated cost was based on the assumption that there would be a fully equipped Air Force on the cessation of hostilities and that only a negligible amount of equipment replacement would be necessary in the first five-year period."[28] This repeated the premise advanced by A/C Guthrie in 1943 and suggested that decision makers might have to juggle the jet fighter decisions of the spring: a research project, yes; operational capability, not necessarily. When the CDC met again the following day to discuss establishments, Gibson announced that he had met with his service advisors and was now able to recommend a 20,000-strong air arm with associated costs of just under $60 million.[29]

Discussions continued over the next month, until it was decided on 24 September that despite the uncertainties of the issue, given the "desirability of having some reference made at the present session of Parliament," Gibson should state that for planning purposes the Air Force was using a figure of between 15,000 and 20,000.[30] Meeting just four days later, the full Cabinet decided that the statement in the House should be prefaced with the caveat

> that, until some estimate could be made as to the nature and extent of Canada's international commitments and the effects of new weapons, it was not possible to assess with any degree of accuracy Canada's defence requirements and, consequently, no final decisions could be made as to the exact size and composition of the forces Canada should maintain in the postwar period.[31]

Gibson tabled the RCAF estimates on 4 October. Starting with the rationale approved by Cabinet, he indicated that the Air Force would have Regular, Auxiliary, and Reserve components, with the Regular component covering all Air Force roles, including bombing, air defence, and transport. Strength would, however, be limited to just ten Regular squadrons, of which two would be fighter units using wartime aircraft. There were criticisms, but the government held fast to its belief that it was too soon to commit to any significant course of action.[32]

Force size, new aircraft, support to industry – all of these issues were moot until the government decided that it was going to continue spending a considerable portion of its budget on defence once the war ended. In this, C.D. Howe, as Minister of Munitions and Supply, appeared to be the voice of experience and decision. And yet, depending on his mood, he could also sound more like the voice of doom. In the early days of 1944, Howe had met with Gibson and the CAS to discuss the future of the aviation industry, particularly whether Canada should have a domestic design capability to meet RCAF needs.[33] Soon after, on 12 February 1944, Howe sent a memo to Ralph Bell in which he indicated that it was too early to say what commitments the government could or would make to the industry: "I suggest that the airplane business in the post-war period must not expect to find itself a ward of the Government. In that position it will be no different from any other peacetime industry. Much time and worry can be saved by accepting this fact now."[34] Howe continued to sound this same general theme throughout 1944, urging all industries to look to the future and organize themselves for peace,[35] but his thinking on aviation had not been missed. Reacting to the industry minister's philosophy, A/V/M Ferrier wrote to the CAS on 28 February that he felt that the previous year's efforts had in effect been wasted. He concluded that, left on its own, the civil air transport sector would be unable to generate enough demand for manufacturers to succeed.[36]

It is likely that word of Howe's views got out, as less than three months later he was taking somewhat the opposite tack. In discussing a submission to the CWC by seven private aircraft manufacturers, he suggested that even though the aircraft industry would shrink at the end of the war, some special assistance should be considered to promote design and development initiatives. A supporting brief indicated that the industrialists' proposal sought financial support through a number of strategies, but, importantly, asked the government to determine its postwar requirements and to place design and development orders with the private manufacturers. The CWC asked the Ministers of Munitions and Supply and of Finance to report back to it.[37]

In the coming months, the politicians would continue to weigh the pros and cons and to watch their bottom line – and a fine line it was between supporting aircraft production and abandoning the industry to the postwar shutdown of the armaments sector. The CDC's change of direction, just weeks after the end of the war, illustrates the point. The CDC revised the purchase quantities for North Star transports at its meeting on 24 September 1945. Although a contract had been signed in March for seventy-four aircraft to meet RCAF requirements, the Air Force now needed only fifty transports and could make do with twelve for fiscal year 1946-47. After a Cabinet meeting the following day, Veterans Affairs Minister Ian Mackenzie (formerly Minister of National Defence), Finance Minister James Ilsley, Prime Minister King's Quebec lieutenant Louis St-Laurent, and C.D. Howe together decided that a contract for the first twelve aircraft should be signed but that the order for the balance should "be the subject of subsequent consideration."[38] It seemed very much a question of defence production if necessary.

Indeed, in Canada, as in most contemporary Western nations, the state acquires military equipment as the result of a long process. The process starts with the definition of national security policy, which, when compared with the threat, permits the development of an adequate military structure, the latter in most cases involving a certain amount of equipment procurement. Staff and war colleges throughout the NATO alliance teach this fundamental process, but at the end of 1945, Canada had not completed any such coordinated analysis. Bits and pieces of the process were underway, but there were overlaps and gaps.

As early as 1944, policy planners had speculated that, with Germany and Japan out of the way, the greatest postwar threat would come from the Soviet Union. In addition, there seemed little chance that Canada and the US would return to their prewar positions of isolation, particularly in light of advances in aircraft capabilities. In May that year, the Working Committee on Post-Hostilities Problems, made up of senior officials from all departments, identified nine areas of cooperation with the US. Airfields and radar systems in the north, along the transpolar route from Russia to North America, were on the list.[39]

On 30 June 1945, the Joint Planning Sub-Committee, made up of members of the three services, completed a study titled "Strategic Factors Affecting Canada's Post-War Military Requirements." The precis noted, among other things, that Canada would have to play a greater role, proportionate to its place in the world, and would have to be prepared to act in concert with either the Commonwealth or the US. Advances in air power were considered a major factor, with two possible effects being recognized: (1) North America was now vulnerable to airborne and air-landed incursions, and (2) there was far less time to mobilize forces than prior to 1939. No nation was identified as a specific threat, but incursions were considered most probable in the North. It was felt that the US would be particularly concerned by such acts of aggression and would want to assist in its own defence as well as that of Canada. A brief list of preparations noted the need for "'Regular' forces immediately available" and for "adequate arrangement for the development and production of military equipment."[40] This was not much of a threat assessment to go on, but it did at least provide a starting argument for maintaining a credible military capability.

Throughout the fall of 1945, the Air Staff worked busily, in conjunction with the Post-War Planning Committee, on a proposal for a postwar air force. A/V/M Wilfred Curtis, then the Air Member for Air Staff and effectively the second in command of the RCAF, sent the draft document to his Chief, Air Marshal Robert Leckie, on 29 November. Leckie was born in Britain and served in the Royal Naval Air Service (RNAS) during the First World War. After a brief time in Canada after that war, he went back to Britain and the Royal Air Force. In 1940, he returned to Canada in conjunction with the British Commonwealth Air Training Plan (BCATP). He transferred to the RCAF in 1942 and became CAS in 1944. Curtis, too, began his flying days with the RNAS. After the First World War, he set up and ran his own successful insurance company in Toronto but remained active in the RCAF Auxiliary and returned to active duty in 1939. After holding senior appointments in Britain, he returned to Canada in 1944 and replaced Leckie as CAS in 1947.[41]

In his assessment, Curtis felt that "there do not appear to be recorded anywhere, adequate terms of reference officially approved by the Government upon which to base our post-war plan, and give us good grounds for future increased requirements."[42] The draft plan, therefore, stated a number of premises that established the raison d'être for the RCAF, some of which would be important to force structure and procurement decisions over the coming months and years:

> 1 The primary function of the Royal Canadian Air Force is the maintenance of an air force in sufficient strength and readiness to uphold national policies and interests and in concert with the Navy and Army to guard Canada from attack.
>
> 5 For planning purposes the Cabinet has approved the strength of the RCAF Regular at 15,000 to 20,000 personnel. In light of the uncertain [security conditions within the world] this plan is based on a strength of 20,000 personnel which is the minimum practicable figure for a small balanced Air Force.
>
> 10 To be effective, the RCAF must be equipped with the most modern types of aircraft available and, as these aircraft become obsolescent, must be re-equipped with up-to-date types.
>
> 11 Aircraft, equipment and facilities are available in sufficient quantity for the initial equipping of Regular and Auxiliary squadrons ... The plan provides, therefore, for the utilization of existing types of aircraft with the intention of a gradual re-equipping, as dictated by developments and in accordance with RCAF operational requirements.
>
> 12 Consequently the aircraft equipment programme of this plan is based on five years for types which are presently available and for which no additional purchases are necessary, such as Harvards, Lancasters, etc. and it is also based on five years for new up-to-date types [such as the North Star].[43]

While overall the force structure called for balance between full-time and part-time units, it was thought that the larger and more complex aircraft should be operated by the Regular squadrons: three heavy bomber, three heavy transport, one photo, one fighter reconnaissance, one fighter-bomber, and one artillery observation. The Auxiliary squadrons would number twelve fighter, two fighter reconnaissance, and five fighter-bomber. Once training and liaison aircraft were factored in, along with wastage, workshop reserve, and a small "unforeseen commitments" factor, the total requirement came to 1,898 aircraft ranging from Lancaster bombers and North Star transports down to gliders. The associated annual operating costs were $53 million, but this did not include capital costs for the replacement of aircraft.[44]

Within the fighter and fighter-bomber squadrons, both Regular and Auxiliary, there would be only two types of aircraft. In keeping with the notion that the end-of-the-war types were adequate for the coming five years, the Air Staff selected, not surprisingly, the most recent variants of the Spitfires and Mosquitoes that RCAF personnel had been operating in Europe.[45]

Postwar establishments for all three services were presented to Cabinet on 19 December. Prime Minister King set the tone of the deliberations by referring to the need to cut costs as quickly and significantly as possible, and to release from service as many men as possible to keep the economy going. The Navy plan called for 10,000 Regular and 18,000 Reserve personnel operating twelve major and many minor warships. The naval budget for 1946-47 (including demobilization costs) totalled $45 million in recurring costs (costs that could be expected annually), with another $30 million in one-time costs. The Army plan included an "Active Force" of 25,000 that would form a cadre for an army of two corps and provide for headquarters and special troops. A "Reserve Force" of 180,000 would provide the troops for a six-division and four-brigade force to flesh out the Regular cadre. The budget for these plans would be $70 million recurring and $74 million non-recurring. As for the RCAF,

> Air Staff proposals provided for a peace strength of 20,000 for the Regular Force, 10,000 for the Auxiliary and 25,000 for the Reserve. The Regular Force would consist of 10 operational squadrons and 8 composite flights, with necessary headquarters, commands and training, maintenance and ancillary units and formations. The Auxiliary Force would comprise initially 19 squadrons, with an additional 9 squadrons at some future date. The Reserve would consist of former active members of the R.C.A.F.

The proposal went on to indicate that estimated annual costs on this basis would be $57 million, of which $45 million would be required for the Regular Force, $8 million for the Auxiliary, and $4 million for the Reserve. Such estimates were subject to a number of necessary qualifications and excluded abnormal commitments, such as the operation of the Northwest Staging Route and associated landlines, and commitments in Newfoundland and Europe. Cabinet agreed that, as long as the finances were acceptable, the Navy and Army could implement their plans as presented. The Air Force, on the other hand, was directed to develop a new plan.[46]

No time was lost in returning to Cabinet with new proposals. Curtis's figures of the fall had included a range of 15,000 to 20,000 Regulars, and two new options were developed by the Air Staff in the first weeks of January 1946. For purposes of comparison, the original force structure of 20,000 was called Scheme A. The second option, Scheme B, was a new proposal and required 16,100; Scheme C was based on a total of 15,000 and was submitted in accordance with Cabinet's direction.[47] Meeting on 6 February, Cabinet considered the new figures:

> It had been found that the only practical way of reducing to the number to 15,000 was by eliminating the bomber reconnaissance squadrons, three of which were provided for in Scheme "A." Since the Chief of the Air Staff did not consider that

> a balanced Air Force could be constituted without combat aircraft for long range reconnaissance, bombing and anti-submarine defence, Scheme "B" had been developed so as to retain two four-engine bomber reconnaissance squadrons. This proposal, while precluding an equitable distribution of units through the provinces, would, in the opinion of the Air Staff, provide a force composed of all essential elements and might be regarded as an acceptable compromise. The studies undertaken had indicated that a strength figure of between 16,000 and 17,000 was the critical level.

Accordingly, approval of Scheme B was recommended; its estimated total annual cost was $59,150,000. Given the wholesale demobilization then underway, it was not anticipated that the Air Force would be rebuilt sufficiently to reach this total establishment for another two years, and the annual cost until that time would be proportionately lower. After considerable discussion, Cabinet "approved in principle Scheme 'B.'"[48] Approval "in principle," of course, left the gate open for either further cuts or expansion. It is interesting to note, however, that although the range of options presented to the CAS by Curtis in the fall had allowed for an air force of 15,000 Regulars, Air Staff calculations for a minimum viable air arm had apparently crept up over the last weeks of the year.

Whatever previous concerns there had been, it was fairly obvious that the government was prepared to stand behind its decision – at least that was the tone and the content of an address given by Colin Gibson to the Empire Club of Toronto on 28 February. The Minister of National Defence for Air outlined the various components of the new Scheme B structure and their associated costs. At over $55 million annually, this was not a cheap operation, but it afforded a "measure of security" and, among other things, offered benefits "from a considerable amount of research which is being undertaken to keep the Air Force abreast of the times."[49] The link back to industry would not have been lost on the industrial elite of Central Canada.

While Gibson was extolling the strengths and potential of the future air arm, senior aviators were sharing details of Scheme B with Britain and the US. On 12 February, Air Marshal Leckie wrote to his RAF counterpart, Sir Arthur Tedder, to explain in somewhat muted terms that his Regular air force was now down to just eight operational squadrons, of which only three were fighters. In the current situation, "I have based all my plans upon the ability to expand rapidly, and any inherent virtue the scheme now has lies in that direction." An attached summary described the key features of the plan and showed that Canadian fliers would be operating Spitfires and Mosquitoes.[50] How odd, then, that just two weeks later, in a similar document sent by Curtis to the US military attaché in

Ottawa, all reference to Spitfires was deleted and replaced with the de Havilland Vampire jet fighter.[51]

The explanation for this sudden shift becomes apparent in the introductory paragraphs of the April 1946 final version of what was now being called Plan B. In the foreword, Leckie called the document the "Peace Plan" and said that it would be subject to continuous change (how right he was!). It began by stating the philosophical posture of the RCAF:

> As it is not practicable for Canada to maintain a large Air Force capable of undertaking war operations on any considerable scale, at short notice, the peacetime RCAF must of necessity be a well balanced nucleus of highly proficient personnel, which is capable of rapid, efficient expansion as quickly as possible as a combatant Air Force.
>
> The RCAF will consist, therefore, of a well coordinated training organization, some squadrons of types designed to provide material for expansion into a fighting force, and the staff and organization necessary to support them.
>
> It has been necessary to plan initially for an orthodox force, but it has been borne in mind that changes will have to be made as technological advancements in aircraft, weapons and the utilization of atomic energy, demand.[52]

Subsequently, the document recognized both the existence of Canada's international associations and the undefined nature of any related security commitments: "This plan is not based on any decisions as to commitments which Canada may be called upon to meet by the United Nations Organization."[53]

The equipment policy for aircraft was laid out in more definite terms:

> To be effective, the RCAF must be equipped with the most modern types of aircraft available, and as these types become obsolescent, must be re-equipped with up-to-date types ... If the RCAF is to remain effective, it must not be forced to rely on aircraft that have become operationally obsolete, notwithstanding their mechanical condition.
>
> Aircraft, equipment and facilities are available in sufficient quantity for the initial equipping of Regular and Auxiliary units, *and this plan does not provide for their re-equipping as the latter depends on factors which are at present indeterminable* [emphasis in original]. The plan provides, therefore, for the utilization of existing types of aircraft, with the intention of gradual re-equipment with modern types as they become available.

The actual equipment plan was based on five years of use of types existing in sufficient quantity such that there would be no need for additional purchases

Table 2.1

RCAF Plan B fighter units

Type		Units	Aircraft per unit
Regular squadrons	Fighter reconnaissance	1	12 Vampires
	Fighter-bomber	1	15 Mosquitoes
	Trials units	2	10 of various types
Auxiliary squadrons	Fighter	5	8 Vampires
	Fighter	2	8 jets
	Fighter	4	8 Mosquitoes
	Fighter reconnaissance	1	8 Mosquitoes
	Fighter-bomber	1	8 Mosquitoes

Source: DHH, file 181.004(D44), "Plan B – Post War Plan for the Royal Canadian Air Force," April 1946, ch. 2, para. 14.04, ch. 3, para. 29.02.

Table 2.2

RCAF Plan B fighter requirements

Unit establishment (UE)	Wastage (3 years)	Workshop reserve	Reserve	Total
79	84	20	–	183
67	79	17	70	233

Source: DHH, file 181.004(D44), "Plan B – Post War Plan for the Royal Canadian Air Force," April 1946, app. G.

and on three years of use of obsolescent types "such as the Spitfire and Mosquito" of which there were sufficient stocks to meet requirements.[54]

The details of the plan called for the units shown in Table 2.1, with the required numbers of aircraft shown in Table 2.2. Even the official plan lacked precision, however, for although the text of Plan B might talk about the Spitfire, specific aircraft needs reflected Curtis's 28 February letter. Indeed, one might speculate that in leaving the type of "jet" undetermined in the case of the Auxiliary fighter squadrons (see Table 2.1), some keen staff officer was thinking well beyond what was possible. One might even posit that, as limiting as the government's restrictions on the Air Force may have been, there was still a thread of optimism and vision both at the staff level and in the hopes of the future head of the RCAF. This is the positive interpretation of this imprecision. The other possibility is that there was just too much uncertainty for a precise statement of what aircraft might or might not be available when the plan was finally implemented. It was perhaps indicative of the rapid changes going on at every level of the RCAF and the government. In November, as the Air Members reviewed the activities planned for the coming year, they agreed that a series of progressive stages would be needed, each about six months long, in order to implement Plan B effectively.

THERE HAD BEEN CONSIDERABLE confusion in moving from a massive war establishment to a smaller peacetime air force, yet the basis of the program seemed logical and had been accepted by the government. The Air Force now had defined a structure and organization. Personnel policies and decisions could follow from these, permitting the manning of units and organizations. As luck would have it, and as will be discussed in the following chapter, there was no need to go out and acquire new airplanes, since these were at least either available or on order. As it was, the Air Staff predicted that the postwar organization would not be in place and operational until near the end of 1947 or later.[55]

3
International and Industrial Alliances

THE FIRST PRIORITY OF the Royal Canadian Air Force leaders was to work within the constraints established by the federal government, but they also worked with an awareness of their American and British allies and of the evolving international security situation. The plans that they developed as 1946 progressed, and the periodic reviews that were conducted, were shaped to some extent by the international political and financial circumstances that Canada faced. At the same time, the abilities of the Canadian aviation industry, acting often as a brake, influenced the Air Force's ability to make good on "Plan B – Post War Plan for the Royal Canadian Air Force." Teasing aircraft from the factories, not just the types available but those that were needed, became a recurring theme.

All of these factors were evident in the decision to buy a new fleet of jet fighters from Britain. Built by de Havilland, the Vampires mentioned in Chapter 2 were obviously not "new Canadian designed jets," but at the beginning of 1946 the option to convert some £3.9 million of British wartime credits into operational aircraft made these diminutive fighters an attractive interim choice. Not only did it provide Canadian pilots with a chance to fly jets, keeping the RCAF at the leading edge of technology, but it also helped balance the wartime ledgers and get the British economy back on its feet. Overall, it was concluded at the 3 January meeting of the Air Council that even if a delay in delivery was likely due to production lags, it would still be advantageous in the long run to take Vampires rather than Spitfires.[1]

The topic did not come before the Air Force leadership again until 11 September, when a report was tabled that reviewed the ongoing discussions with the Royal Air Force on the use of Canada's aircraft credits. It was shown that approximately £2 million was available for Vampires and that this would purchase just over eighty aircraft. Since the operational requirement (without wastage or any reserves) called for seventy-nine aircraft, this option worked out very tidily. Indeed, perhaps the figures were too good; one is left to seriously wonder whether planners had not developed the preceding April's Plan B based on what £2 million would buy. Delivery dates remained a concern, since apparently no aircraft were available immediately.[2] In any case, the Air Members were aware that although the Vampire suited the original vision of a single-engine fighter, it did not meet the current Canadian philosophy, which called for a twin-engine design. Pragmatically, they decided that the Vampire could be used to fill the gap until a Canadian twin-engine fighter became available.[3]

Discussion resumed at the next Air Members meeting on 23 September 1946, when Curtis tabled a wastage chart that called for a total of 144 Vampires by 1951, a much more optimistic prediction than had been suggested in the figures tabled in April. Perhaps for this reason he remained interested in the delivery schedule of the domestic fighter, the CF-100, and the Air Member for Research and Development (AMRD) was able to state that at the current rate of development, the prototype would fly by fall 1948, with operational deliveries to the RCAF beginning the next year. More debate followed as to the suitability of the Vampire, but the Chief of the Air Staff (CAS) suggested that the process of using the British war credits was too far along to stop. Curtis recommended accepting the Vampires and informing the government of the need for more aircraft in two to three years.[4]

A final review of the Vampire question took place two days later, on 25 September. The de Havilland aircraft was not an all-weather fighter, but no British or American jet then in existence could meet the current Canadian operational capabilities,[5] and the Air Members, particularly the CAS, appeared happy enough with the British aircraft, as it gave Canada a jet fighter and led towards orderly replacement with an unspecified type (presumably the CF-100) around 1951. It was decided to accept the Vampire to the limit of the British credit and to fill the balance of the jet requirement with British-manufactured Meteors.[6] There appears to be no explanation of why the wartime Gloster Meteor would even be considered when a superior Canadian design was to be ready within twenty-four months. It was perhaps indicative of the rapid changes taking place at every level of the RCAF and the government. At least the Meteor was an aircraft with which Canadians had some experience.

During the year, the Air Staff devoted considerable attention to the question of standardization with Canada's two principal allies, the United Kingdom and the United States. As a member of the Commonwealth, Canada had shared the doctrine and equipment of the RAF; all RCAF personnel and units serving overseas had been integrated into wartime RAF structures. At the same time, since 1941 Canada had been a partner with the US in the defence of North America, through the Permanent Joint Board on Defence (PJBD).

Continuation of this relationship with the US seemed certain. The minutes of the 19 December 1945 Cabinet meeting record that the Cabinet Defence Committee (CDC) had recently received, through the PJBD, proposals from the US to review the existing plan for defence of North America based on the ABC-22 bi-national defence arrangement of 1941. At the first postwar meeting of the PJBD, the American representatives had specifically referred to their government's desire to carry on with the relationship. A joint planning staff, subsequently known as the Military Cooperation Committee (MCC), was charged with development of the joint appreciations.[7] Cabinet members were reminded that a 28 February 1945 decision by the Cabinet War Committee (CWC), as it was then called, made reference to the desirability of continuing defence relationships with the United States, particularly with regard to the Soviet Union and the extensive forces it was maintaining. Cabinet considered the continuation of joint defence planning to be appropriate and recommended that such planning take place at the Chiefs of Staff Committee (CSC) level, "it was felt that joint planning should begin as soon as possible in order that US intentions might be known, and their effect estimated upon the plans for Canada's postwar forces." Significantly, the ministers gave their approval "on the understanding that any new plans for joint defence would be submitted to the government for decision."[8]

It was almost a year later, in November 1946, when Cabinet met to make these very decisions, even though Prime Minister Mackenzie King had asked that priority be given to a comprehensive defence review as early as May of that same year.[9] During the year, the PJBD, through the MCC, had developed a Joint Appreciation and Outline Plan that identified the real – if alarmist, in the opinion of some – possibility of a significant attack on North America by the Soviets. This outline had permitted the preparation of the Joint Canadian–United States Basic Security Plan during the summer, which included the development of an air defence scheme for the protection of the continent.[10] The appreciation was the first item tabled at the 14 November session of Cabinet, a session devoted to defence issues.

In the ensuing discussion, King voiced his agreement with a coordinated defence framework. He indicated that "the defence of Canada was inseparable from that of the United States. This had been the accepted policy in both countries since before the war." Nonetheless, King went on, he had already had a discussion with President Harry Truman on 28 October and now felt that "the importance and urgency of the issues involved emphasized the necessity of early discussions between the two governments at the diplomatic level." What ultimately became Recommendation 35 of the PJBD called for "close co-operation" between Canada and the US in such fields as standardization of equipment. Although King was privately supportive, he was his usual political self in Parliament when discussing the matter in February 1947, speaking of a "limited liaison" that included interchange and standardization but that respected the "control of either country over all activities in its territory."[11]

The service heads had come to the November Cabinet meeting ready to present their plans and associated costs.[12] The RCAF would soon be involved in joint planning of an air defence scheme that "would be very extensive and involve very large financial commitments. It was unlikely that it would be fully supported by the current [air force program and budget]." The reasons were apparent: the Plan B version of the RCAF was organized, as Chief of the Air Staff Air Marshal Robert Leckie had reported to his British counterpart the previous year, as a nucleus around which rapid expansion could occur. "The current programme provided for only eight operational squadrons requiring personnel of some 4,000 and headquarters, administrative and training units, all of which would come within the approved ceiling of 16,100. At present the strength of the permanent force was approximately 12,000." At barely three-quarters of its authorized size, the RCAF was not well positioned for any new undertakings.

After further discussions, Cabinet agreed that though the notion of joint planning was acceptable, it would be inappropriate to endorse the joint appreciation submitted through the respective service chiefs until intergovernmental talks could take place at the diplomatic level. Further, it was thought that "joint planning with the United States should not proceed beyond the present stage, pending the forthcoming discussions and pending agreement between the two governments as to the lines upon which further planning should proceed and joint measures to be undertaken." It was decided that for the government to have a means of comparing the PJBD estimate, "the Chiefs of Staff be directed to prepare forthwith a joint defence programme for the immediate future – including a joint appreciation and joint plan," paying due attention to both the contents and status of the PJBD plan and unique Canadian factors. As the meeting continued, discussion turned to establishments. It was noted that the defence of North America appeared most closely linked to the structure and roles of the Air Force. It was therefore decided that a review of Army and Navy requirements should be conducted. King emphasized that there was only a limited amount of money in government coffers and that funds spent on defence would not be available for the considerable postwar social programs on which the Liberals had embarked. Finally, Cabinet noted the urgency of conducting a Canadian national estimate along with a review of establishments so that the government would be best prepared for the upcoming discussions with the US.[13]

In preparation for these sessions, revised plans were developed and submitted to the CSC on 1 December. The Army and Navy held fast to their original concepts, although both agreed that a defence-of-North-America scenario did fall heavily to the RCAF. In their views, however, it would not be possible, given the scope of the problem, to conduct a proper estimate in less than several months. The Air Force opinion was different. Air Commodore (A/C) C.R. Dunlap, the Deputy Air Member for Air Plans (Organization) (D/AMAP/O), underlined the fact that the currently accepted defence plan had been adopted before the present threat and the limitations of the United Nations had been fully appreciated, and before the increasing importance of air defence had been recognized. It was very timely and urgently necessary, in his view, to make immediate adjustments to the 1947-48 plans to take into account these changes.[14] Thus, on 9 December, when the final document was presented to the CSC, it was accompanied by an independent document from Dunlap, who believed that an increase in RCAF manning was critical. Surprisingly, the CAS took a contrary view, stating that there was no need for additional fighter units and that efforts had to continue focusing on planning for the complete air defence system previously conceived.[15] The talks took place on 16 and 17 December, and the Canadians were surprised and pleased afterwards when the Americans changed their approach to one that did not call for the immediate implementation of the Basic Security Plan. Firmness was still the watchword, but no hostile actions were expected for five or six years.[16]

Any air defence system would have to make use of the fighter squadrons already approved in Plan B. As seen previously, there were various options for equipping these units, all of which relied on the use of British-made airplanes. This was perfectly reasonable given that the RCAF had operated mostly British-designed aircraft during the war. Even before the end of hostilities, the two Chiefs of the Air Staff had been corresponding on the issue of coordinated design and manufacture and, by extension, use of any bilateral products. In a 23 May 1945 letter from Leckie to Sir Charles Portal, wartime chief of the RAF, the Canadian airman stated, "it is our desire to retain some units of the aircraft industry and to manufacture in Canada the aircraft required by the Royal Canadian Air Force. With this object in view we have already issued two specifications for aircraft to be designed in Canada; these are a twin engine trainer and a high performance Jet Fighter." Replying at the end of September, Portal was "delighted" and specifically interested in upcoming winter trials.[17]

During 1946, Britain was particularly keen on coming to an understanding with Canada and the US on the standardization of equipment. At the 5 September 1946 meeting of the Chiefs of Staff, Leckie's Army counterpart, Chief of the General Staff (CGS) Lieutenant-General Charles Foulkes, tabled correspondence from the UK Defence Committee that proposed the standardization of equipment between Britain, Canada, and the US. The CSC agreed that the concept as described was in Canada's best interest and that the proposal should be forwarded to the CDC with the proviso that Britain and Canada make individual representations to the US. On 24 September, Foulkes reported that during a recent visit to Ottawa by Field Marshal Viscount Montgomery, the Chief of the Imperial General Staff, it had been revealed that the British had already approached the Americans, who had found the concept suitable – indeed, the matter had received the support of President Truman and the US Joint Chiefs of Staff. In Ottawa, Montgomery briefed the Prime Minister and the Minister of National Defence, Douglas Abbott, who subsequently authorized the Chief of the General Staff to enter into discussions with Washington. The Chiefs of the Air Staff and Naval Staff were to make similar arrangements.[18]

By the end of 1946, it seemed that the defence and security agendas had moved forward effectively. All the necessary actions for translating the nation's security needs into defence requirements and an acquisition strategy had taken place, if in a somewhat haphazard manner. National security and defence analyses had been done; an air force structure had been developed and approved. Alliance arrangements had been considered, in terms of both coordinated plans and coordinated resources. In theory, the RCAF could now develop an effective and systematic acquisition program and, perhaps in conjunction with British and American requirements, go to industry with a shopping list for future designs.

But theory and practice would not quite match up. We have seen that the RCAF had already started Canadian aviation manufacturers on the road to developing new types, particularly a new fighter. Indeed, although 1946 had been as tumultuous for the aircraft industry as for the nation, the new firm of Avro Canada had begun design and development work in order to complete the new fighter within the 1948 time frame.

Avro had its beginnings before the end of the war, when C.D. Howe met with the well-known British aviation leader Sir Roy Dobson of Hawker Siddeley and worked out a deal to transfer control of Victory Aircraft, a Canadian Crown corporation, to the British firm. No significant postwar markets could be developed, however. Trans-Canada Airlines, the national airline, would not commit to buying transports. The irony was all too apparent: long-range transport was the very element of the aviation sector that seemed best suited for growth and that the government was most interested in supporting. When A.V. Roe Canada was activated on 2 November 1945, the new operation controlled 1 million square feet of plant space, but the sales department had no orders for aircraft. Dobson was not deterred and stated in a press release, "for a period, the Canadian Company will be a design, research and development affair with no aircraft being produced. We are putting into Canada a team of designers." He went on in a somewhat bittersweet fashion: "We have not gone into Canada as a money-making organization; we have gone in to spread development of the science of aeronautics and to give Canada a basic industry which in our opinion she badly needs. Canada will become the aircraft production centre of the British Empire within 10 years." Howe apparently found that "the whole plan is very satisfying from the standpoint of Canada."[19]

Despite having no production orders, Avro was able to turn a profit by doing piecework and then by overhauling and converting the Lancaster bombers that had been built by Victory Aircraft. Meanwhile, a group known as the Initial Projects Office had been set up at Avro to look at unofficial schemes. One of its primary tasks was to review the RCAF's requirements for a new jet fighter.[20] What would become the CF-100 was first discussed in September 1945, close to a year after Stedman had won his battle to develop a long-range fighter prototype. Avro Canada supervisor Fred Smye, who had worked for Ralph Bell and C.D. Howe during the war, set up a meeting at which he planned to give representatives from the British parent firm some reason for optimism and to show government officials that Avro was committed to a Canadian operation. The RCAF was represented by the Air Member for Research and Development (AMRD), Air Vice-Marshal (A/V/M) A.L. James, who laid out technical specification Air-7-1-Issue 1, which delineated the Air Force's requirements for the new fighter. One of the British representatives, W.W.W. Downing, was apparently surprised that the aircraft seemed underequipped for Canadian conditions and recommended that the specification be revised to require a twin-engine, two-man aircraft.[21] A new specification, Air-7-1-Issue 2, was soon produced. It read in part,

> The aeroplane shall be powered by two gas turbine jet propulsion engines and shall provide for a crew of two. It shall be of all metal construction with a pressurized cabin ... The range in still air with built in fuel tankage at maximum gross weight shall be sufficient to permit the following operation: Taxi and run-up 4 minutes, takeoff 1 minute at takeoff RPM, climb to 40,000 feet, cruise to radius of action of 650 nautical miles, combat 15 minutes at 490 knots at 40,000 feet, return cruise 650 nautical miles, descent 10 minutes from 40,000 feet, approach 7 minutes idling RPM. The operational ceiling shall be not less than 50,000 feet ... The sea level rate of climb shall be not less than 10,000 feet per minute ... The maximum true air speed in level flight at 40,000 feet altitude shall be not less than 490 knots (.85 mach).[22]

A contract for one non-flying and two flying prototypes was signed in October 1946, almost two years after Cabinet had approved the Turbo Research plan and associated expenditures. Curtis had played a major role: "The difficulties were great. However it was decided to give A.V. Roe Limited the job ... The decision was made on my advice and I have never regretted it."[23] On the strength of Cabinet's decisions and on the formal agreement, Avro general manager Walter Deisher was able to announce to a gathering to Toronto businessmen on 27 February 1947 that "we have a contract to supply the government with jet-propelled fighters which will be as fast or faster than the 606 m.p.h. Gloster Meteor."[24]

Behind the scenes, the RCAF's leaders were fully committed to jet fighters but could see that there were limits and real difficulties. In March 1946, well after Avro had begun to put together its proposal but well before it would be approved, the Air Members had reviewed progress in Turbo Research's engine development. It was now apparent that funding, a constant concern, could be a problem if a new source of money was not found to replace recently cancelled war appropriations. Since jet engines were still new, however, the CAS believed that this was the perfect opportunity for Canada to get into development on an even playing field: "The meeting agreed that there was no question as to the advisability of having facilities for production of aircraft and engines in Canada. *The dominant factor in any such decision must be economy of production* [emphasis added]." A/V/M James gained his colleagues' support for a proposal that the RCAF become directly involved in sponsoring turbine engine development.[25] This made sense: earlier control of the Turbo Research project by the Department of Munitions and Supply was for the purpose of getting the technology introduced into Canada, but now it was time for the Air Force to become more involved not only in the new fighter but also in its motive power. This involvement began five days later, when James met with his counterparts from across the public service. The Air Force's position was simple: Canada needed a jet engine capability for defence. Although there was no apparent disagreement with this view, the Air Force's notion was tempered by the other participants, who felt that, with preliminary research underway, the job of development and manufacture belonged in the private sector. The consensus was that the government should redirect the work to industry but with an investment of $12 million. Howe was not prepared to give away the money, but Dobson wanted business and in April 1946 took on the engine project as a strategy for selling airplanes.[26]

This was a start, but the RCAF's involvement did not end here, and the Air Staff now found itself with two sources to consider, though at this point neither was ready for testing or manufacture. Correspondence from Turbo Research's chief engineer, K.F. Tupper, to A/V/M James, the Air Member for Technical Services (AMTS), in April referred to recent developments concerning the TR-3 and TR-4 engines. In mentioning the latter, Tupper appeared to indicate that Avro was moving towards designs other than those stated in the specifications. Having reviewed the letter, James sent a memo to his deputy, in which he acknowledged Turbo Research's concerns, at least implicitly. He suggested that the specifications for the engine and the aircraft might have to be amended or even rewritten.[27] There is little doubt that this strategy would have caused some concern: certainly, from today's perspective, operational specifications and not designers' penchants should define aircraft performance.

By the end of 1946, there had been real progress, but not all was smooth and positive. Correspondence from the RCAF Resident Engineer at Avro signalled that there was some confusion and delay with the development of the TR-5, the engine that would come to be known as the Orenda and power Avro's new fighter. Avro personnel, it was reported, wanted to wait for the program to be better defined before committing themselves to specific performance figures. At the end of January, however, Fred Smye was able to advise that, "in accordance with recent discussions," the company intended "to commence tests of the derated TR5 engine in December, 1948, and to have this engine prepared for flights in August, 1949, at a rating of not less than 5,500 lbs. thrust." Further, Avro intended to have the 6,500-pounds-thrust version ready for flight by August 1950. The same letter indicated "very tentative flight dates" for the CF-100, suggesting that the first prototype could be flying by August 1949 and the second before the end of that year.[28] So much for the AMRD's 1946 prediction of a flying prototype by the autumn of 1948. Though it was too early to say, it appeared that Avro had bitten off quite a mouthful.

At first glance, the situation at Montreal's Canadair was broadly similar to Avro's experiences. The decisions made in 1943 to procure a long-range transport had led to the job being given to Canadian Vickers in Montreal, a firm that had been building aircraft for the government since the early 1920s. Initially, the plan was to produce seventy-five aircraft: fifty for the RCAF and twenty-five for Trans-Canada Airlines. As we have seen, however, orders were cut back as time passed. In mid-1944, Vickers decided that it could no longer continue building both ships and aircraft. This left the door open for employees of the aircraft facility to form their own firm, which, with government support, took over the Vickers operation on 11 November 1944. The firm was called Canadair, a contraction of the name Canada Air proposed earlier.[29]

With the agreement of the American company Douglas Aircraft, Canadair was to build a derivative of the successful C-54/DC-4 cargo plane to fill the government's needs. The company began vigorously buying up all available C-54, and subsequently C-47/DC-3, components.[30] With these stocks in hand, work on what was now called the North Star progressed rapidly, and a first flight was achieved on 15 July 1946. Although of some concern, the shrinking North Star orders were balanced by a coup on the DC-3 side of the operation. At the end of the war, Canadair had learned that the US government had directed

Douglas, which had first designed the aircraft, to end its DC-3 production. Douglas fully agreed, as it wanted to dump its inventories and move on to the more modern DC-6. With Douglas out of the way, and having bought up all remaining stocks, Canadair quickly became the world centre for refurbishing of the famous transport.[31] Compared with that of Avro, Canadair's condition at the close of 1946 looked most promising.

IN THE FIRST FULL year of peace, the RCAF continued to refine its structure and define its needs, within the economic constraints imposed by the aftermath of the war and the need to prepare for a new and looming threat to North America. Senior aviators considered the most pragmatic options for weaving together need and opportunity; as a result, they became the catalyst for maintaining and even improving an aircraft manufacturing capability. And although there had been little inclination to develop a combat aircraft in 1944, the seed of a fighter requirement – and a jet fighter at that – had now been sown. Indeed, whether the CF-100 flew in 1948 or in 1949, the fact that there were plans and deadlines at all was no small achievement.

4
Caught Flat-Footed

By the opening days of 1947, the Canadian government had accepted that there was a real external threat to national security and that something would need to be done about it. This admission and resolve would not, however, mean an opening of the public purse strings.

The primary focus of military analysts and planners remained on the possibility of Soviet incursions that would, they believed, come across the Pole. For the moment, however, the threat was in no way clearly defined, at least not in the minds of the politicians, and a periodic review system was instituted to ensure a sound basis, at least in theory, for making decisions. Even when the potential for conflict began to grow, there was little impact on Canadian air power and Air Force capabilities. Instead, throughout 1947 and 1948, RCAF leaders conducted a concerted, if disorganized, effort to redefine an air force structure, to find funding and acquisition strategies, including getting the most out of wartime credits, and to give substance to a domestic fighter capability.

Having been directed by the government to assess the immediate future with respect to defence tasks and structures, the Chiefs of Staff Committee (CSC) spent the closing days of 1946 preparing a Joint Appreciation and Plan for the Canadian Armed Services that the minister tabled at the Cabinet Defence Committee (CDC) meeting on 9 January 1947.[1] Canada's four thematic military commitments were laid out in the following order: ensuring Canadian security; participating in a "world force" under the United Nations; providing a mobilization capability in the event of war; and participating, if it were deemed to be in the interests of Canada, in a major war outside of North America. The appreciation also specified ten measures in relation to Canadian security, including the need for a complete air defence system for North America. Intriguingly, the study then went on to articulate only this last measure in any detail, indicating that there were currently serious shortcomings to be resolved if an effective "in being" system was to be put in place. Though stating that it was "not considered necessary to increase air interceptor forces during the forthcoming year," the Joint Appreciation concluded, paradoxically, that the lack of adequate fighter forces was "a major deficiency."[2] Following up on their own conclusions, the service chiefs discussed specific measures at an early February session of the CSC. Among these was the preparation of an "Air Interceptor Plan," which would involve the establishment of a series of airfields with associated command-and-control facilities and radar systems.[3]

The reality was that there was not much money to do anything. Minister of National Defence Brooke Claxton reported to Cabinet on 14 January 1947 that the services would be capable of "normal" operations in the upcoming fiscal year with a budget of $200 million plus another $38 million for "special commitments."[4] On that same day, however, discussion of the same issue at the CDC meeting, with its more limited attendance, had been somewhat less positive. The service chiefs had explained what could and could not be accomplished if the defence budget was reduced to this level. For the RCAF, it meant implementing a new organizational structure, Plan E, that offered a strength of 12,100 and cut the number of aircraft in Regular operational fighter squadrons from twelve to eight; the Auxiliary squadrons came away even worse off. The end result was a fighter force that would be effectively cut in half, with a strength of just sixty aircraft.[5]

This belt tightening did not mean that the government was ignoring the seriousness of the emerging defence situation. Since assuming the defence portfolio on 12 December 1946, Claxton had worked long and hard to coordinate the three services and form a coherent defence policy. Born in 1898, he served in the artillery during the Great War and entered politics in 1940. Before being named to the defence portfolio, he had been Minister of National Health and Welfare.[6] He believed that Canada would have to be ready for two theatres of operation: the Canadian North and Western Europe. He felt that attacks on Canada would be only diversionary in nature and that forces would not be sent to Europe until after the start of hostilities, and then only once adequately prepared. Expensive, large standing forces were thus unnecessary, but technical standards would need to be maintained.[7]

Claxton tabled two issues at the CDC meeting of 11 February 1947. He thought that it would be useful for both the CDC and the full Cabinet to receive periodic updates on the CSC's Strategic Appreciation and Plan: "Since the organization of the Armed Forces could only be studied in the light of the general strategic situation, it was important that these studies be related [to the problems in question]." Prime Minister Mackenzie King found merit in this approach, and the CDC endorsed the process. Claxton then went on to explain for his colleagues the difference between plans and implementation programs. Plans were just tools to enable a nation to organize security requirements. Implementation programs, involving the commitment of human and financial resources, were of greater importance and these would be brought to the government for approval. At this point, the Chief of the General Staff (CGS) proposed that the Canada-US Bilateral Appreciation and Basic Security Plan be brought forward and reviewed in conjunction with the annual review of the Canadian Joint Appreciation and Plan. This treatment of the two documents was found acceptable.[8] Claxton's explanations and his colleagues' comprehension of the differences now enabled the services to get on with the planning details but ensured that the elected representatives would make the final decisions about implementation and, by extension, resources.

By the middle of March, the preliminary draft of the fall report to the CDC had been put together and was presented to the CSC. An intelligence appreciation indicated that for the next ten years there was "little danger of war being precipitated inadvertently." External Affairs, it was mentioned, had conducted its own appreciation, which agreed with this assessment. The staff thought, however, that the likelihood of conflict would grow in the ten- to twenty-five-year forecast period, since, it was believed, the Soviet Union would continue its drive for dominance. From this estimate, it was presumed that any short-term attack on North America would be largely diversionary in nature and that, in consequence, Canada should be prepared for two defence roles: the defence of North America in conjunction with the United States, and possible UN actions under the control of the Security Council. In terms of defence funding, it was thought that the current level of activity was sustainable with the existing establishments. The staff writers also considered, however, "that certain long term weaknesses would result and would affect capability for eventual implementation of the Basic Security Plan."[9]

The CGS objected to focusing on just these two roles, reminding those present that there were two other, previously stated, roles that needed to be considered: provision of a mobilization organization (in this case a permanent force of adequate size to undertake training of reserves should expansion be ordered) and maintenance of a capability for offshore operations. In any case, he argued, it would not be necessary to brief the government on these since, as previously decided, the executive need be involved only in implementation decisions. The Chief of the Air Staff (CAS) was in general agreement but felt that the notion of being prepared for operations outside North America was a significant departure from the existing plan and should be highlighted to the government.[10] His analysis would prove prescient.

Despite the earlier decision not to review the strategic situation and plans until the fall, the CDC received an update on the new intelligence picture on 1 April.[11] As at the 17 March presentation to the CSC, it was stated that there was little likelihood of any "planned" hostilities and that if war did break out, any actions against North America would be diversionary in nature. Lester Pearson, the newly appointed Under-Secretary of State for External Affairs, was concerned, however, that the global situation, rather than becoming more stable, was now less certain following the Communist actions in Greece and Turkey and the resulting US counteractions. Discussion turned to the implications of these developments for force structure, but the CDC decided to await the formal review scheduled for September before making any decisions.[12]

The Chiefs of Staff had, however, put forward an update on 24 March based on the previously imposed reductions. For the fighter force, the numbers put forward were worse than the January figures. The two new Plan E interceptor squadrons were to be equipped with two Vampires and two Harvards each! The fighter reconnaissance squadron previously established with twelve Vampires now had just eight Harvard trainers. Cuts to the Auxiliary squadrons had been made, and at least four units had no aircraft at all and would not be established for the moment.[13] It is possible that these figures were intended to shock the politicians, for there could be a great difference between the unit establishment (UE, the number of aircraft a unit was entitled to have; the term is still used today) and actual holdings, which might be higher or lower than the UE because of temporary redistribution or, as was apparently the case here, pending deliveries. One gets the impression that the figures used were in fact just interim holdings pending the arrival of the Vampires.

Despite these frequent reviews and interpretations, the central elements of the plan remained constant, and Claxton used these themes when he delivered the 1947-48 Defence estimates to Parliament on 9 July. He stressed that there were three purposes for Canada's military:

1 To defend Canada against aggression.
2 To assist the civil power in maintaining law and order within the country.
3 To carry out undertakings which by our own voluntary act we may assume in co-operation with friendly nations or under any effective plan of the collective action under the United Nations.[14]

Despite this simple pronouncement, Cabinet, Minister, and services were caught in a fairly dense fogbank, with currents and eddies taking them in many directions. Less than two years after the end of the war, and with economic pressures demanding frugality and prudence, decision makers could also see the need for, or at the very least the desirability of, a philosophy of capable security.

The competing factors of threat and money and, to a degree, inter-service rivalry all contributed to making the definition of a precise force structure problematic. For instance, on 12 May 1947, the Current Plans and Estimates Committee of the Air Member for Air Plans (AMAP) took a long look at the process of building a new air force using Plan E. Of the three options, the favoured one was to build a mobilization plan structure based on a strength of

16,100. The committee chair, Air Commodore (A/C) C.R. Dunlap, thought this approach reasonable given the uncertainty of developing models for the other two options: a larger force structure identified as simply "16,100 plus" and another of 12,100, the latter being the actual Plan E size. Throughout the summer, there was constant movement back and forth at the staff level with no clear indication that direction had been provided. Initially, it seemed appropriate to safeguard the number of units even if, when operating with a force of 12,100, these would be manned with far fewer personnel than the normal establishments; later, it was thought prudent to return to the larger figures of Plan B.[15]

For the RCAF in 1947, the question of force size and capability was based largely on the Air Interceptor and Air Warning (AIAW) annex to the Basic Security Plan.[16] The threat picture on which the AIAW was based was possibly exaggerated both from a Canadian and even an American perspective, but perhaps it was better to be too concerned than otherwise. For the Americans, who were wrestling with the creation of a United States Air Force and the forging of an integrated Department of Defense, as long as the Canadians were approaching the problem earnestly, it was good enough for the moment.[17] And the matter of air defence did continue to count heavily in discussions.

Presenting the subject at an early June meeting of the CSC, the CAS thought the AIAW annex "constituted a satisfactory and adequate plan for the air defence of Canada, utilizing techniques and facilities which were now known and available. It was true, of course, that implementation programmes could not be prepared unless they were related to some over-all plan." Dr. Ormond Solandt, chair of the Defence Research Board, agreed: "It was obvious that such a plan could not be implemented for many years to come. Its implementation, therefore should be arranged so as to provide an integrated defence system at all times capable of operating as a whole." In this respect, he said that the Air Force would require a balance of facilities, detection means, and aircraft. "It would be undesirable" to build all of the facilities and leave them unequipped.[18]

The Basic Security Plan was presented to the Chiefs of Staff in detail on 26 June 1947. It called for extensive defensive assets around the major industrial and population centres of North America. Additional capabilities, such as airborne early warning and control of interceptors, the ability to convert from manned to unmanned interceptors, and a ratio of two interceptors per bomber, were also included. In the discussion that followed, the CGS remained of the opinion that though the defence of North America was important, efforts should, for a variety of reasons, focus more on the primary theatre of potential operations, which for the moment was the Middle East. Looking at the issues from a different perspective, Arnold Heeney, Secretary to Cabinet, suggested "that the central question for the Chiefs of Staff, as the Government's military advisors, should be whether or not the plan proposed was the best plan for the defence of Canada." He seemed to sense that the CGS was looking at the issue from an army perspective.[19] In any event, the CSC decided to give the plan further consideration, and on 4 September the air defence appendix was reviewed again and found acceptable. It was decided that the complete plan needed to be reviewed and that the distinction between the plan and any implementation program needed to be spelled out through the Military Cooperation Committee of the PJBD. The plan could, however, be structured in a such a way as to permit a preliminary phase that would include training, reconnaissance, and similar preparations, and that would minimize costs to the extent possible by using existing facilities.[20]

Defining the threat during this period must have been like shooting at a moving target. On 2 September, the CSC's Joint Planning Committee presented the CSC with a review titled "Roles and Relative Sizes of the Canadian Armed Services." The document's assessment was that the air threat was now more strategic than tactical and that by 1952 the Soviets would have the ability to conduct attacks with up to five hundred B-29-type heavy bombers carrying a mix of conventional and atomic and chemical weapons. It was estimated that after 1957 the Soviets would be capable of attacking with up to a thousand "high speed" jets with a radius of action of five thousand miles. These aircraft would carry a mix of weapons and could employ air-launched missiles similar to the V-1 rockets that the Germans had used against Britain in 1944. By comparison, the intelligence staff noted, the Soviet navy and army posed a very limited threat to Canada.[21] From this analysis, it should have been evident that the primary role of the RCAF must be the air defence of North America.

At its 4 September meeting, the CSC reviewed a document from the MCC that indicated that "there were no changes of substance which warranted revision at this time of either the appreciation or the plan." Lester Pearson, and probably others, had trouble accepting this view. Pearson felt that "while the present world situation might not involve a change in the plan itself, the emphasis to be placed on defence should be governed by the international situation, and such improvements or deterioration as they occur." The CSC agreed to advise the MCC that it could not accept the view that the world situation was unchanged. At the end of September, the CSC re-examined the threat situation. In reviewing the inter-service Joint Intelligence Committee's latest assessment, it voiced some concern that the period of stability was forecast, as always seemed the case, to run for ten years. The CAS opined that this was "not entirely satisfactory" and argued that a specific end date should be established.[22]

All of these reviews and reports led up to the previously directed fall 1947 presentation to the CDC that had been agreed to in the late winter discussions of the CDC and the CSC. The Minister of National Defence and the Chiefs of Staff appeared before the Cabinet committee on 28 October armed with their findings and recommendations. Although acknowledging that the world situation had deteriorated, their presentation still reflected the notion that there was little chance of war in the coming decade. In this light, the planned implementation scheme focused largely on preparations through various activities such as mobilization planning, mapping and charting of the North, training, and equipment standardization. In particular, the CAS outlined the need for a trial air defence warning system.[23] The committee went on to consider the defence program for the coming year. Claxton and the military leaders argued that since they were having difficulty meeting even the reduced manning authorized in the previous review, these limits should now be cancelled, although the ceilings would still be applied. Some increases to the Reserve components were proposed, and the CAS planned to add five new squadrons, although it was estimated that three years would elapse between the time approval was received and the time the units would achieve operational status.[24] Aircraft procurement was not a big part of the program, but funding would be required for contract activities in preparation for purchases the following year. Particular reference was made to the continued work on the CF-100, which had been "specifically designed to meet the needs of the Basic Security Plan."[25] Prime Minister King had some problems with these paper increases, noting that Britain was just then in the process of making large cuts. Claxton replied that Canada had very quickly reached its peacetime establishments after the war and that perhaps all that the Prime Minister was seeing was Britain's somewhat slower adjustment.[26]

The CDC met again the following week and accepted the proposals, based as they were within the limits of the existing manning ceilings and the additional figures identified in the Reserve unit increases. At the same time, it approved the air defence trial.[27] The RCAF had not achieved all it wanted, but Air Force recommendations had formed the basis for the decisions made. Among the Air Staff there must have been at least some reason for satisfaction.

Although the CDC had not placed much emphasis on matters of aircraft design and production, discussions were taking place at the staff level regarding the creation of an Industrial Defence Board (IDB). The Air Force position was firmly in line with that first enunciated by the original Air Board thirty-five years earlier, now tempered by the less than total success of aircraft procurement during the war. The inter-service Joint Air Policy Committee commented on the IDB's terms of reference at the end of 1947. In carrying out the functions defined in its terms of reference, the board would in fact be deciding which types of aircraft should be designed and built or built under contract in Canada.[28]

A final version of these terms was presented to the CSC on 3 February 1948. According to the terms of reference, the IDB should

- examine the aircraft industry and its potentialities for development;
- ensure that the Armed Services, Trans-Canada Airlines and Canadian civil firms are supplied as far as possible with suitable types of Canadian-built aircraft;
- ensure that the supply of aircraft to the Armed Services and essential transportation services continues in war.

[The board would thus]

- decide which types of aircraft should be designed in Canada;
- decide which types should be built in Canada under licence;
- decide which firms should be allotted repair contracts; and [to what degree repair work should be done by civilian firms].[29]

The CSC found these recommendations, as far as they went, to be valid and "suggested that the Minister be advised that the Chiefs of Staff considered that these studies should be undertaken ... as a matter of first priority."[30] On 19 April, the question reached the Cabinet table, and the politicians had no disagreement with the establishment of the Industrial Defence Board.[31] Once again, the RCAF had successfully promoted the notion of air power as a fundamental element of national power. At the same time, however, the one great limitation was that the terms of reference restricted the activities of the IDB to coordinating Canadian industry, thus missing out on the synergies that would have come from working with the Americans.[32] In addition, optimizing the balance sheet was never far from the politicians' minds.

Indeed, although defence issues had held the attention of Cabinet throughout the winter of 1947-48, discussions had been related more to budget trimming than to force structure or procurement strategies. There remained the very real concern that there was only so much money to be had for advancing the government's various postwar programs and that scarce dollars spent on defence would not be available for important social initiatives. There was also the matter of appearances. Douglas Abbott, the Minister of Finance and former Minister of National Defence, wanted to get the overall budget down from $2.3 billion to under $2 billion and had an initial go at the defence program in early January.[33] Three follow-on sessions then took place between 19 and 23 February.

At the first of these meetings, Abbott reported that the Treasury Board had reviewed departmental estimates, and it appeared that the federal budget for 1948-49 would be $2.016 billion, with defence spending of $252 million. The

Finance Minister wanted to know whether the defence requirement was in reality inflated, since the Department of National Defence (DND) had managed to spend only $190 million of its $244 million budget for the 1947-48 fiscal year. Now, because the DND budget was tied to defence policy, it seemed appropriate to wait for the presence of the Minister before discussing the matter further.[34]

On 20 February, Claxton explained to his colleagues that the current underspending was in no sense tied to inflated figures but was actually a result of the services being below their authorized establishments and was further compounded by the unavailability of certain equipment for which purchase had been authorized. If all the activities forecast for the coming year actually took place, DND would spend about $250 million. Included among these was the "A.V. Roe contract," for which he provided no details. Claxton went on to suggest that, given the current world situation, cuts in defence did not seem advisable. He also noted that Canada was spending less per capita on defence than the US, Britain, France, and "most other countries." He further indicated that "it was almost certain that, during the coming year proposals for substantial additional projects would be urged by the United States." Despite these explanations and arguments, Abbott appeared determined to present a budget with the same total dollar value as the current one and could not do so if defence projections remained at $250 million. He suggested a number of options for funding the DND budget, and Cabinet asked the two ministers to see what could be done.[35]

Discussions were held immediately, and on 23 February Abbott returned to Cabinet with a special clause for inclusion in the budget. To get around the problem, the budget documents would state,

> To provide for the orderly establishment and organization of the Defence forces of the Army, Navy and Air Services on a peacetime basis, and to authorize total commitments for this purpose of $255,514,584, including authority, notwithstanding section 29 of the Consolidated Revenue and Audit Act, to make commitments for the current year of $227,082,515, and commitments for future years of $28,432,069, against which commitments it is estimated that actual expenditures will, in 1948-49, not exceed $207,082,515.

It was a construct that any Liberal would have been proud of – a sort of "spending if necessary" approach. But Claxton was prepared to accept this wording since Treasury Board officials had projected that DND would be unable to spend more than $232 million, although his department felt that spending could hit

$240 million. Cabinet approved the funding formula as presented; Claxton had his money.[36]

Just how quickly things could and would change, and just how important the money could be, was apparent from a brief Cabinet discussion just two months later, on 21 April. Claxton reported on the "rapid deterioration of relations with the USSR" and how this was precipitating actions in both the US and Britain. And "while no change in the nature of the Canadian defence programme was being recommended at present, the rate of preparation was being accelerated." Cabinet noted this shift with approval.[37]

Part of this acceleration would include increased production. At Claxton's request, a memo to the IDB on 4 May laid out the strategies the three services had been using up to that point with respect to industrial mobilization. The RCAF paragraph began by saying that there could be no effective air force without a manufacturing capability to back it up. At the end of the war, it had been accepted that defence needs and surplus equipment did not justify new production, and so the industry had been kept alive with maintenance and overhaul work. In recognition, however, that this would not be enough to ensure the aviation sector's ongoing viability, it had been decided that new design and manufacturing activities were needed; these had led to the new fighter and jet engine projects and to the healthy state of the industry. Responses from the other services were not in the same league: in relative terms, the Navy had done nothing and the Army but little.[38]

It was fine to look to the future for the development of a purpose-built Canadian-designed fighter, but there were serious shortcomings in the present. A/C H.B. Godwin, the Deputy Air Member for Air Plans (Plans) (D/AMAP/P), advised his superior on 4 May that he considered the current state of the RCAF to be less than satisfactory. Referring to the small numbers of Vampires and Mustangs (the acquisition of Mustangs is discussed later in this chapter) held by the RCAF (eighty-five and thirty, respectively) and the lack of war stocks, he said, "it is my appreciation that this fails to form even a nucleus of a fighter organization." He went on to recommend the expeditious establishment of nine Regular fighter squadrons of twenty-five aircraft each, for air defence purposes, these being augmented by eight Reserve squadrons. He also recognized the importance of an aircraft industry and so wanted the fighters for these squadrons to be produced in Canada. Somewhat prophetically suggesting a 1953 production date, he suggested that when these new fighters did become available, any single-engine interceptors (presumably the Vampires) in service at that time could be transferred to the Reserves. The build-up to this structure would, according to the proposed schedule of Plan E, take place between 1949 and 1953. That was fine for the future, but the AMAP, Air Vice-Marshal (A/V/M) A.L. Morfee, advised the CAS on 2 June that, again based on Plan E, the best the RCAF could muster in a short-term emergency would be five air defence squadrons of twelve Vampires each.[39]

These sorts of predictions no doubt formed at least part of the catalyst for renewed discussions about defence spending at the Cabinet table. On 18 June, the Minister of Finance explained how he, Claxton, and their staffs had recently looked at the defence estimates vis-à-vis the current world situation. Whereas the Department of National Defence had recruited up to 85 percent of its authorized personnel establishments, "in neither the Army nor the Air Force did these provide anything much in the way of 'forces in being.'" DND, he suggested, should be able to recruit to 100 percent of its authorized ceilings. Abbott was also persuaded that the three services and the Defence Research Board should be authorized supplemental estimates of some $45 million over the next two years. Cabinet, with Prime Minister King in the chair, agreed with these proposals.[40] More spending had indeed become "necessary."

While Cabinet was loosening the purse strings, the Air Force planning staff continued to fret. On 29 June, Godwin repeated his concerns to the AMAP. He said that, basing their calculations on the current defence policy, which focused on the defence of Canada, his staff estimated that there was a fighter requirement for 9 Regular and 8 Auxiliary (9 + 8) squadrons of 12 aircraft each, in addition to 3 (2 + 1) fighter-bomber and 1 (1 + 0) fighter reconnaissance units, also of 12 aircraft each. He repeated his arguments about the deficiency of fighters and fighter production, this time commenting that the problem was common to the Western nations and underscoring that the US and Britain would be unable to supply Canada in time of crisis. He went on to say that a new plan being developed – to replace Plan E, which was itself only now coming into effect – would enable the fighter units to build up to a UE of 25 aircraft within twelve months of mobilization. He asked that the Air Members approve the new plan for planning purposes and that the Air Staff to "initiate measures sufficient to ensure a continuous supply of fighters."[41]

The gravity of the situation became all too clear by the summer of 1948. It was all well and good to look at increased funding and new aircraft, but the new fighters were years away and the problem had to be confronted now. The first new plan since Plan B was adopted at the end of 1945, Plan E was an attempt to put scarce resources to best use. The scheme's introductory notes emphasized that it deviated "considerably both in size and scope" from its predecessor. Yet Plan E still had significant financial, and hence manpower, restrictions, and it was thought that these would not be resolved before the summer of 1949. The document's introduction (which was considerably shorter than that of Plan B)

TABLE 4.1

RCAF Plan E fighter units

Type		Units	Aircraft per unit
Regular squadrons	Fighter	2	8 Vampires, 4 Harvards
	Fighter reconnaissance	1	8 Mustangs, 4 Harvards
Auxiliary squadrons	Fighter	7	8 Vampires, 4 Harvards
	Fighter	1	12 Harvards
	Fighter	5	No aircraft

Source: DHH, 181.004(D45), "Royal Canadian Air Force Plan 'E' (Plan E 1948-49 with Amendments to 11 August 1949)," n.d.

stated that the plan could not "be regarded as providing more than a framework upon which to build in time of emergency." It was acknowledged that though operational squadrons should contain eighteen aircraft, Plan B had limited the number to twelve, and Plan E would further reduce these units to eight operational aircraft. Changes from Plan B included dropping the Mosquito and the introduction of limited numbers of Mustangs. Plan E called for the units and aircraft establishments shown in Table 4.1. The Regular fighter squadrons were to be grouped in an Interceptor Fighter Wing, which would form a trained nucleus for air defence of the "main industrial areas," in line with the AIAW concept.[42]

Even these frugal needs could not be fulfilled without difficulty. A 7 July 1948 memorandum from the AMAP to Curtis outlined the Plan E aircraft requirements compared with current holdings. The RCAF owned 28 Mustangs and had 10 in service, against an operational requirement for 36. There were 81 Vampires on the books with 23 in service, against a requirement for 57. Although Curtis's immediate preoccupation focused not on fighters but on numbers of long-range Lancaster bombers for a new reconnaissance unit, he was well aware of these fighter shortcomings.[43] Working with Claxton, he had already presented a request to the CDC for the purchase of an additional 27 Vampires to ensure adequate stocks to cover increased operational needs (presumably the fighter wing for the air defence trial system) under the Basic Security Plan and attrition until 31 March 1951. Basing his estimate on current holdings, current and projected flying rates, and a planned wastage of one aircraft per 1,000 flying hours, Curtis projected that the RCAF would start to lose operational capability by the end of 1949. If ordered quickly, these additional aircraft would therefore begin arriving just in time to cover the shortfall.[44] When the item came up for discussion at the end of July, the Minister of Finance wondered whether it might not be a waste to buy additional aircraft of a type that could be obsolete by 1951. Curtis convinced the committee that such circumstances could not have been foreseen and that the aircraft was currently a good one. The purchase was approved, with $4 million to be found in the defence program.[45]

The lack of fighters was again a hot topic in the fall. The acting (and soon to become) AMAP, A/V/M Dunlap, asked A/C Godwin on 18 September to prepare a list of deficiencies that could be turned over quickly to the minister and the government. Referring to the joint plan to deal with emergencies that might arise between that date and the following summer, Dunlap asked Godwin to pick a few of the most critical items and develop these before doing a more comprehensive review of requirements. Just two days later, Dunlap's other staff division provided a response that must have pleased both officers. A/C W.A. Orr, the Deputy Air Member for Air Plans (Organization) (D/AMAP/O) presented a comprehensive list of aircraft needs through 1953. Orr's memo indicated that "the requirements for fighter aircraft have already been sent, along with the supporting data, to the CAS for immediate consideration." Moreover, "cognizance has been taken of the current fighter situation and our urgent requirement for a defensive force and replacement aircraft for other roles have been deferred, where possible, in favour of an increased fighter procurement programme." Overall, the proposal called for the purchase of 320 Vampires and 342 CF-100s.[46] On 30 September, Dunlap expressed his own feelings to Curtis. His main concern was finances: "Taking into account all the factors and at the same time bearing in mind the current monetary situation prevailing between the US and Canada, it appears to me that the correct number [of fighters] to be purchased during the fiscal year 1949-50 is sixty (60)."[47] Clearly, the RCAF leaders were well aware of the larger national and international tensions, and they recognized the requirement to balance security needs against the economic health of the nation. The problem was that the product of this calculus did not amount to much.

Fighter requirements had been examined at two CSC meetings on 28 and 29 September. Initially, the service chiefs reviewed a summary submitted by the Joint Planning Committee that pointed out that the air defence structure suffered from the lack of a suitable fighter aircraft and that "it was hoped that arrangements could be made to produce a modern US-fighter type in Canada."[48] This was the first formal discussion of this concept, but the idea had its basis, as we shall see shortly, in wartime experience and previous discussions of standardization, which had, among other things, sought to avoid duplication between the allies.

Meeting with the CSC on 29 September, the CAS identified those Air Force requirements for the following year that should be forwarded to the Canadian Commercial Corporation (a government purchasing organization, which we shall discuss shortly):

> The most urgent requirement among Allied Air Forces was fighter aircraft. Canada was in a particularly weak position in this respect and there was an immediate need to put some of these aircraft into production. Only when a suitable number of additional aircraft had been produced would the Air Force be able to plan adequately and efficiently for the first year of mobilization. Provision for this aircraft production was therefore an essential part of the Air Force programme for the next fiscal year.

Looking at the overall program, he continued:

> One of the things which required an early decision and would affect defence policies at once, was the priority to be attached to the defence effort in any particular field. It was known, for instance, that within six months of any war breaking out, the United Kingdom would require substantial assistance in respect to fighter aircraft. If this assistance were not provided and the United Kingdom were unable to successfully defend itself, there would be no requirement for [naval convoys or army expeditionary forces].[49]

Curtis might offer solid encouragement, but Orr's proposal for six-hundred-odd fighters was clearly far from what the RCAF had procured, or had even thought of procuring, in the previous eighteen months. What types to buy, in what numbers, and, of course, with what money had been recurring themes. In this sense, history almost seemed to be repeating itself. As in the interwar years, the RCAF had, since the fall of 1945, been making do with limited funds and any procurement opportunities that presented themselves. The conversion of British war credits into Vampires was a case in point. A similar exercise had resulted in the procurement of thirty American Mustangs – the very successful but dated P-51 – the previous year. On 27 March 1947, Cabinet had approved the purchase, which was funded with a prepaid balance for US war surplus stocks.[50] To be sure, there was nothing wrong with these aircraft as a stopgap measure, but these small-scale war credit purchases were not helpful when trying to put together an effective air program.

Although the services had not always liked the wartime acquisition process, with the Department of Munitions and Supply acting as the government's purchasing agent, the politicians had been happy with the outcome, so in 1947 it seemed reasonable to repeat the success of that system. Indeed, it was Claxton who rose in the Commons on 2 July to voice his support for the new purchasing agency, the Canadian Commercial Corporation, a branch of C.D. Howe's Department of Trade and Commerce: "Our thought is that it is of fundamental importance that we should maintain in peace-time an independent civilian organization which is capable of being expanded to meet the needs of an emergency in war." It was appropriate, he felt, to structure defence purchasing on the success of Munitions and Supply during the Second World War.[51]

One of the features of the wartime program had been coordinated production between the allies and the RCAF, and the government had already agreed in principle that this was the preferred means of equipping the Air Force and fostering a domestic production capability. As seen in Chapter 2, as early as the summer of 1945, the Chiefs of the Air Staff of the Royal Air Force and the Royal Canadian Air Force had discussed the issue of coordinated design and manufacture. On 12 February 1947, Canada and the US had signed a Joint Statement Regarding Defence Cooperation, calling for the "encouragement of common designs and standards in arms, equipment ... and new developments."[52] Discussions and agreements of this sort ultimately led to Curtis's policy, stated in the minutes of the 4 June 1948 CAS staff conference, that "any *design and development of aircraft in Canada should be complementary to programmes in the United Kingdom and the United States, and should under no circumstances duplicate other programmes*" [emphasis in original].[53]

There had been cautions, however. Some months earlier, in preparation for the visit of General Carl Spaatz, Chief of Staff of the newly independent US Air Force, the Air Member for Technical Services (AMTS) had sent a briefing note to the CAS on 14 February 1948 outlining some issues regarding aircraft manufacture and procurement. In general, he supported the notion of having an integrated production capability with the US, since joint procurement would help keep unit costs down. He cautioned, however, that there might be a negative impact from such an arrangement: Canadian needs could be swallowed up even when production was taking place in Canada. Referring specifically to the aircraft and engine work at Avro, he said that "we should prove our ability before inviting them to see what is going on."[54]

There was no question that the senior aviators were concerned with shaping the course for the RCAF, weaving together the various national and international factors that could not be ignored if decision makers in Cabinet were to be satisfied. With regard to buying aircraft, considerable thought had gone into purchasing decisions, but, with the exception of the war surplus acquisitions of the

TABLE 4.2

Fighter operational requirements

Characteristic	Day fighter	All-weather fighter
Speed	500 knots at FL450	478 knots at FL350
Rate of climb; minutes to altitude	10,000 feet per minute; 10 minutes to FL450	Engine start to FL400; not more than 10 minutes
Service ceiling	At least FL500	At least FL410
Radius of action	At least 400 NM	Range 2,000 NM; radius 1,000 NM

Note: The units of measurement are taken directly from the operational requirements and will not be familiar to some readers.

- A day fighter generally operates in daylight conditions, when the enemy aircraft can be seen and engaged with the naked eye; an "all-weather fighter" has sufficient capability (usually on-board radar) to track and engage an enemy aircraft when flying at night or in cloud.
- "FL" or "flight level" refers to altitude in hundreds of feet. For example, FL450 equals approximately 45,000 feet.
- "Knots" is the term used for speed expressed in nautical miles per hour.
- A nautical mile (NM) equals 6,000 feet, as opposed to a statute mile of 5,280 feet.
- "Rate of climb" and "minutes to altitude" are critical for fighters that have to climb rapidly, often from a "ground alert," in order to engage approaching bombers.
- "Service ceiling" refers to the maximum altitude at which the aircraft can be operated effectively. In the thinning air, flight controls lose their effect and aircraft become sloppy.

Source: LAC, RG 24, vol. 5394, RCAF file 60-1-76, Aircraft Operational Requirements – Future Aircraft, Acting AMAP to AMOT, "Operational Requirements Future Aircraft," 23 June 1948.

Vampires and Mustangs, not as much emphasis had been placed on what types to purchase or build. True, there was the research and development work on what was now commonly referred to as the CF-100, and the various force structure plans talked about having squadrons organized and equipped for various roles, but not until the summer of 1948 did the AMAP get down to fine detail by publishing a series of Operational Requirements (ORs) that laid out the performance capabilities for all major aircraft types needed by the RCAF.[55] These specifications were deemed valid until 1951 and included four fighter types: day interceptor, night fighter, ground attack fighter, and all-weather fighter. The salient characteristics of the day and all-weather fighters are shown in Table 4.2, along with an explanation of the terminology.

The Air Member for Operations and Training (AMOT) minutes for 14 July pointed to the ORs as fulfilling a long-standing necessity to codify needs,[56] and over the course of the summer many constructive comments and refinements were proposed. The most common of these suggested that there was no need for a unique ground attack capability and that the day fighter could be suitably modified to handle the task. The night fighter OR was described as an "interim" requirement, to be used only until the all-weather (AWX) fighter was available.[57]

If these were the first OR statements from which aircraft could be designed and manufactured, how did Avro happen to be working on its model XC-100 and the TR-5 engine for the previous two years? And what had it accomplished?

The truth is that Avro had been concentrating on a project that it considered more lucrative than the Air Force's jet. Work had been going on for over a year on putting a four-engine jet transport in the air. The design was the C-102, known simply as the Avro Jetliner, and it was a good one. As it turned out, the Jetliner was almost the first commercial jet transport in the world, being beaten to the air by the de Havilland Comet by just a few weeks. The Jetliner had huge potential in the civil aviation sector, and in the broadest sense it very well satisfied the Canadian vision for air power, but lack of support and funds from Trans-Canada Airlines meant that the Avro management had little time available to worry about the CF-100.[58]

Although it could be argued that the Jetliner was a significant and important contribution to the larger definition of Canadian air power, the senior aviators were nonetheless more interested in their fighter's development and were happy when in the middle of 1947 Avro began devoting greater effort to the new interceptor. A new chief engineer, John Frost, brought in from de Havilland in England, became the main design engineer, and the project staff was greatly increased. By the end of the year, the mock-up was starting to look like a fighter.[59]

In January 1948, while Frost was in England looking for ejection seats and other components, his designers discovered what appeared to be an aerodynamic design flaw. The cure involved repositioning the engines within the wings, which in turn involved redesigning the wing spars, the main structure around which the wing was constructed. When he returned to Canada, Frost was gravely alarmed, fearing that a weakness had been created, but he was overruled.[60] By the time the jet was ready to fly, some two years later, the wing spar question had still not been settled.

Work on jet engines progressed somewhat more quickly since Avro wanted to use the power plants in both the CF-100 and the Jetliner. The previous year, Cabinet had been briefed on the progress that had been made and the financial arrangements that Avro was seeking. At a session on 23 April 1947, Avro officials advised Cabinet that the firm was ready to go ahead with full-scale development;

the ministers approved up to $3.5 million in additional funds if warranted.[61] This was, after all, a remarkable achievement for a nation that had never to this point produced an aircraft engine.

Now, in the late winter of 1948, the company was set to conduct the first static test of the TR-4 Chinook engine. Smye wrote to A/V/M James on 1 March 1948, advising him that the engine was coming along well. Although test reports showed that there were some problems left to be rectified, the first run was anticipated to be a success.[62] The actual first start-up and engine run took place on 17 March in preparation for the official run on 24 March. On both occasions, the engine performed well, even better than some of its contemporaries.[63] Nonetheless, another year would pass before the TR-5 Orenda would be ready.

In the days following the Chinook test, the government provided additional funds to Avro to help accelerate development activity. Howe had already obtained $1.5 million for the firm in October 1947.[64] Now, in the following spring, it was Curtis who pushed the approval of an additional $3.5 million over and above what had already been provided between his and Howe's recommendations, Avro would actually receive $5 million rather than just the $3.5 million that Cabinet had promised the previous year. In a letter to Claxton, Curtis explained that since the project was now "well along" and since it had been the aim of the development work on engines to eventually establish a manufacturing capability in Canada, it was time to make the necessary infusion of hard cash. Curtis was convinced that spending the money now rather than waiting for additional development work would ultimately speed up the company's progress by as much as six months. Claxton forwarded Curtis's recommendation to Howe, who, having recently visited the Avro facility, replied that he was "greatly impressed by the progress being made." He felt that if the additional money would speed up the program, then it was warranted.[65] Indeed, it was Howe who sponsored the request at the CDC meeting on 15 April. He reported that the development of both the engine and the aircraft was about 40 percent complete and that the additional funds would permit accelerated development. The Minister of Finance was cautious, however, and asked whether the money would really have the desired effect. There is no indication of any discussion on this point, but the item was passed.[66] The amount was not significant, but the support for the program was an indication of the desire of many people to see Canadian defence production and readiness increased. Curtis's memo to the Minister of National Defence had caused a distinct ripple.

Like Avro, Canadair found that its best chance of survival lay in the commercial market. Never before involved in building fighter aircraft, the firm devoted all its development energy to producing the North Star. Although the aircraft was not a runaway success, it was good enough to win contracts from the British Overseas Airways Corporation (BOAC) and Canadian Pacific Air Lines, which, along with overhaul work, kept the firm solvent. It was the hope of increased commercial sales, as much as anything else, that led the firm to expand plant capacity in 1947-48.[67]

THROUGHOUT 1947, THE government was convinced that its priority lay in getting the nation back on a healthy peacetime footing. This meant that defence policies and spending would have to follow the lead of finances and the economy. By late 1947, however, and through the first nine months of 1948, the situation changed radically as the Soviet threat became more real. Defence activities, from policy making to force structuring to aircraft acquisition, began to take on new significance. The sad truth was that by 1948 the reductions enforced in 1946 and early 1947 had left the RCAF with an appallingly limited capability. Funding now appeared safe, though not without the occasional debate, and initial concepts were in place for an expansion program. Reliance on domestic production for long-term needs seemed appropriate, but after three years of relative neglect, there was still not much to show. The many instances where the CAS and his staff developed plans and briefed and convinced the politicians of the best course for the Air Force show clearly the air marshals' crucial contributions in making the best of the many constraints that they faced, as well as their ability to recognize and develop opportunities.

5
Facing the Threat in Earnest

THE AUTUMN OF 1948 saw the beginning of a period of significant realignment of Canadian security policy. Government and military leaders were ready to move ahead as quickly as possible with a reasonable rearmament program. The catalyst – discussions that eventually led to the formation of the North Atlantic Treaty Organization (NATO) during the following year – meant that there was now a reason and, more importantly, an obligation to rebuild a credible military.

A transformation of such great magnitude was easier said than done: old problems had not simply disappeared. Defining force structures and needs, as well as determining sources of aircraft and purchasing mechanisms that would permit purchases from the nation's allies, proved as challenging as designing and building a jet-age fighter in Canada. None of it came easily. As the Royal Canadian Air Force built its options, the Air Staff sagely recognized and addressed the major problems confronting it. When the domestic fighter program lagged, they turned to the next best source for aircraft, picking a fighter and supply strategy that proved remarkably successful.

On 8 October 1948, the Cabinet Defence Committee (CDC) gathered to consider a significantly different strategic review and defence program than those that had been presented in previous years.[1] The most recent intelligence appreciation indicated that the likelihood of accidental war was greater than in the past and that the risk would not diminish "until the Western Powers have strengthened and coordinated their forces and have succeeded in redressing the military balance in Europe." Focusing on the dilemma that had become increasingly evident in the preceding months, the CDC considered re-equipping the limiting factor in addressing the situation. The new requirements presented to the politicians had been developed based on the existing long-term Basic Security Plan and on a short-term strategic plan designed to address any emergency that might arise before July 1949.

Presentations and discussions at the full Cabinet meeting two days earlier had already sensitized the CDC members to many of the themes and concerns that were presented on 8 October. Reporting back after their participation in discussions in Washington, Minister of National Defence Brooke Claxton and Lester Pearson, now Secretary of State for External Affairs, believed that there was a solid basis for participating in a new security organization but that such participation would come with some responsibilities. Pearson suggested that Canada's involvement might call for greater military efforts in terms of force size and defence supplies, both of which would require a larger defence budget. And although his colleagues might not be enamoured of increased spending on the military, there appeared to be little choice, since such spending would probably become necessary in any case should the world situation deteriorate. Claxton looked at the question from an equipment perspective but one that took into account Canada's fiscal and international interests: "The possible implications as regards equipment were very important. Industrial preparations would be required and these would be helpful. If it were possible for us, in return for US types, to release present UK types of weapons and supplies for use by European allies, this would be of mutual advantage both from the military and economic points of view." Their colleagues were generally supportive of these exigencies and responses. The minutes show that "the Minister of Finance suggested that the obligations of Canada under such arrangements would make it necessary to re-examine carefully the nature as well as the extent of Canadian defence expenditures in order that the Canadian contribution would be the most effective and suitable to our resources and circumstances." This would be a legitimate course of action, Pearson suggested, since the US was going to be doing the same thing. Neither St-Laurent, now Acting Prime Minister, nor Cabinet appeared to have a problem accepting this concept of participation, and it was agreed that Canada would inform the other nations of its intentions.[2]

Although strategically these developments had a positive thrust, the air appendix of the papers placed before the CDC spelled out the immediate bad news. Canada had some eighty Vampire and twenty-nine Mustang aircraft that "in the event of an emergency ... could be concentrated into [one Mustang and four Vampire squadrons and] would represent the entire fighter force which we could use to protect Canada. There would be no aircraft left to form an air expeditionary force, or to accompany the Canadian Army overseas." Discussions within the Air Plans branch in September led to the estimate that the RCAF would need some five hundred additional aircraft grouped into thirty-two squadrons in order to respond effectively to the growing Communist threat. It was recommended that work start immediately on a variety of actions, including full-scale production of the long-range fighter and ordering of sufficient numbers of single-engine fighters to cover the shortfall until Canadian production could be established. The air marshals had not forgotten the lessons of the war, however, and reminded the politicians that these actions would have an added benefit. The proposed procurement strategy would, they felt, put Canadian industry in a good position for mobilization in the event of war.[3]

Minister of Trade and Commerce C.D. Howe agreed with the RCAF's procurement ideas. He "observed that the development of the twin-engine fighter was an approved project and the placing of a production order was a logical outcome of the development phase. With regard to the US-type fighter, it was reasonable to investigate procurement. Presumably capacity could be made available at de Havilland's plant for Canadian production."[4] The CDC agreed to examine the financial implications of the entire plan and further agreed that the Chief of the Air Staff (CAS) should informally investigate acquisition of an American fighter. As we shall see, the Air Force had already begun looking seriously at North American Aviation's F-86.[5]

By the end of October, discussions with the British indicated that there was not as much chance of a short-term emergency as had first been thought; the potential for trouble seemed to be most acute beginning in 1956.[6] Nevertheless, the CDC reviewed the air requirements in detail on 30 October.[7] Curtis wanted production of 100 CF-100s, purchase of fifty-six F-86s as a stopgap measure, and a scheme to produce the F-86 and the C-119 transport in Canada. There followed considerable discussion, since the expanded program amounted to $195 million, more than double the existing program of $88 million. Of the increase, close to $47 million was for new aircraft. Howe was somewhat concerned by the high initial costs but attributed them to front-end loading of development expenses by the firms in question. Claxton felt that the most urgent items in the program were indeed the purchase of assembly-line tooling and the confirmation of a pre-production order for ten CF-100s. Equally important was the acquisition of a first batch of F-86s from the US, with a follow-on authority to manufacture the type in Canada. The CDC decided to approve the funds needed for tooling for the CF-100 and agreed that the 1949-50 defence estimates should include the pre-production run of ten aircraft. It also agreed that Howe should formally investigate the F-86 situation during his upcoming trip to Washington.[8] This shift to a US design was fully in keeping with Cabinet's thinking earlier in the month.

In Washington, Howe met with US Defense Secretary James Forrestal and reached an agreement that would make it possible to manufacture the F-86 under licence in Canada using US Government Furnished Property (GFP), including engines, instruments, and other special components.[9] It was a repeat of the assembly approach that had worked well during the harried days of the Second World War but that would once again prevent Canadian industry from getting involved from the ground up. Moreover, the move to a US model was a fairly significant change in direction from the ties with Britain that the Vampire exemplified. In fact, Howe carried with him a document that explained why Canada would rather buy American:

> By reason of the different standards, techniques and procedures employed by Canadian industry, aircraft of United Kingdom design have to be re-designed and re-engineered to the extent that the aircraft produced in Canada have to have [logistics] pipeline support from this country. Aircraft of United States design can be made in Canada without such changes and both aircraft and components can be absorbed into the normal pipeline. Since the Royal Canadian Air Force must be capable of operating with the United States Air Force in the defence of North America, the advantages of using equipment that can be supported by the industries of Canada and the United States far outweigh any other consideration.[10]

Without mentioning the details of his discussions, Howe made a general statement on 18 November, while still in the US capital. He indicated only that there would be significant coordination of defence production and that there was a likelihood of Canadian aircraft being built from US patterns.[11]

Howe's powers with respect to defence production were detailed in an Order-in-Council that was approved shortly after his return from the United States. Order-in-Council PC 5700, dated 8 December 1948, gave him as Minister of Trade and Commerce certain fundamental powers with respect to defence procurement.[12] Specifically, he had control of funding for "Vote 418 respecting research and development of jet engines and aircraft." Moreover, another section gave him the "powers, duties and functions" previously exercised during the Second World War by the wartime Department of Munitions and Supply, an organization that, as described earlier, had been led by none other than C.D. Howe himself. A year and a half later, in the fall of 1950, as a result of the outbreak of the Korean War and an unparalleled build-up of defence procurement activities, a Department of Defence Production (DDP) was created,[13] and the Munitions and Supply powers were transferred to it on 22 March 1951.[14] In simple terms, the requirements staffs of the services would set down the operational needs, and then DDP would work with industry "to determine the source of supply" and manage the delivery.[15]

But that was in the future, and throughout 1948 the task of procuring defence supplies from the US was a particularly vexing one. Extensive work by bureaucrats on both sides of the border could not seem to solve the problem. In July, the Air Staff learned that the Americans were working on a revised trade bill, one that would still, however, need Congressional approval.[16] Awaiting this decision, Air Vice-Marshal James, the Air Member for Technical Services (AMTS), provided Curtis with a review of previous unsuccessful attempts to open up defence trade between the two nations. He made reference to a May 1946 proposal called the "Inter-American Military Cooperation Act," which had not passed. A subsequent proposal, HR 3836, was still under consideration, and although it did not specifically allow or disallow procurement or transfer of government property, US Air Force officials believed that Canada could participate in any resulting agreement.[17] There was still no resolution by October, and all three services made their frustration known to the Canadian section of the Permanent Joint Board on Defence (PJBD). The RCAF felt that considerable work and progress had been made but that "this inability of Canada to procure military equipment of types used by the US Armed Forces is the greatest single obstacle in the satisfactory implementation of [coordinated defence] plans."[18]

These disappointments contrasted dramatically with the cooperation that had occurred during the war, discussed earlier in this book. The wartime Hyde Park Agreement, in which Canada and the US had sought to achieve maximum defence production effectiveness through minimum legislative bureaucratic barriers, was supposed to serve as the model for the postwar period as well, but the Americans quickly reverted to their protectionist philosophy and would neither sell nor, as we shall see, buy from Canada. What little they were prepared to release could be had for cash only, and this was not feasible given the balance-of-payments situation discussed previously.[19]

Finally, in the early weeks of 1949, James, working with the Counsel General of the USAF, discovered a workaround that State Department lawyers also considered viable. Section 421, Title 22 of the United States Code authorized the President to "from time to time, when he deems it in the interest of national defence, authorize the head of any department ... to enter into defense [procurement] for the government of any country whose defense the President deems vital to the defense of the United States."[20] This would permit Canada to purchase a significant quantity and variety of defence supplies. The aviation requirement did not immediately include any aircraft, but overhaul work, spare parts, and specific air equipment such as radars were needed. Of particular importance, as the Air Member for Air Plans (AMAP) noted to the Canadian section of the PJBD on 2 February 1949, it opened the door to the supplying of US Government Furnished Property for the projected manufacture of F-86A aircraft in Canada. Under the terms of the legislation, the USAF could act as the purchaser/supplier for the RCAF and Canadair.[21]

By the end of January, there appeared to be both political support and the necessary plans and mechanisms for expanding and re-equipping the RCAF to meet the growing threat. On 4 February, however, Claxton met stiff resistance when he presented his defence estimates to Cabinet. The "principal new features" in the services' programs included three items: (1) the purchase of US-type aircraft, (2) the construction of new facilities, and (3) the start of construction of up-to-date anti-submarine warfare ships. Cabinet decided, however, "that the Cabinet Defence Committee explore further the proposed 1949-50 Defence programmes with a view to recommending reductions therein to Cabinet at the next meeting."[22] Four days later, Claxton returned to Cabinet but, appearing to lack his normal resolve, indicated to his colleagues that they, of course, would have the final say in defence spending. "The Cabinet, after discussion, agreed the sum of $438 million be provided for in the Defence estimates 1949-50 to cover programmes for which commitments could be made, it being understood that the cash requirement would not exceed $375 million."[23] Mackenzie King had by this time stepped down as prime minister, but spending if necessary remained an effective stratagem.

Perhaps Cabinet was still feeling the pinch of the balance-of-payments problem. On 2 March, Deputy Minister of National Defence C.M. "Bud" Drury formally advised the CAS that Cabinet, at its 25 February meeting, had considered the matter of purchasing thirty-six F-86 aircraft through the USAF pending manufacture of the type in Canada and had decided to defer a decision until a resolution to the existing exchange difficulties could be found.[24] Perhaps Canada could offer its own aircraft in exchange for American products – this notion was presented by General Andy McNaughton, the Canadian representative to the PJBD, at the board's 17-18 March meeting. Reporting back to the CAS on 21 March, the AMAP indicated that General McNaughton had done an "excellent selling job" when he proposed the CF-100 and the Orenda engine as possible items of interest to the US.[25] There is little doubt that the senior officers realized the importance of such reciprocal purchases to the viability of Canadian industry and the creation of a useful mobilization base. Of course, there was no CF-100 to offer at the moment, so this would have to wait.

The easy movement of defence materiel would not be achieved overnight. Only with the passage of the Mutual Defense Assistance Act (originally the Mutual Assistance Act) by the US Congress on 6 October 1949 did the pieces of a coordinated system begin to fall into place. From that date onward, Canada and the other allies could benefit from access to US producers. Many American bureaucrats and politicians realized that their Canadian partners in defence would grow stronger if the US were to buy Canadian materiel. Thus, in April 1950, after visits from a number of Canadian delegations, the US Munitions Board accepted the need for reciprocal processes for the purchase and sale of defence materials, and in May, Congress finally relented on the Buy American policy, and the Secretary of Defense indicated that the US would buy $15-20 million in defence supplies from Canada.[26] The US had at last approved the mechanisms for defence procurement that, unknown to it at the time, would be sorely tested in the following months. Moreover, an avenue for buying F-86 components and selling CF-100s was now available to Canadian manufacturers.

The overriding context for all these discussions was the formation of what would soon become known as the North Atlantic Treaty Organization. Initial discussions had taken place in the spring of 1948. Britain, the US, and Canada saw the need for some type of defence alliance given the apparent impotence of the United Nations. Momentum built during the following year, until twelve nations, including Canada, met in Paris to draw up the North Atlantic Treaty in April 1949.[27] When the treaty came into effect on 24 August, it provided little clout for a military alliance.[28] Not until the following year, at a conference at the Hague, was a military capability established. The Medium Term Defence Plan called for the development and deployment of the NATO Integrated Force by 1 July 1954.[29]

It was within the context of NATO that the Canadian government revisited in some detail the whole issue of equipment spending and balance of payments in the final weeks of 1949. As an instrument of foreign policy, Canada's treaty role had been negotiated by External Affairs, and only afterwards was the military able to begin detailed analysis of the implications.[30] Claxton briefed the CDC on 23 November, reminding his colleagues that warfare was now dependent on equipment that could not be produced overnight. A long-term model had been developed, and it was now necessary to seek government approval for funding levels so that the plan could be refined and implemented. The idea of a five-year plan found favour, but there was concern about the associated costs, which totalled close to $2.4 billion. The Air Force portion was approximately $1.2 billion and included requirements for 204 F-86s and 112 CF-100s. Moreover, as the initial step in the process, the RCAF now sought immediate approval for the first 100 F-86s and 10 CF-100s. Despite these high figures, the CDC found the five-year concept worthy of further refinement by National Defence and Finance officials.[31]

On 21 December, Claxton briefed the full Cabinet on the recent meetings of the Defence and Military Committees of NATO. He said that there was good resolve and confidence, but that in the short term the European nations lacked the wherewithal to withstand any aggression. Part of the problem was a shortage of equipment, and it was likely that Canada and the US would be presented with a list of deficiencies and asked for help. He thought it would be better to state immediately what Canada could do to help, rather than be asked for something that it would prefer not to provide. Potential assistance could include training facilities for European nations in Canada, dispatch of Canadian units to Europe for training from time to time, supply of raw materials, and supply of military equipment. Because of the current US "dollar content" in Canadian products and the problems of balance of payments, the last option appeared the least likely. The report was noted by Cabinet, and Prime Minister St-Laurent mentioned that the Atlantic Pact had been created as a deterrent body and that, to be effective, the deterrent would have to be "sufficiently impressive."[32]

Doubtless with this encouraging thought in mind, Claxton returned to Cabinet on 18 January 1950 with his estimates for the upcoming year.[33] He reported that as a result of several recent meetings, the CDC had concluded that to support all the activities and commitments incumbent in the North Atlantic Treaty would require a defence budget of $614 million.[34] This amount was still, in per capita terms, well below the amounts projected by the US and Britain. The Minister of Finance remarked that since the government was not in the habit of delivering deficit budgets, $160 million would have to be cut from the overall estimates. The Minister of National Health and Welfare objected: this new defence budget was $42 million over the current defence estimates and reflected Canada's disproportionate growth in defence over the previous three years. It appeared that the government could not manage both heavy defence spending and the social programs that it had introduced in recent years. Prime Minister St-Laurent intervened, stating that although a comprehensive review of defence issues was needed, it would not be seen in a good light if Canada were to back away from its treaty obligations. There was much additional discussion, but it was finally agreed that for 1950-51, the Department of National Defence estimates could be set at $425 million and that this amount would be considered the peacetime maximum, which was not to be exceeded except in case of a deterioration in world stability. This worked out to $31.50 per capita and totalled 18 percent of the national budget. Although still below the per capita rates of the US and Britain, it was a remarkable increase over prewar figures.[35]

Yet not even this princely sum, the RCAF staff concluded, was adequate for fielding a viable air arm. The Air Force was to get roughly $165 million each year for five years, a planning projection that had been agreed to by Claxton. At a special meeting of the Chiefs of Staff Committee (CSC) on 31 January 1950, the service chiefs reassessed the nation's defence needs and capabilities. There were three requirements – territorial defence of North America, the possible provision of reinforcements for other regions, and participation in the development of a strategic air offensive plan – but the money provided was not considered adequate to cover all three. It was unlikely that the funds would permit any force structure increases; rather, spending would have to be concentrated on equipment. "In this regard it should be made clear to the Cabinet that any aid which might be made available by the Canadian Government for Western European countries should not cause a reduction in the development of the Canadian Armed Forces." When it was Curtis's turn to speak, he spelled out the impact of financial limitations on the Air Force:

> The proposed allocation of funds would result in a very considerable reduction in the plans for the defence of Canada insofar as the Royal Canadian Air Force was concerned. He wished to go on record as stating that the RCAF plans under review involved a serious calculated risk. No air defence in depth could be provided within the limitations imposed and the fighter defence would be confined to the more important target areas.

Specifically, this meant that the Air Force would be reduced from a recently approved structure (discussed below) to five Regular and ten Auxiliary fighter squadrons, with the rest of the Service barely a shell. Aircraft attrition was such that even this financially constrained organization was problematic. Although the purchase of F-86s was now moving ahead, it was no sure cure for the problem.[36]

The whole question of force structure, with all its combinations and permutations, had appeared to consume the Air Staff over the previous fifteen months. Part of Curtis's presentation to the CDC at the end of October 1948 had been the proposed force structure that could be implemented once aircraft were purchased and squadrons formed. His new fighter arm would, at that point, jump from five composite squadrons, operating the combined resources of Plan E's obsolescent aircraft, to a force of seventeen Regular and Reserve units operating modern jet aircraft.[37] By December 1948, this new force, which, according to the figures presented, would be operational by 1953, was being discussed routinely. But Curtis did not like to associate the new structure with a 1953 implementation date, since he wanted this new organization in place without delay. Rather than refer to a "1953 Plan" or a "modified Plan E," the AMAP suggested that this new structure be called "Plan F."[38]

No sooner had Plan F been adopted than yet another phasing option came into play, this one centred on 1956. In an extensive plan dated 1 March 1949, the AMAP staff laid out the aircraft procurement schedule for F-86s and CF-100s that covered the years 1949-50 to 1955-56. Overall, the plan called for 356 F-86s (the first 56 purchased in the US) and 380 CF-100s. Domestic production of the F-86 was planned for 1950-51, with CF-100 deliveries beginning the following year. Between the two types, approximately 400 fighters would be delivered by the end of 1953. The staffs had made a number of assumptions. Figures were not really solid after 1953, and it was suggested that by that time there would have been significant developments in air defence practice and equipment that might necessitate revisions to the plan.[39] Given all that had happened in the previous four years, these were reasonable assumptions.

The covering memos of A/C Godwin and A/V/M Dunlap offered some cautions. These were significant requirements, and there was a need to look for economies. Perhaps, suggested Godwin, fighter squadrons could be based in groups of two or more to save on infrastructure. Dunlap wondered, without stating specifics, what savings there might be from "the elimination of non-essential functions currently performed." Godwin was particularly concerned about the financial viability of this new plan, and just days later, on 11 March, convinced that it was unmanageable, he proposed reductions.[40] His modifications to the 1 March proposal cut the fighter funding almost in half, from $540 million to $291 million. He believed that this scaled-down effort could still preserve the operational needs of the Air Force. He called for the Reserves to be equipped with an "operational trainer," which would be replaced by 250 first-line fighters from the US on mobilization. In reference to the aircraft industry, his plan, he said, would include one factory producing a first-line fighter with another manufacturer contributing the fighter trainer. Overall, Godwin sought reductions in all areas of air activity in order to achieve fiscal practicability. These were cautious words indeed, and they offer clear evidence that the senior aviators understood well the limitations of the nation and the government. They were not simply out to build an air power empire.

Godwin was not alone. A 14 March review of the proposal by the Directorate of Operational Requirements (DOR) expressed similar concerns over funding, or rather lack of it. The review found that there was not enough money to permit both the equipping and manning of the proposed organization, and it came out firmly behind placing the emphasis on equipment: "To compromise on operational aircraft is a retrograde step unless the RCAF is willing to accept the long equipment build up period after hostilities commence."[41]

The minutes of the Air Members meeting of 14 March 1949 show the maturity of the senior aviators' reasoning. On the one hand, it was thought desirable to present the government with a comprehensive accounting of what the complete Air Defence System, which was what Plan F was for all intents and purposes, would cost. On the other hand, it would be essential to bring down the requirement as much as possible to get the costs to an affordable level. The Air Member for Operations and Training (AMOT) suggested that two options should be prepared: a limited plan that was likely to be acceptable and a full-scale plan to be "used as an ultimate goal that the RCAF should strive to attain." At the same time, however, the Air Member for Technical Services (AMTS) thought that it would be worth waiting "until the full effects of the Atlantic Security Pact were known. The Atlantic Pact was quite likely to have some bearing on the composition and forces which would be required and available for the Air Defence of the North American Continent." For the time being, the Air Members decided to prepare a minimum essential four- to five-year plan, "the object being to obtain formal Government approval for an Air Defence System and to obtain financial approval for a four or five year programme for the RCAF."[42]

The planning staffs moved quickly to develop detailed options. A staff check dated 5 April 1949 shows that for Plan F, although the war establishment fighter squadrons would remain at twenty-five aircraft, the peace unit establishment (UE) would consist of just twelve jets, and only eight for Auxiliary units. The text indicated that the rate of build-up of the Regular squadrons would increase under Plan F, compared with Plan E, and that the differentiation previously planned between Regular and Auxiliary units would be done away with when units came up to full strength. Additionally, all units were to contribute to interceptor tasks and subsequently take on ground attack as a secondary role.[43]

Work was also underway on the full version, which included "all the extras," and this was ready for discussion by the Air Members on 25 May:

> The proposed Long Range Plan was based on the assumption that Canadian aircraft factories would be capable of producing sufficient fighter and maritime-type aircraft. It was also assumed that the RCAF would build up to a strength of 120,000 by M [mobilization] plus 1 year. A strength of 120,000 was considered adequate to support 50 Squadrons comprised as follows:
>
> - 29 Fighter Squadrons
> - 6 Maritime Squadrons
> - 5 twin engine Transport Squadrons
> - 4 four engine Transport Squadrons
> - 2 long range Tactical Reconnaissance Squadrons
> - 2 long range Bomber Squadrons
> - 2 Tactical Bomber Squadrons.

This Long Range Plan was divided into three phases: Phase I – Plan "F" (peacetime force); Phase II – M (mobilization) plus one year (including the Basic Security Plan force); and Phase III – M plus three years (estimated wartime force).[44]

These requirements were fine for North American defence, but the nagging question of what, if any, forces should be earmarked for deployment to Europe was becoming more and more critical. In August 1949, with the NATO agreement now in place, Claxton briefed Cabinet on the Chiefs of Staff Committee's thinking on the question. Canada, it felt, should not seek an active role in European defence. If defence arrangements were regional, then Canada should continue to work with the US, and, like the US, Canada could reasonably limit its participation in Europe to an observer role.[45] Paradoxically, within the previous seven days, the Air Members had met twice to discuss the deployment of forces to Europe, generally in the form of a fighter wing of three squadrons.[46]

These concerns did not show up when the final version of Plan F was published in November, but the document did clearly stress the need to develop the air defence capabilities of the RCAF. To achieve a fighter defence capability ready for immediate use, "it will take several years to produce the equipment and to train the personnel in its use. Thus, cognizance must be taken of requirements for future years when producing the current annual plan." This was not to the exclusion of other capabilities, and, in both Curtis's foreword and the introductory paragraphs of the plan, mention was also made of the need for maritime forces and for a tactical force to support the Army in dealing with lodgements in North America. There was no suggestion, however, of the need to deploy forces overseas; rather, much attention was paid to the air defence of North America, to the planning that had been done in conjunction with the United States, and to the need to have the plan implemented by the end of fiscal year 1953-54 in order to meet the projected threat. As originally presented at the end of October 1949, the Interceptor Force considered necessary to deal with this threat was to consist of seventeen squadrons (nine Regular and eight Auxiliary) and the associated air control and warning units and communications systems. Fighter squadrons would have the secondary role of supporting the training of the Mobile Striking Force in peacetime training activities, but there would be no purely fighter squadrons assigned to the RCAF Tactical Force.[47]

The government's security policies and financial capabilities, along with the RCAF's force structure, continued to influence the types and quantities of aircraft that the planners could hope to acquire. Curtis had made it clear in his presentation to the CDC at the end of October 1948 that the Air Force was after a mix of F-86s, ideally manufactured in Canada, and Avro's CF-100.[48] Some 250 F-86s would be needed, he had said, along with 300 CF-100s if operational needs, as defined by Plan F, were to be fully met. Strangely, these totals, particularly as they apply to the F-86s, do not agree with figures found in the actual Plan F document. The November 1949 version of Plan F makes clear that the F-86s were seen as a stopgap and nothing more; the plan called for 311 CF-100s and just 8 F-86A models. In fact, if CF-100 production went as planned, there would never be more than 80 of the American-designed jets needed at any one time.[49] The RCAF may well have felt that wastage would be of such proportions that it would have to purchase 250 aircraft to meet the various contingencies called for by the phased introduction of Plan F organizations. The actual reason for Curtis's figures is unclear, but there can be little doubt that the pace of change made the identification of a precise and definitive final force structure and the associated acquisition schedules a virtual nightmare. Similarly, though Curtis may have known what he wanted, options, questions, and controversy surrounded the equipping of the Air Force.

The choice of the F-86 as the "standard jet day fighter for the RCAF" was explained in an AMOT report tabled by A/V/M Roy Slemon at the Air Members meeting on 7 January 1949. The document, entitled "Fighter Aircraft Procurement Policy for the RCAF," described the Air Force's need for both all-weather and day fighters, but it had been drawn up primarily "to assemble in one paper all the deliberations and arguments [that] have led to the selection of the North American F86A as the standard jet day fighter for the RCAF." With the all-weather requirement to be met by the CF-100, the bulk of the report dealt with the question of equipment standardization. It was explained in clear terms that although it had been appropriate to operate British aircraft both during and immediately after the war, such was no longer the case. Canada must be able to operate alongside the Americans, and there was no more operationally effective way to do this than by employing the same equipment. Moreover, it was considered important, regardless of a design's origin, to manufacture the aircraft in Canada, and here wartime experience had shown that British and North American engineering and manufacturing practices were simply not compatible. These conclusions should have led to the obvious decision to adopt the F-86 over any similar British designs, but the planners recognized that the Vampire Mark 3s that the RCAF was operating now were "very satisfactory aircraft" and that it would therefore be remiss to eliminate the suggested replacement Mark 7s without at least comparing their flying qualities with those of the F-86. Both, it turned out, had operational strengths and weaknesses, and the issue then came down to one of short-term and sustained availability and compatibility: the F-86 won in both cases. The CAS was very comfortable with this reasoning and directed that the report be forwarded to the public relations directorate (DPR). He felt that "the public should be aware of the reasons for standardizing on United States equipment."[50]

Indeed, the issue was topical during the year, particularly after Howe's Washington announcement the previous November. In March, DPR responded to the *Ottawa Citizen*, explaining the rationale for choosing the F-86. The basis for the decision lay in the certainty of supply. It was better to have a North American source than an overseas one. It was pointed out that building both engine and aircraft in Canada was better yet – the CF-100/Orenda combination, for example, was pretty much the optimal solution.[51]

Subsequently, DPR prepared a long article for the November 1949 issue of the RCAF's *Roundel* magazine and forwarded a copy of the text to the minister's office. The article went to great lengths to point out the desirability and importance of choosing a North American product for the RCAF if the Service was to be able to maintain its aircraft strength at full capability and to work closely and efficiently with the USAF. The piece concluded, "our present policy is aimed at allowing the RCAF to play its full role, taking advantage of Canada's particular geographical position and industrial potential. The F-86 is the fruit of that policy."[52] But what had become of the Avro angle?

There had never been any question, public or otherwise, about acquiring the CF-100, but from November 1948 until late 1949 there was a fair bit of discussion at the director level about the employment of the aircraft in the ground attack and reconnaissance roles. Group Captain (G/C) C.L. Annis, Director of Air Operations (DAO), was convinced that the CF-100 had potential in these areas, but whereas the reconnaissance role seemed most plausible, the ground attack/fighter-bomber function appeared problematic, given the need to find weight offsets for bomb and/or rocket loads.[53]

At the end of 1949, the discussion was elevated to the Deputy Air Member for Air Plans level, where it was agreed that the viability of using the CF-100 in either of these roles should be looked at only after the aircraft was flying and performance characteristics had been considered. On 17 November 1949, A/C W.E. Bennett, Deputy Air Member for Air Plans (Organization) (D/AMAP/O), wrote to his counterpart in Plans reviewing the suitability of all fighter types for the fighter-bomber task. He indicated that the Mustang was capable of the task, whereas the Vampire was not. The F-86 was capable of carrying bombs and rockets, whereas the CF-100 could not do so without modification. He concluded that since the smaller F-86 would represent the least loss and would at the same time have the best chance of survival, "it is not considered wise at this time to consider the CF-100 further." He pointed out that in any case there was no requirement in Plan F for any fighter-bomber aircraft.[54]

This discussion of roles for the CF-100 was already well underway before a specific operational requirement had been issued. Eventually, one was published on 22 June 1949. It was a curious document. Introduced as the first operational requirement for the CF-100, ORI/1-27 consisted of just two pages and did not set out any performance data for the aircraft. One presumes that the requirements of the previously issued OR/4 All Weather Interceptor Aeroplane (mentioned in note 55 in Chapter 4) were to be used. ORI/1-27 began,

> Pursuant to RCAF requirements for an aircraft to perform all weather fighter duties, the CF100 aircraft has been selected and is to be prepared to the detailed

requirements set forth herewith. The primary role of the CF100 is to be all weather fighting. The aircraft is for Regular Squadron use in any part of the world.

The original document shows clearly that the last sentence had originally been composed using the phrase "in Canada."[55] A second version of ORI/1-27 was issued on 10 February 1950, "incorporating all policy decisions" and retaining the "any part of the world" statement.[56] Officially, the RCAF might not be considering operations in Europe, but some bright staff officer could see the implications of the NATO agreement.

It is significant that the initial ORI/1-27 statement of requirement was not definitive. The fighter-bomber role aside, there was more work in progress in an attempt to define avionics, navigation aids, and, through the summer of 1950, an autopilot.[57] The litany of second thoughts did not end there. In June 1950, the issues of long-range ferry tanks and ejection seat/survival equipment were raised,[58] followed soon after by questions of weapons loads for the all-weather and tactical fighter roles (ORI/1-35, issued on 15 June 1950). The latter role was not dropped until four years later, according to a related document[59] but probably generated considerable staff activity in the interim. The dual trainer ORI/1-28 was issued in early 1950, and development of this new ORI took additional staff time in the summer, with much effort devoted to sorting out appropriate radar systems and ejection seats.[60] A fourth operational requirement, ORI/1-31 for a photo reconnaissance version of the CF-100, was issued on 8 July 1949.[61] Late that year, however, it was realized that the aircraft could not effectively provide a strategic reconnaissance capability and that, in any case, Plan F did not include a reconnaissance requirement.[62]

If these requirements were finding their way to Avro in dribs and drabs, one can easily conclude that the contractor was not solely to blame for the delays that were starting to occur. Indeed, writing to the firm in early July 1950, Curtis took some responsibility for Avro's difficulties: "It is realized that these changes will upset your planned progress on the pre-production aircraft, and will probably cause considerable scrapping of the fabrication already completed." Nevertheless, he asked the firm to "please consider these new requirements, in all their implications, as speedily as possible."[63]

Before we leave the topic of operational requirements, it is appropriate to mention briefly the statement of requirement for the F-86. Several drafts of ORI/1-23 were circulated in the first half of 1950. The preamble stated that the F-86 had "been selected to meet [the] requirements [of an] aircraft to perform day interception and tactical duties." The aircraft's primary role would be as a day fighter, but it would also be called on to provide tactical support for ground forces. The latter function would require the ability to carry bombs and rockets.[64]

The most important theme to emerge from the conceptualizing during the summer and fall of 1949 centred on the use of the two aircraft to satisfy the needs of the Air Force. When Curtis had first tabled his plan in the fall of 1948, there had been no thought, or at least no serious thought, of deploying forces outside Canada. Now the situation was different, and the RCAF had to be ready for an overseas operational commitment.

Initially, it appeared that the F-86 would be the better choice for such duty, since "from the point of view of logistics alone, it would seem that these squadrons should be equipped with F86A's so as to be able to take advantage of US supply lines. This was one of the factors which influenced the thinking of the Air Members ... when it was decided that one mobile wing of 3 regular fighter squadrons would be equipped with F86A's."[65]

Strangely, within weeks of that pronouncement, the senior aviators modified their opinion. Discussions on 3 August pointed to the CF-100 as an option for providing assistance to the North Atlantic allies: "It was the consensus of the Air Members that the best contribution would be the operation of a Canadian fighter base which would ultimately be manned by three fighter squadrons including CF100 (all regular squadrons participating on a rotational basis between Canada and the European Theatre)."[66] On 5 August, the issue was again raised and the choice of the CF-100 was confirmed: "A brief discussion was held on the role of the Mobile Fighter Wing and the type of aircraft best suited to that role. It was generally agreed that the Mobile Wing should be capable of carrying out all weather operations particularly night fighting. The Air Members decided, therefore, that all mobile squadrons should be equipped with CF100 aircraft."[67]

When it was issued later in the fall, Plan F did not mention the deployment of forces to Europe, but it did underline two themes. First, although the subject was not discussed specifically in the document, the Air Defence annex clearly laid out the phased introduction and withdrawal of various types of fighters to and from service.[68] The F-86 would serve with the Regular units only until sufficient numbers of CF-100s were available, which was predicted to occur in 1952-53. Reserve squadrons would begin receiving limited numbers of the F-86 in 1951-52, building up to eight aircraft by 1953-54, but the war establishment of the Reserve units was shown as CF-100s. The RCAF thus planned to use the F-86 as a short-term and low-cost remedy to an aircraft shortfall.

The seriousness of this shortfall was readily apparent. Three squadrons were due to become operational beginning in the summer of 1949 and going into the following fiscal year, but there were no aircraft. Rather than delay, drastic measures were recommended. The AMOT proposed that the first unit, 421 Squadron, be allocated Vampires, by taking these aircraft from the Reserves. The other two could use Harvard trainers pending the delivery of F-86s.[69] Just where were these new machines?

In a briefing paper at the end of October 1949, the CAS assured the CDC that the aircraft were indeed coming.[70] The F-86 situation looked promising, maybe even better than planned. During the initial talks with North American Aviation, makers of the F-86, C.D. Howe had doubted that Canadair would be able to do more than assemble American parts; both he and the North American Aviation president were concerned that the Montreal firm would not be able to handle the complex wing shape and the challenging manufacturing process. Curtis, on the other hand, had been convinced that Canadair could actually build the aircraft from scratch,[71] and his instinct was proving to be correct.

Production had begun in August 1949 with the assembly of a crated F-86A. There was to be a follow-on test run of 10 aircraft, but this number was expanded to 100. Unfortunately, North American was busy building the aircraft in the US, so all tooling for Canadian manufacture would have to be produced by Canadair. Also complicating matters, the specifications for the version selected by the RCAF, the F-86E, were not available, so the first 20 Canadair aircraft had to be built to the F-86A standard and converted later. Despite these significant challenges, excellent progress was made, and the first flight took place just one year after the arrival of the first crated fighter.[72]

While assembly of the F-86 was underway, in October, part of Curtis's October, 1949 presentation to the CDC dealt with progress at Avro: "The development of an RCAF all weather fighter (CF100) is well ahead of expectations. A contract has already been placed for ten pre-production models; three of these will be delivered during the fiscal year 1950. Barring unforeseen difficulties, production models should be ready for delivery to operational squadrons in 1952."[73] The first flight of the CF-100 took place on 19 January 1950, more than six months before that of the F-86. The pilot was Canadian Bill Waterton, who was working for the parent firm Hawker Siddeley and was arguably the British Empire's most qualified jet aircraft test pilot. The flight went well except for the failure of the undercarriage to retract. Informed of the overall success, Sir Roy Dobson headed for Canada to see what Avro had created. He arrived in time for the third test flight, and apparently Waterton decided to give him a show. The abnormal result of some rather normal manoeuvring was a flexing of the wing main spar where the previous redesign had been necessary due to engine repositioning. Some skin panels were damaged and it was concluded that the spar would need reinforcing. More problems arose during the course of the year as the aircraft was flown for the Americans in May and at the Toronto Airshow later in the year. During the latter event, the wing spar once again let go, this time with a "sharp thunderclap," according to Waterton. Although he had probably not been any harder on the aircraft than any other test pilot might have been, he became the scapegoat for airframe shortcomings that were purely the result of the design difficulties discussed in Chapter 3.[74] He returned to his position in Britain shortly after the Toronto incident, but the wing problems did not go away and continued to plague the CF-100.

By the end of 1949, the RCAF, in concert with the nation's political leadership, was well along in responding to the growing Soviet threat and in realigning defence priorities and force structures following the formation of NATO. Air Force leaders had shown their sagacity on several occasions, focusing their efforts on the overriding need to define, develop, equip, and field a viable fighter capability for North American defence. They had also begun examining the question of assigning forces to the European theatre. Particularly significant was the air marshals' realization that funding was of fundamental importance and that money was, regardless of the threat to the nation, a finite commodity. The government could be expected to give only so much to defence activities, and it was up to the RCAF to make the most of scarce resources.

In translating needs into development and manufacture, the airmen had shown good judgment as well. Curtis had trusted in Canadair's ability to build the F-86 from scratch; his confidence was now paying off and would reap additional benefits later. Faith in Avro's abilities remained unshaken, for the moment at least. If there was doubt in anyone's mind that the CF-100 would meet the RCAF's needs, it would emerge with the outbreak of the Korean War and the arming of the European alliance.

6
And So to War

ON 20 JUNE 1950, as North Korean forces prepared to invade the South, Cabinet approved Minister of National Defence Brooke Claxton's choice of "Canuck" as the official name of the CF-100.[1] Ironically, just as it was christening the Avro jet, the catalyst for an unimaginable growth in the F-86 program was about to capture the world's attention. Nothing had prepared the nation for the impending crisis. To be sure, there had been an acknowledgment of the Soviet menace, and plans were in place for a gradual build-up in defence capability, but threat estimates still predicted several years of relative calm. All of this was about to change, and change radically.

Within weeks, the services would be asked not just to deal with the Korean problem but also to look at sending significant forces to Europe. The Air Force would have to find ways to accelerate and expand its procurement plans and to assist its allies with their shortfalls in fighters. NATO would seek to close an alarming capability gap. As long as peace prevailed, there would be time to act. NATO policy could be reviewed and fresh decisions made about how much more to spend and what additional forces could be deployed with those new funds.

Throughout July, as the world watched the continuing retreat of South Korean and American forces, the service chiefs prepared emergency responses for the government. Finally, in a three-day session spanning the first week of August, Cabinet discussed the Korean crisis in detail. In answer to both the threat and calls for action, Claxton advised his colleagues that an accelerated defence program was envisaged. The Royal Canadian Air Force would grow to a total of twenty-eight squadrons by the end of 1953. Acquisitions would include CF-100, F-86, and, in the short term, additional Mustang fighters. More aircraft meant increased funding, but in view of the gravity of the world situation, Cabinet approved the overall plan in principle, satisfied with the details that had been presented.[2]

These deliberations on finances and force expansion, as well as later re-evaluations of force structure and European basing, were influenced by actions in the United States. At the end of July, the Americans had approved a defence budget of between $25 and 30 billion, with a fresh $10 billion for Europe.[3] Now feeling pressure to act, the Canadian government, in addition to increasing domestic defence spending, passed the Defence Appropriation Act, which authorized another $300 million "for the production, acquisition, repair and provision of equipment, services, supplies and facilities, for the use of the defence forces of Canada and those of any part of the North Atlantic Treaty." Stating a maximum amount was a sage approach, for it demonstrated a significant and firm support for the alliance while limiting the extent of Canada's financial involvement.[4] This initiative permitted the Minister of Finance to report to Parliament on 6 September that the new moneys would permit a "large increase in the production of defence supplies and equipment ... so urgently needed now." Similarly, Canada's representative to the NATO Council of Deputies had indicated just days earlier that Canada was ready to do its part and "in respect to military production urged NATO to state [its] specific requirement."[5]

Money was useful but placing forces in Europe might be better, and there was no lack of pressure in the fall of 1950 for Canada to send units to the Continent. The possibility appears to have been first mentioned at talks in Washington in early September. Not long after, Winston Churchill rose in the British House of Commons to suggest that Canada's share of the NATO field army would reasonably amount to two or three divisions. In Canada, Prime Minister Louis St-Laurent spoke about these suggestions on 13 September: "Our present view is ... that the most effective immediate contribution Canada can make to the joint strength in Europe ... is in the provision of arms and equipment."[6] The Americans continued to apply pressure through the winter of 1950-51. Canada should, according to an internal US document, be able to spend another $500 million on defence and field a light bomber force in addition to the fighters already under discussion. Claxton and St-Laurent resisted these proposals, waiting to see how well the nation could manage the promises of the previous year.[7] There was a simple reason why Canada could not let its guard down, now or later: aside from the US, it was the only country paying its own way. Other countries that were being supported financially by the Americans were quite prepared to set their force goals and equipment plans at as high a level as the US would underwrite. In one way, though, Canada was like the US: neither nation's spending on NATO contributed directly to the defence of North America.[8]

NATO, too, was working on its options, and these were made known to the member nations, including Canada, by the end of September. Claxton would later say that "NATO owes the fact that it has built up its strength to the communist aggression in Korea."[9] On 12 October, the Cabinet Defence Committee (CDC) met to examine anew the NATO Medium Term Defence Plan. Claxton opened by submitting that countries could no longer say that they might or might not field certain forces. Rather, by signing on to the plan, which called for operational capability on 1 July 1954, each nation had at the very least a moral obligation to meet any such commitment. Since Canada was paying its own way, unlike the European nations, which were using US funds, it was critical that the politicians understood these commitments. Should the financial obligations seem too great, alternative plans would need to be proposed. Indeed, it appeared that the 1951-52 costs might be higher than anticipated, and the same could be true for the following years. The minutes recorded Claxton's unease: "In these circumstances if we were not prepared to assume substantially greater obligations it might be necessary ... to indicate quite clearly that Canada was not prepared to go beyond the defence programmes for 1951-52-53 that had already been approved by the government." Prime Minister St-Laurent and Minister of Finance Douglas Abbott were also concerned about committing to the long term when there seemed to be no clear definition of what that involved. For the moment, though, Abbott felt that Canada should say that until there was a clear identification of the requirement, it would provide only such funds as had already been budgeted. Adding his views, Lieutenant-General Charles Foulkes, the Chief of the General Staff (CGS), suggested that, since the overriding priority of NATO was to build up the defence of Western Europe, where the first and main attack was expected, it was up to the government to decide what portion of its alliance obligations it would fulfill now or by 1954.[10] Perhaps the politicians need not have been so worried, for as autumn progressed more and more Canadians, eventually reaching 53 percent of the population, came to consider the threat of war as the nation's most serious problem.[11]

Discussion of Canada's contribution to the Medium Term Defence Plan did not end in October. A long and very wide-ranging meeting of the CDC was held in the closing days of 1950.[12] China had now entered the war in Korea, and it was even more critical, in the view of both Claxton and Secretary of State for External Affairs Lester Pearson, for defence to get top priority. Their contention was that the threat would not peak in 1954: it had already arrived.[13] Claxton opened the 28 December meeting by comparing US and Canadian efforts. In the current fiscal year, the Americans were spending $22.5 billion, representing 9.5 percent of their national income, 47.2 percent of their government spending, and $148 per capita. By comparison, Canada was spending $700 million, representing 5.7 percent, 29.6 percent, and $51.40, respectively. In terms of manpower, the Americans would soon have 23 of every 1,000 citizens in their active forces, compared with Canada's 4.5 per 1,000.[14] Without saying it in so many words, Claxton was sending a clear message that Canada could and must do more.

He then outlined what that more should be. For the RCAF, it entailed increasing Orenda production to the limits of the facility and then looking for more facilities. F-86 output should be increased to fifty aircraft per month. Discussion of these two themes continued. Claxton pointed to the worldwide shortage of jet engines, and Howe thought that Avro should be able to produce 100 engines per month. Chief of the Air Staff (CAS) Air Marshal Wilfred Curtis speculated that it might take up to two years to reach this level, by which time he hoped that Avro would also be capable of producing twenty-five CF-100s per month. Claxton felt that increasing F-86 production would give NATO greater access to the only fighter that appeared capable of facing off with the Soviet MiG-15, and he pointed out that Britain wanted almost four hundred of these aircraft (a story we shall turn to presently). If the US would come through with the Government Furnished Property (GFP), Canadair could provide these aircraft. Howe confirmed that the plant capacity could handle it. The money for the aircraft would come from the $300 million included in the Defence Appropriation Act. Overall, Claxton said, these expanded activities would enable Canada to meet its obligations under the Medium Term Defence Plan, which included sending eleven fighter squadrons to Europe.[15]

This looked expensive compared with the relatively frugal structure of Plan F, and when it was added to the Army's requirement to send a full brigade to Germany, the overall defence bill was frightening. Some of those present at the meeting thought that stationing forces in Europe during peacetime made no sense, but many others supported this strategy. One proponent of the Air Force was J.W. "Jack" Pickersgill, St-Laurent's special assistant and head of the Prime Minister's Office, who believed, along with others, that the RCAF offered the best deterrent and the best demonstration of national commitment and excellence.[16] Although the CDC expressed some reservations about the politics of NATO force structuring, the plans for an expanded Canadian role were approved.[17] The Finance Minister's control over defence spending and priorities was, for the moment at least, at an end.[18] Claxton, Howe, and Curtis had spelled out the key issues surrounding policy, force structure, procurement, and production as clearly as possible in a period where the threat of world war made perfectly defined projections of future strategies difficult, to say the least.

During the following months, Cabinet and the CDC became more and more involved in force structure and finances than in policy. Indeed, the grand strategy had been set: Canada was a full participant in the North Atlantic Alliance. What was needed now was to keep close watch on how the nation would make good on its obligations, to ensure that the force structures and financial commitments did not add up to more than the country could bear. Throughout January 1951, as the Speech from the Throne was being written, Claxton discussed with Curtis Canada's level of participation and its ability to meet the force goals of the Medium Term Defence Plan's Integrated Force. He asked Curtis to first look after the squadrons earmarked for the defence of Canada and also to ensure that the Air Force could provide a minimum of six squadrons overseas while attempting to come as close as possible to the goal of eleven squadrons.[19]

For public and political consumption, he could appear more assured, and his approach during the debate after the Throne Speech on 5 February showed his resolve. Laying out the challenges facing the nation, he noted that the Air Force would get priority, for both home and European service. He announced that the RCAF would consist of forty Regular and Reserve squadrons, with eleven of the former being stationed in Europe, and that these forces and the supporting schools and units would need some three thousand new aircraft. In doing so, he indicated that the European air division would fly both the F-86 and the CF-100.[20]

By the summer of 1951, NATO had recognized that there were systemic gaps between national funding and force structure goals. The North Atlantic Council had created a number of interim organizations to analyze what individual nations were contributing and, naturally, to see whether they could do better. One of these, the Temporary Council Committee (TCC), was established and functioning by September, and its first report came out in November that year. The analysis concluded that Canada could do more, suggesting at that point an additional $250 million. Earlier, a submission to the TCC had stressed that Canada was at its limit, pointing out that the funding projection for the following fiscal year, 1952-53, was estimated at $2.4 billion, or 13 percent of GNP; surely no nation could be asked to do more. That message had been delivered by Abbott and had not gone over well since, in reality, he had said that Canada's economy was doing well but that increased defence spending would affect domestic standards of wealth. Pearson, on the other hand, was not opposed to more spending, but perhaps something in the range of $150 million would be more tolerable.[21]

Measuring financial options took up significant time and energy through 1951. Meeting on 17 April to examine the entire defence budget and mutual aid package, the CDC was somewhat taken aback to learn that of the $361 million allocated to Mutual Aid for 1951-52, only 9 percent was for actual contracted production. Some $272 million was intended for the provision of surplus wartime British pattern army equipment to a number of European partners. Since statements had been made to the effect that Canada was to be an arsenal of democracy, it seemed that more needed to be done on the manufacturing front. At the same time, the CDC was loath to commit more funds than the combined 1951-52 spending package of $1.875 billion. It was agreed that Canada would be prepared to take on additional production, such as a British order for F-86s, but that this would have to come from a revamping of the existing spending plans, not as additional spending.[22] Curtis was so informed before leaving for Washington for an upcoming meeting with his NATO air force counterparts.

The Washington meeting was one of several from May through July during which the government undertook yet another intensive review of the air program. A shortfall between planned and projected NATO air force capabilities had been identified by alliance planners, and the air force chiefs of the four major powers – the US, Britain, France, and Canada – met in Washington and then in Paris to discuss what could be done to close the gap.

The meeting in Washington took place on 30 April 1951, and Curtis reported back to the Chiefs of Staff Committee (CSC) on 10 May. He returned home from the US capital with a hypothetical requirement for literally thousands of aircraft. He set out a proposal for Canada to provide an additional 289 operational fighter aircraft over and above the 203 previously requested. The resulting force structure would require twenty-four rather than eleven squadrons for the Integrated Force. The CSC noted this item and asked Curtis to prepare a paper outlining the detailed resource implications.[23]

The issue was on the CSC agenda on 23 May, at which time the Air Force presented the full details of the proposal, one that was nothing short of colossal. The RCAF contribution to filling the gap would call for one additional fighter squadron, a division of light bombers (in lieu of 200 additional fighters), and a transport squadron. A total of 790 F-86Es would be needed to satisfy the fighter needs, including reserve, operational training, supply pipeline, and wastage. A total of 364 light bombers, 16 long-range transports, and over 600 trainers would also be needed. The additional costs would come to $700 million over the 1952-55 period. This plan drew criticism from Lieutenant-General Guy Simonds, the new CGS, who stated that the gap also existed for Army and Navy capabilities. The CSC finally agreed to prepare a paper for the CDC, outlining the situation and the resource requirements that Curtis had brought home from Washington.[24]

On 29 May, the CDC confirmed that Curtis must participate in the follow-on meeting in Paris, since it would be an inexplicable about-face for Canada not to take part in these talks after complaining that it had not been consulted in the preparation of the Medium Term Defence Plan. Reinforcing this perspective, Curtis advised the ministers that General Dwight D. Eisenhower, in his role as Supreme Allied Commander Europe (SACEUR), had sought to include Canada in these talks but without having to invite all the other NATO nations. Although Eisenhower had not been generally successful in bringing Canada to the table, it was obvious that Canada had to take up this one invitation. Thus, after the usual discussion about the nation's inability to make additional commitments, the CDC approved Curtis's participation. He was advised that "he could, within the authorized financial and manpower programme, explore the possibility of making adjustments within the existing programme" but that the government could not undertake additional financial responsibilities, certainly not before re-examining its land and sea commitments.[25]

Claxton took these decisions to the full Cabinet one week later, but he added a significant twist. In view of NATO's persistent urging of Canada to help fill the gap in aircraft numbers, the CAS, during the Paris conference, would explore how Canada might make a larger contribution, within the existing ceilings on personnel and funding, by deploying only one aircraft type.[26] Although the origin of this stratagem is not apparent, since it had not been discussed by the CDC, it would not have taken an observer long to realize that Canada could contribute more F-86s than CF-100s for the same overall cost (and, as we shall see, with much less difficulty).

At the end of June, Curtis was back and ready to brief the CDC on the results of the Paris meetings. Even though he had advised Eisenhower that Canada could not take on any additional commitments, this had not stopped the allies from identifying Canada as a source of aircraft and units. NATO, Curtis reported, wanted Canada to ensure

> the allocation to the Integrated Force of a division of 12 fighter squadrons with 300 front-line aircraft; a division of 12 light bomber squadrons with 192 front-line aircraft; and one long range transport squadron with 16 aircraft to be based in Canada. The F-86 requirements [for aircraft operated] outside Europe would be 297 aircraft for operational training, squadron build-up in Canada and attrition for the period 1951-54. To this would be added the Integrated Force requirements of 800 aircraft as contained in the Paris Plan bringing the F-86 requirements to a total of 1,097 aircraft including a 100 percent war reserve of 300 aircraft not required after 1954. Thus the current procurement of 790 F-86's would be sufficient until 1954. On the same basis, the procurement of light bombers would be 514, less a war reserve of 192, or a total of 322 up to 1954. (Present Canadian air commitments to the Integrated Force were 11 fighter squadrons with 203 front-line aircraft and 587 for reserve, etc.).
>
> The production for NATO countries of F-86 airframes up to Canadian capacity, [was] estimated to be about 1,800 – apart from the aircraft mentioned [for Canada] and airframes possibly required by the United Kingdom.[27]

These requirements, in addition to manpower and support infrastructure, including flying training organizations with their own aircraft requirement for over six hundred trainers, went well beyond the production that had been previously authorized, and the government was ill prepared to take on these commitments despite the confidence of RCAF and Department of Defence Production (DDP) staffs that they could be met. Without knowing what the bill for the Navy and Army would be, and feeling that the country had shouldered enough already, St-Laurent asked that Claxton's reply reiterate that Canada could undertake no further obligations for 1951-52 and was not prepared to consider commitments for future years.[28]

The proposals that Curtis had brought back from Paris underscored a recurring theme of efficiency through the common use of a small number of aircraft types across the alliance. The whole question of standardized equipment had been around since before the end of the Second World War, and many cooperative schemes were presented for discussion within days of the outbreak of the Korean hostilities. Visiting Ottawa the previous July, Air Chief Marshal (A/C/M) Sir Ralph Cochrane, Vice Chief of the Air Staff (VCAS) of the Royal Air Force, had met with the CSC and described how the US Air Force was interested in the British Canberra medium bomber, which had proven to be quite capable during prototype flights. According to Cochrane, the USAF's concern was whether the aircraft could be produced, if needed, in North America. Cochrane opined that this might be an opportunity for Canada, given its industrial efforts of this type during the war, to contribute to the allied effort. He also made particular mention that the engines used for the Canberra, Rolls-Royce Avons, had been used in the first of the CF-100s, so the Orenda should also fit into the Canberra. Although no decisions were made, the door was left open to Canadian manufacturing participation should the USAF opt for the Canberra.[29]

The Air Members had met some ten days before Cochrane's visit to consider not just the Canberra but also a follow-on to the CF-100.[30] That the RCAF leadership was thinking about a replacement fighter seems nothing short of an amazing display of optimism when one remembers that the second prototype of the CF-100 had yet to fly. In considering their strategy, the air marshals, somewhat surprisingly, believed that finances would not be a problem in designing and fielding a replacement for the CF-100, but they were concerned about NATO standardization and wanted confirmation that designing such an aircraft would not be a duplication of work already underway in Britain or the US. The concern was not so much about money but about the more pressing need – to the Air Force at least – to ensure that the limited number of design personnel available to Avro would not be duplicating work being done elsewhere within the alliance.

The possibility of building both the CF-100 and the F-86 for the RAF was presented to Claxton in late October 1950. The British CAS, Sir John Slessor, who had just completed a visit to Canada, was interested in acquiring both types.[31] At a special meeting with the Air Members on 11 October,[32] he had been keen to find out just how closely the CF-100 would meet a similar RAF operational requirement. Should it not be possible for Canada to send an aircraft to Britain for evaluation, Slessor was prepared to dispatch a team to Canada to look at the fighter. He also hoped that Canada would be able to equip the aircraft with Orenda engines, since Britain was short of the alternative Rolls-Royce Avon. All this coordinated investigation and evaluation was, according to Slessor, of the greatest importance, for if by chance the British were trying to develop a fighter capability that already existed in Canada, they were wasting limited design resources. The two air force chiefs apparently thought along the same lines in this regard.

Shortly after Slessor's visit, however, it became apparent that what the RAF really wanted was the F-86. Slessor had been to Washington, too, and had been told that the RAF could obtain the aircraft through Canadair. GFP and engines would come from the US, and the aircraft would be built by Canada.[33] This cooperative venture quickly ground to a halt, however, because the plan did not satisfy the policy of the US Joint Chiefs of Staff, which precluded the purchase of interceptors by foreign nations through the MDAP. (The Mutual Defense Assistance Act, mentioned earlier, was frequently referred to as the Mutual Defense Assistance Plan, hence MDAP.) In fact, by prior agreement, Britain was supposed to be the primary NATO producer of interceptors, and the US did not want to set a precedent by bailing out the designated alliance supplier and then later having to help other member nations as well.[34]

The response of the Canadian government was not much more positive than that of the Joint Chiefs. On 8 December, Claxton sought Cabinet's support for building 380 F-86s but met with opposition. Cabinet's logic was that even with this request coming from a Commonwealth country and presuming US co-operation, Canada would undertake the work only if the request came formally from NATO. Echoing alliance concerns, the ministers reiterated that the policy on who supplied what aircraft had been previously agreed to and would now have to be applied to any and all NATO partners, including the British, regardless of the situation.[35]

If it had been simply a matter of securing NATO approval for the plan, the problem would have been easily solved, but such was not the case. Even after the political situation was finally resolved in mid-1951, there was still the frustrating conundrum of engines. Britain was counting on the Americans to provide the engines for the jets in the same way that Canada needed US engines for its own first batch of F-86s, but the Americans were not in a position to make good even on their commitments to Canada, let alone add to the bill.

Having presented the broad lines of the scheme in December, Curtis was obliged to return to the CDC on 20 February 1951 with a less satisfactory update.

He indicated that the RCAF had requested thirty-five sets of GFP per month through the USAF and that the RAF had requested an additional fifteen sets in order to build 392 jets for Britain, but that the British had now been informed that these were not available. The RAF had then asked whether Canada could provide complete aircraft but had been told that this, too, was impossible. Slessor had since advised Curtis that his staff was also attempting to reallocate British-built Avon engines in the hope that they could be mated with the F-86. Curtis continued his briefing, stating that in discussions with General Hoyt Vandenberg, his USAF counterpart, on 16 February he had learned that engines were in such short supply in the US that it would be impossible to raise the RCAF allocation from the eleven per month originally agreed to. Curtis had been able to coax the USAF into giving him twenty per month, and with these numbers he felt that the F-86 program could progress at a reasonable rate and would not be far behind schedule by the end of 1952. Squadrons would be activated as planned but would have to make do with fewer aircraft initially. Howe observed that the Orenda, particularly given its production delays, did not seem to be the cure-all for this problem. Only 100 were likely to be built in 1951, and although production should jump in 1952, all of these engines were slated for the CF-100.[36] It was great to have two world-class aircraft, one of which was eagerly sought by the RAF, but without engines the alliance was very far up the proverbial creek, with no means of propulsion in sight.

By late summer of 1951, a solution of sorts had been worked out. The British would get their airplanes, but in 1953 instead of 1951; this was the best that the Americans could manage. Canada's contribution was not small, however, and the CDC revisited the entire issue on 12 September. The committee was briefed on the financial implications of the scheme and asked to approve the allocation of some $71 million of Mutual Aid money for the fabrication of the F-86 airframes. The ministers were told that after much negotiation, Britain had been able to obtain the needed GFP from the US and now wanted formal indication that Canada would provide the airframes, as it had been promising all along. Deliveries would take place at a rate of about fifty per month starting in June 1953 and would enable Britain to field six squadrons as part of the Paris plan. Howe said that there was no problem filling this order, and Claxton confirmed that the Mutual Aid money was available.[37]

With the plan to meet RAF needs settled, the ministers turned to the question of how Canada could best meet NATO needs. Claxton felt that it would be better for Canada to make direct force contributions, as these would put Canada in a better light. From the financial viewpoint, it already appeared that Canada would have to increase its allocations to something like $5.9 billion to make good on its obligations, and if the expanded Mutual Aid sums were added to this, the costs would be that much higher. At several points during the discussion, Prime Minister St-Laurent said that he was very comfortable with the idea of providing aircraft rather than complete units. If this was an important contribution that Canada could make, "he would not be anxious about NATO criticism." "It appeared wiser to make contributions that would be in the best interests of NATO as a whole than to try to make the best showing for Canada by contributing large forces." This approach was seconded by Howe and Pearson, the latter seeing the contribution of these aircraft and the six RAF squadrons as a valuable increase in NATO capability. Returning to the F-86 question, Claxton's deputy minister, C.M. "Bud" Drury, mentioned that the British were looking at fielding their own fighter and that the F-86 was only a stopgap. Curtis then advised the CDC that there would probably be a difference of about one year in the availability of the two fighters, with the F-86 coming first. This prompted Pearson to again say that providing the aircraft by the end of 1953 (that is, before the 31 July 1954 target date for the Integrated Force) would be a valuable contribution. The committee deferred a final decision on additional funding until the Minister of Finance could be available, but it approved the plan on 2 October.[38]

In the early days of the RAF deal, Curtis had laid out the situation in a memo to the chairman of the Chiefs of Staff Committee. Of particular importance was his preamble, in which he explained the concerns and thoughts of the British leadership. From discussions and correspondence, Curtis had concluded that the British were

> gravely concerned over the lack of suitable aircraft to counter the latest Soviet types appearing over Europe. It will be noted that the only suitable types are those currently in production in Canada, namely the F86E and the CF100.
>
> The fact that our present facilities for production of the F86 are greater than those of the CF100 has influenced the UK request. Sir John Slessor was extremely interested in the CF100 and would have included some of this type had we been able to provide them next year.[39]

These same factors were to influence Canadian plans and decisions during 1950 and 1951.

There is little doubt that Canada and its new NATO allies were caught off guard by the Communist invasion of South Korea. The larger Red threat had already been recognized, and Canada and its armed services had been preparing for the possibility of armed conflict, but the scale of those preparations could be compared to those of what C.P. Stacey has called the "Rule of the Dollar" period in the first months of the Second World War, when the Liberal government of the day had ensured that defence spending did not become too demanding.

The summer of 1950 saw the government accept that defence was its number one priority, much as had been the case almost exactly ten years earlier, when Britain had been alone in Europe against the Axis, but this did not mean that Cabinet was ready to forget cost limitations altogether. It was not blind to the needs of the services, but, in the case of the RCAF at least, it would leave it to the Service leadership to figure out the best way to put squadrons in the air from what was little better than a standing start.

1 Louis St-Laurent (left) and Lester Pearson at an early United Nations meeting. Their leadership took Canada onto the world stage, providing the national strategic framework within which the Royal Canadian Air Force would become a dominant element. *Source:* Library and Archives Canada

Clockwise from top:

2 In the immediate postwar period, Canadair took over the rights to the Douglas C-54 design and from it produced North Star transports for the RCAF. *Source:* Canadian Aviation Museum

3 The Avro Jetliner first flew only weeks after the de Havilland Comet, thus becoming the world's second jet transport. It also occupied the business plans and design staff at Avro. *Source:* Canadian Aviation Museum

4 A 418 Squadron Vampire being pushed into the hangar. Although not big, the Vampire gave Canada access to jet operations by using up wartime cash credits from Britain. *Source:* Canadian Aviation Museum

AVRO
Jetliner

EDMONTON 418
AM-A

AW

Top to bottom:

5 Once the Cold War hit, the RCAF was ready to buy whatever could be had. The Mustang was not a jet, but once US foreign military sales could be arranged, it was a well-proven and inexpensive stopgap. *Source:* Canadian Aviation Museum

6 The big engineering challenge, which some feared would be more than Canadair could manage, was the relatively complex centre section of the Sabre's wings. *Source:* Canadian Aviation Museum

Counterclockwise from top left:

7 With the centre section construction challenge behind them, Canadair began turning out jets even faster than called for by procurement plans. *Source:* Canadian Aviation Museum

8 The first of almost two thousand F-86s rolls out of the Canadair facilities at Cartierville in suburban Montreal. *Source:* Canadian Aviation Museum

9 Wilfred Curtis and C.D. Howe (seen behind the engine intake cowl from this angle) were on hand for the first official run of the Chinook engine. The follow-on Orenda would be used in the CF-100 and power Canadair Sabres to the pinnacle of NATO day fighter performance. *Source:* Canadian Aviation Museum

10 Seen here with another Chinook engine is Sir Roy Dobson of the British firm Hawker Siddeley (centre). There was little doubt that the parent company was keen on Avro Canada's successes, but in the end the Toronto facility would have to make its own way through the heavens. *Source:* Canadian Aviation Museum

12 ***(facing page, bottom)*** Design changes forced the modification of the main wing spar on the "Clunk," as the Canuck was nicknamed, and this in turn contributed to major problems with weaknesses in the wing assembly. *Source:* Canadian Aviation Museum

11 C.D. Howe, Brooke Claxton, Bill Waterton, Wilf Curtis, and unknown (R to L) at the acceptance of the first CF-100 in October 1951. The Canadian-designed and manufactured jet, which had been a central theme in Air Force postwar concepts as early as 1943, was finally a reality. Test pilot Bill Waterton is the centre of attention. *Source:* Canadian Aviation Museum

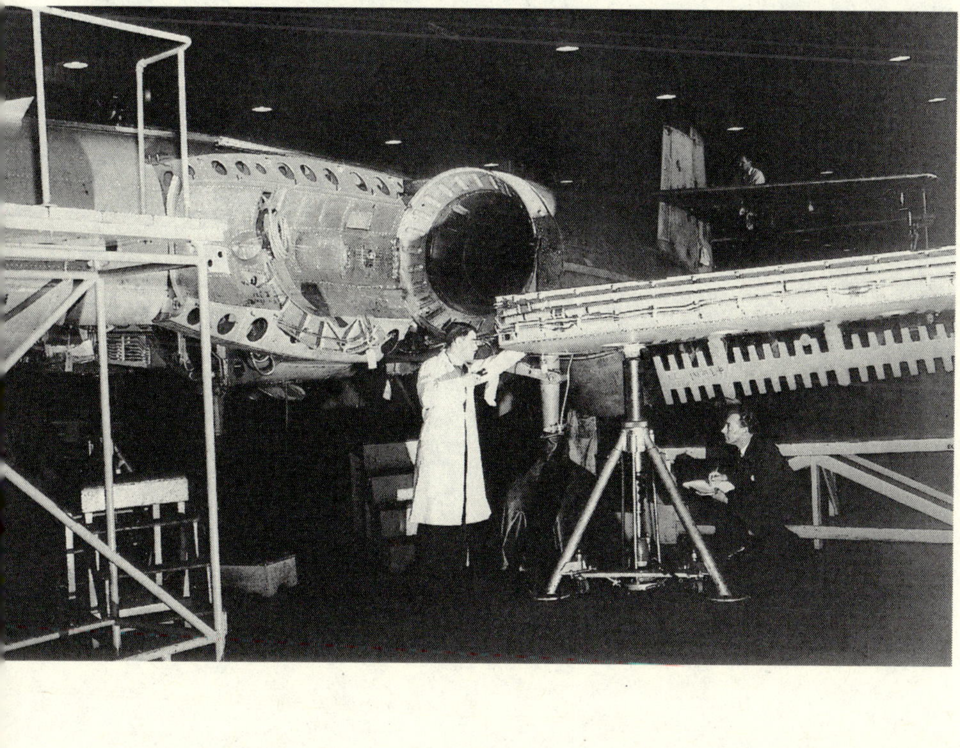

13 The CF-100 assembly line. Mass production was slowed by repeated design changes coming from the RCAF, and production numbers would lag dangerously. C.D. Howe considered cancelling the program. *Source:* Canadian Aviation Museum

15 *(facing page, bottom)* Sabres for the Luftwaffe nearing completion. The Royal Air Force was also a ready customer when British designs were not available to meet the growing threat early in the Cold War. *Source:* Canadian Aviation Museum

14 The finished product, with its pre-production lightning bolt on black paint, sits outside the final assembly hangar at Malton, Ontario. *Source:* Canadian Aviation Museum

16 A Canuck Mk 5 in Belgian service. Despite efforts to sell the aircraft to the RAF, the US Air Force, and even the Colombian government, Belgium was the only international customer. *Source:* Canadian Aviation Museum

7
Juggling Numbers

As Atlantic Alliance commitments were being addressed at the strategic level, and the allies were attempting to resolve the coordination of fighter production, Royal Canadian Air Force planners were looking hard at how best to accelerate expansion within the RCAF to ensure that both Canada and central Europe would have the fighter defences that the Canadian government had agreed to. Strapped into their "mahogany bombers" in Air Force Headquarters in Ottawa and grappling with all the changes that needed to be built into the fighter force structure, these planners must have felt very much as though they were engaged in high G-force combat manoeuvres.

Since early 1950, the Air Staff had been working with a new force structure model, Plan G, that would make optimal use of the funding decisions previously approved by Prime Minister St-Laurent and his ministers. Within weeks of the outbreak of the Korean War, this scheme would be revised at least three times. The original plan had been developed in recognition of the limited resources that were available and hence was a fairly modest proposal. In fact, Plan G had included just five operational fighter squadrons.[1] Immediately following the invasion of South Korea, an accelerated program had been approved and put into play. Then, on 1 September 1950, staff planners produced a third version, combining the original and accelerated versions and referring to them as Target Position A and Target Position B, respectively. Even this was not the final iteration. During the final days of August, work had already begun on a fourth option, which was presented as Target Position C and quickly renamed Plan H. Wrapped up in this twisting series of adaptations were aircraft requirements that changed with mind-numbing speed. The following paragraphs describe events that spanned only a six-month period.[2]

On 12 July 1950, Curtis explained in a memo to the Air Members that the CDC had scheduled a special session in light of the situation in Korea. He indicated his intention to propose a very modest acceleration in the current air program, with an additional proposal for the formation of two or three more fighter squadrons, one of which could be offered for service in Korea. In the same memo, he confirmed that the Americans had 100 Mustangs for sale.[3]

On 17 July, Minister of National Defence Brooke Claxton asked a special meeting of the CSC what, besides supporting Korean operations, the services might be able to manage to improve local defences generally.[4] Curtis wanted to see aircraft and engine production stepped up and explained the Air Force's wishes the next day at a special session of the CSC. Besides changes to the existing plans for long-range transport and maritime patrol squadrons, he recommended that 100 Mustangs be purchased without delay and that production of both fighters be accelerated: the F-86 to seven per month and the CF-100 to five. He also wanted the Orenda production facilities expanded so that up to fifty engines per month could be built should this become a requirement.[5]

These recommendations were probably based on, and were certainly in consonance with, a series of staff checks collectively called "Planning Korean Situation" that had been presented to the Air Member for Air Plans (AMAP) the previous day. The staff discussed aircraft supply and made special reference to the Reserves. The impending delivery of the Mustang was seen as good news. The aircraft was considered still operationally sound and good for both permitting pilots to maintain their fighter skills and providing valuable fighter support for ground operations. As part of the package, an estimate had been done on the cost of sending one Mustang squadron and one transport squadron to Korea. The total annual cost was placed at $22 million, with another $12 million to cover the initial setup. More importantly, the document called for the immediate acceleration of both the CF-100 and F-86 programs as well as the manufacture of Orenda engines.[6]

The Mustang purchase was arranged in a matter of days. Following Cabinet approval, the office of the Secretary of State for External Affairs contacted the Canadian ambassador in Washington on 19 July. He in turn was asked to contact the US State Department to request the purchase under the Mutual Defense Assistance Act (MDAA). Contracts were drawn up and the State Department approved the deal at a cost of $2,507,700. Deliveries could begin in August and were to be completed by November.[7]

Reacting to the crisis in Korea, the Air Staff were busy adjusting the force structure plan that had been under development since the beginning of 1950 as Plan G. When Claxton had announced in January that the total services budget for the coming fiscal year would be $425 million, the RCAF had been authorized just $169 million, which would fall to $165 million in the following years. Claxton had also decided that RCAF personnel strength would not rise above 18,278. It was these resource caps that had caused the planners to develop the original Plan G.

Now the fighting in Korea had precipitated expansion and acceleration in defence preparations. The RCAF document published on 1 September included both the original and modified versions of the Air Force structure, calling these

Target Position A (the original Plan G) and Target Position B, respectively. The biggest growth was in fighters. Target Position A had included three single-engine jet and two twin-engine jet units, whereas Target Position B had six single-engine and three twin-engine jet squadrons. To these Regular units were added two more Auxiliary fighter squadrons. These were part of an overall operational force of sixteen Regular and twelve Auxiliary squadrons. The Regular units were to be at war establishment strength and the Auxiliaries at half strength by 1 December 1953 or sooner. "All Regular Force Squadrons are to be liable for duty under NATO or UNO [United Nations Organization] in accordance with agreements that may be entered into from time to time." The plan stated that the RCAF would keep its previous tasks but was now assigned two others, all to be carried out within the alliance context. The new duties were to provide reinforcements and to contribute to the strategic offensive. In preparing for the full suite of tasks, there were three stated priorities. The first was to establish an effective air defence mechanism for "home or overseas"; the second referred to the defence of Canada, both at sea and on land; and the third dealt with the reinforcement of NATO.[8]

The specifics of Target Position B were impressive compared with the thinking of just a few months earlier. For the fighter element, this meant an increase in strength from three to six F-86 squadrons at 25 aircraft each, and from two to three CF-100 units at 18 aircraft each. This in turn translated into accelerated aircraft production – 10 F-86s per month, for a total requirement of 352, and 5 CF-100s per month, for a total of 134, including the pre-production aircraft. Also included in the 1 September revision were the 100 Mustangs from the US. Target Position B required that all nine jet squadrons be fully operational by 1 April 1953 and that three F-86 squadrons be stationed in Britain in order to gain experience over European skies. After considering the variety of operational and personnel factors involved, the plan proposed equipping the ten Auxiliary squadrons with a mix of 10 jet fighters and 4 Harvard trainers each. To support both the Regular and Auxiliary units, Target Position B came up to a total requirement, with some aircraft being used only in the interim, of 370 F-86s, 77 Vampires, 139 CF-100s, and 150 Mustangs.[9]

The new totals thus called for a Regular build-up from two 12-aircraft single-engine jet squadrons on 1 April 1950 to six 25-aircraft single-engine jet squadrons by 1 December 1953, with an additional three 18-aircraft CF-100 squadrons to be ready by the middle of 1954. At the same time, the Auxiliary force would need 120 single-engine jets, although the type was not stated.[10]

Even before this presumably finalized version of Plan G was ready for approval, the planners were thinking that it was not adequate, and they presented a new proposal, called Target Position C, on 23 August; essentially, it called for a doubling of the Regular component of the RCAF. That same day, Air Commodore (A/C) H.B. Godwin, the Deputy Air Member for Air Plans (Plans) (D/AMAP/P), floated a study brief outlining the possible expansion of the Air Force from twenty-eight to forty-two squadrons. After reviewing Target Position C, the CAS gave his approval and the document was given a new name – Plan H. The following are extracts from the briefing note that accompanied the proposal:

> The RCAF is currently working to a Force of 16 Regular and 12 Auxiliary Squadrons as shown in Target "B" of Plan "G" – Revision. This paper outlines the RCAF Requirements to build up to 30 Regular and 12 Auxiliary Squadrons by 1 Sep 53, with the buildup of a Group of 9 Fighter-Interceptor Squadrons overseas (3 wings of 75 a/c each) completed by this date. One wing of 3 Interceptor Squadrons will be available in Canada in Reserves [sic] for NATO and UNO assignments. This force is referred to as Target Position "C."[11]

The brief went on to describe the specific increases from Plan G to Target Position C:

> Increments to Plan "G"
> Air Defence Command – The following are provided above Plan "G": –
>
> a In Canada
> - 2 Fighter-Interceptor Squadrons
> - 3 Fighter-Interceptor Squadrons available for reinforcement of home or overseas forces
>
> b Overseas
> - 1 Group HQ
> - 2 Wing HQ
> - 6 Fighter Interceptor Squadrons
>
> In terms of aircraft the Target C needs until the end of 1953 are:
>
> - SE [single engine] Regular 1 squadron – 25 aircraft
> - SE Auxiliary 3 squadrons – 28 aircraft
> - SJ [single jet] Regular 8 squadrons – 200 aircraft
> - SJ Auxiliary 7 squadrons – 56 aircraft
> - TJ [twin jet] Regular 3 squadrons – 54 aircraft.[12]

When converted to production figures, this structure amounted to twenty-two fighter squadrons requiring 578 fighters for air defence. Almost all of this increase was due to additional F-86s; the CF-100 requirement remained at 134.[13]

Now that a structure had been accepted, at least up to the level of the CAS, attention could turn to equipping the units. Neither Plan G nor its replacement, Target Position B, had been specific about actual aircraft models, at least not in all cases, and Plan H, too, used only generic aircraft types. Resolving this lack of precision and, to be blunt, lack of aircraft occupied the Air Staff for most of the following year.

On 6 September 1950, the Directorate of Requirements (DOR) prepared a table showing the aircraft requirements for the "accelerated Plan G." There were three types of fighters. The "Fighter Interceptor Jet" duties were to be met by the Vampire, of which 74 were on strength (with 3 yet to be purchased), along with 370 F-86s (with 352 on order); the total of 447 aircraft (77 + 370) comprised the stated operational requirement until 31 March 1954. For "Fighter All Weather Jet," there were no aircraft available, but 124 CF-100s were on order to fill an operational requirement for that number. The "Tactical Fighter" was identified as the Mustang. Of these, there were 27 on strength, an operational requirement of 150, and plans to acquire an additional 100.[14]

This was by no means a definitive statement of needs, and throughout the following month the Air Plans staff examined the merits of the two prime players in the fighter force. A paper circulated within the AMAP branch in October 1950 discussed the proportion of F-86 and CF-100 fighters that should be stationed in Canada and in Europe. The paper, and additional minutes, concluded that though the CF-100 was the better all-weather interceptor, the F-86 was cheaper to build and operate and would be more quickly available in the coming years. A/C Godwin, the D/AMAP/P, added a matter-of-fact but nonetheless significant comment on 25 October: "Plans call for all [weather] fighters for [Regular squadrons] in Canada. We could not get them. We have F86E and will get CF100's. These we must use but the plan is still the same." In a final comment on 31 October, the Acting AMAP, A/C J.G. Bryans, confirmed that although the equipment plan for all North American–based Regular fighter squadrons called for the CF-100, F-86s would be used in the interim. He, too, went on to say that this in no way altered the existing plan.[15]

Given the pace of change, it is not surprising that the staff had concerns about what the current plan was or how to make good on aircraft needs. They explored the negative aspects of the issue, and their findings were not reassuring. A staff check done for Godwin at the end of November concluded that the medium-term requirements were beyond the logistical capability of the nation and that, in the case of aircraft production, help would be needed from a foreign source (presumably the US).[16]

This information could not have been well received; certainly, it did not accord with the desire to expand even further. In fact, Claxton wanted to know what more the services needed in the short term rather than over the next four years. On 27 December, the CSC met at Claxton's request to consider what could be done during the next eighteen months, rather than by the middle of 1954, to address the threat. All three services recommended the implementation of "Programme 'B'" (not to be confused with Plan G's "Target Position B"); the RCAF would require 350 additional F-86s in order to bring the Reserve squadrons up to a war establishment of 25 aircraft each, with a 25 percent operational reserve.[17]

The rising aircraft figures were attracting some negative attention at this point. At the 16 January 1951 CSC meeting, the Chief of the General Staff (CGS), Lieutenant-General Guy Simonds, was critical of Air Force plans. When he questioned the apparent high cost of the F-86s, Curtis took the opportunity to explain the rationale for the long-term aircraft acquisition plan. In essence, it called for providing all Regular and Reserve fighter squadrons in Canada with the CF-100, after which 1 Air Division units in Europe would receive this same type. The F-86s initially sent overseas would be brought back to Canada for training purposes. Curtis explained the need for the F-86s in the short term: "If full scale production of the F86's did not go forward now, no first-line fighters would be available for the defence of Canada, and in fact for Europe, until the C.F.-100's were available in quantity, which would not be until after 1952."[18] The pragmatic reality of this approach forestalled further discussion, and the CSC agreed to release the figures of all three services' programs to the Departments of Trade and Commerce and Finance.

The desire to see the Air Force equipped largely with CF-100s was reiterated just days later in Cabinet. The expanded defence capability needed to meet the requirements of NATO, and home defence called for a considerable Air Force structure and building program. For the defence of Canada, there would be 19 interceptor squadrons, each equipped with 18 CF-100s. In addition, there would be 2 Reserve tactical fighter squadrons, each equipped with 18 CF-100s. For the Integrated Force there would be "7 fighter-bomber squadrons, each with 16 CF-100's (equipped with F-86's until 1954-55); 1 fighter reconnaissance squadron with 16 CF-100's; 3 fighter-interceptor squadrons each with 25 F-86's."[19] Aircraft requirements would total 790 F-86s and 728 CF-100s. Although the central thrust of moving slowly to an all CF-100 fleet clearly mirrored Curtis's comments of the previous week, these numbers far exceeded those included in the plans prepared by the staff.

During these same months, Avro was actively marketing the CF-100 to the US Air Force. A unique design was, of course, an advantage, not just for the manufacturer but also for the parent nation's economy. Writing to C.D. Howe on 14 August 1950 to express his thoughts on Avro's two products – the CF-100 and the Jetliner – Sir Roy Dobson was particularly positive about the CF-100. Stating that it was the best all-weather interceptor in existence, he wondered about its international marketability:

> I am interested to know that you think there is a chance of selling it in the States. I feel that in spite of its excellent qualities, it will only be sold to the States under negotiations between the two Governments. The same remarks apply possibly to the Western Union and Benelux countries.
>
> My opinion is that with a little energetic and careful handling we can recoup all our development expenditure with the CF-100, and its adoption by the U.S.A.F. or the R.A.F., or the Western Union, would firmly establish Canada in the fighter field.[20]

Howe's response did not address these concerns; perhaps he was already a little leery of the Avro product.[21]

Neither Howe's nor the government's position on marketing the CF-100 would deter Avro from doing its best to interest the Americans. An internal Trade and Commerce memo dated 18 November 1950 from T.N. Beaupré, the executive assistant to the minister, to Deputy Minister M.W. Mackenzie detailed a recent Avro sales foray to the US. The firm had sent Fred Smye and others to Washington and to Wright-Patterson Air Force Base, where the USAF aircraft development agencies were located, to market the CF-100. "Apparently AVRO felt that the R.C.A.F. contract is not big enough to be profitable, and according to Macdonald [R.D. Macdonald, the Trade and Commerce Special Representative in Washington] the Americans are pretty enthusiastic about the plane." Beaupré then drew a significant, and ultimately accurate, conclusion: "I presume that if Canadair also get on the band-wagon and try to sell the F-86 to the Americans there will be an immediate competition for engines, instruments, components, etc."[22]

Smye sent his version of events to Howe's office two days later. He reported that he had just completed a meeting with a USAF evaluation board at Wright-Patterson Field on 15 November. The Americans had had extensive talks with the Avro team and apparently concluded that the aircraft, though being deficient in forward speed, was still a good all-round combat aircraft. Smye went on to say that he was not sure the aircraft would be recommended for purchase and that any decision was likely to include "semi-political considerations" (which, unfortunately for the historian, he did not reveal) in addition to operational factors. If the USAF was interested, Smye had offered aircraft beginning in November 1952 and building up to a rate of 10 per month by June 1953. These deliveries would be made against a total requirement of 225 aircraft.[23]

What he had not mentioned was the weakness of his delivery schedule. Macdonald reported back to Beaupré in early December. He had just returned from Wright-Patterson. The Americans were quite cooperative but firm at the same time: yes, they liked the CF-100 but would be able to use it only if it was available before September 1952.[24] It would not be, so in the end the Americans did not acquire the Avro fighter.

In the early days of March 1951, the RCAF made a quick but remarkable about-face and began to extol the F-86 for Europe, as opposed to a wholly CF-100 equipped force. Throughout the spring of 1951, there was considerable activity in developing the structure of the RCAF contribution to the Allied Air Forces in Central Europe (AAFCE). It was generally accepted that the primary role of the Allied Air Forces would be to counter the Soviet air threat, which meant that their central mission would be to gain and maintain air supremacy. On 8 March, A/C Godwin in a note to the AMAP described the roles of the RCAF contingent as "air-to-air combat, close support and reconnaissance. The ideal situation is where one type of aircraft is suitable for all three purposes."[25] The concept called for eight squadrons of sixteen aircraft each and three others of twenty-five; this structure reflected the 24 January Cabinet discussions. Although Godwin and his planners would have preferred eighteen aircraft per squadron, the AMAP was definite on the split but allowed that twenty-five aircraft might become the norm. In any case, there was full agreement on the use of the F-86E as the aircraft of choice.[26]

On 22 May, Curtis wrote to the CSC to identify the advantages of this single-aircraft strategy and to propose that the Air Division's functions be coordinated as much as possible with USAF organizations in Europe. He pointed to the existing coordination in North America, the commonality of equipment, and the moves towards the integration of certain logistical activities.[27] Indeed, after a reconnaissance in Europe earlier in the month, the Air Member for Technical Services (AMTS) had advised the other Air Members that the Americans would be happy to see the Canadians working with them. It was therefore decided that "in view of the Canadian-US Air Defence Operations in North America and the consequent development of common doctrines, tactics and training, it would be desirable for the RCAF and the USAF to work together on the [European]

Continent."[28] It is clear from this focus on the USAF that senior staff and commanders realized that if the RCAF was to collaborate with the USAF, the use of a common aircraft would have a positive impact on the operational effectiveness of both air forces. If F-86 Sabres could be had in large numbers and with minimal delay in the face of a real threat, it would obviously be more advantageous to have these aircraft rather than the still-to-materialize CF-100 Canucks.

These shifts in policy had been formally recognized when the Air Staff published Plan H on 1 April 1951. The document's preamble explained how, at the urging of the RCAF to make a larger contribution to NATO, the government had approved what amounted to a doubling of the air arm on 21 January. Though acknowledging the primacy of North American air defence needs, Plan H recognized the requirement for an air division in Europe. This organization would have twelve squadrons of F-86 aircraft; units would have sixteen aircraft each by August 1953 and a full complement of twenty-five by June 1954.[29]

Plan H included a number of policy guidance statements. Recognizing that the situation of the nation would change as the years went by, it stated that although overall long-term security goals did exist, specific requirements would have to be submitted to the government annually in accordance with normal practice. Within this context, the RCAF's emphasis for the immediate future would be on the establishment of a "modern Air Defence Force" to such an extent that no other major equipment would be procured until the air defence requirements had been met. The plan had mobilization overtones, and it was necessary to recognize its impact on the Defence Industrial Base. Aircraft and other related material would have to be acquired from Canadian or US sources in order to optimize industrial potential. From the standpoint of aircraft procurement, the details of Plan H called for the use of CF-100s only in Canada by the end of the implementation phase, with a similar reliance on just one type, the F-86, in Europe.[30]

AMAP staff published a forecast aircraft establishment for Plan H on 19 April. The table laid out the requirement for 517 CF-100s, of which 380 would be employed in Canada-based air defence squadrons, with the remainder in training and support units, including two Reserve tactical bomber squadrons. A total of 227 F-86s were listed, including the 203 slated for the eleven NATO squadrons. Again the remainder were allocated to training and support.

Thus, as the summer of 1951 arrived, the RCAF had a reasonable idea of what aircraft it needed and in what quantities. Over the preceding twelve months, there had been something approaching pandemonium in developing the policies, structures, and requirements that would meet Canada's national and alliance security needs and obligations. The same degree of chaos could be seen in the aircraft design and production activities that paralleled the planning.

At Canadair, where there was no requirement for design work, production moved smoothly from initial assembly to actual production-line work in just six months, and the first F-86 Sabre 2 was completed on 31 January 1951.[31] This variant, of which some 350 would ultimately be produced, was, like the US-manufactured F-86A, powered by an American-made General Electric engine, and it was an excellent aircraft. When sixty Sabre 2s were supplied to the USAF for operations in Korea, the American pilots found them superior to the parent North American Aviation version, and there was apparently "considerable competition" to fly the Canadian machines.[32] All things considered, the initial fruits of the Canadair program were a complete success.

As previously discussed, one of the improvements planned for the Canadian-built F-86s was the use of the Avro Orenda engine. There was no doubt that this would greatly improve the fighter's performance; at the same time, the use of a Canadian engine would be a coup for the nation. Employing the Orenda for both the CF-100 and the F-86 would require an increase in production, however, and Curtis had begun working on this issue in September 1950. Perhaps anticipating the success of such a union, the CAS had written the Minister of National Defence on 23 September to recommend the expansion of the Orenda program from the approved 50 engines per month to a full 100 units.[33]

The first test flight of the new F-86/Orenda combination took place in California on 5 October,[34] and Curtis provided an update to Brooke Claxton two weeks later. The AMTS had just visited the US, and the "Americans were extremely enthusiastic over the reports they had had of the performance of the Orenda in the F86 ... If the engines were available now they could be sold immediately." They were not, and Curtis continued his appeal, saying that it was crucial that production be expanded to 100 engines per month, with options to go to 150 to 200 if necessary. When the two men discussed the matter on the same day, however, they decided to take no action until there were actually orders for additional engines.[35] Even after this, Curtis was not comfortable, and by January he was again looking for reasons to increase production. Meeting with the Air Members on 20 January, he stated that 100 engines per month would not satisfy domestic needs and that "we should press for a rate of production that could at least meet our own needs."[36] The data in Appendix B show that Avro reached this rate of production only towards the end of 1953.

Lack of engines and the slow progress on the Orenda continued to dog deliveries of both types of aircraft through the first half of 1951. In early May, the AMTS briefed the Air Members on the CF-100 delays. The production of the Mark 3 was being held up due to engine shortages.[37] Then in June Avro's Paul Dilworth had to explain to Canadair that the RCAF had directed that all available engines would be used for the CF-100. Avro would do everything it could to help Canadair, but the first engine intended for the Sabre production line should not be expected before the end of October and possibly not before the end of the year. A "second" engine would follow four to six weeks later.[38]

This was but one of Avro's difficulties: almost every aspect of its operation in Malton, Ontario, was in chaos to some degree. The underlying problem was that the company had a strong design team but lacked the expertise and experience to effectively turn the design into production capability and on-time deliveries. The wing spar failure of the first prototype had caused considerable angst and delay during the summer and fall of 1950. The following spring, the program suffered a catastrophic loss when the second prototype crashed, killing both crew members. Although the cause was probably hypoxia, which led to loss of consciousness, and not an aircraft-related fault, this did not become apparent for some time, and the stress on management was intense in the meantime. By the fall of 1951, Howe had decided that he would have to appoint his own experienced man to the job held by Walter Deisher. Crawford Gordon, who had worked for Howe during the Second World War and was currently the Department of Defence Production's Director of Production, was his choice.[39]

Gordon's first days on the job were probably happy ones because the company was finally ready to deliver the first of the ten pre-production aircraft. The ceremony took place in Ottawa on 17 October 1951, and Howe's remarks were positive: "This aircraft is a notable Canadian achievement marking as it does a new milestone in Canada's industrial progress ... a triumph of skill and ingenuity ... I am satisfied that Canada will lead all countries in the production of this type of aircraft." Also present, Curtis was equally upbeat: "Five years is a short time for any country to produce from the planning stage to production a modern fighter aircraft."[40]

Had that aircraft been free of major teething problems, the two men's pride might have been well founded, but such was not the case. After the ceremony, the fighter was immediately transferred to the Central Experimental and Proving Establishment in Ottawa, a standard practice for all new types, to undergo normal evaluation. The usual problems were identified, but the wing spar problems also recurred, and it was decided that Avro would have to fix the fault.[41] The aircraft was returned to Malton by Joe Schultz, who later became the RCAF's Director of Flight Safety. He reported, "when I landed at Malton, it was an interesting sight; rivets and things were hanging on to the bottom of the wings through the cracks. Engine nacelles scratched because wings flexed. Engine bullits bent thirty degrees. Quite a mess."[42]

Quite a mess indeed, and one that did not go unnoticed. Throughout October, the Avro situation was featured in many Canadian newspapers. On 6 October, a *Financial Post* article examined the company's problems in detail. Describing how and why it had ended up in its current predicament as a result of trying to build three new products at once – the CF-100, the Orenda, and the Jetliner – the article noted that the company had undertaken a great challenge but concluded that it had done some remarkable things. Had the firm failed? Not according to management, who believed that it had designed and produced three completely new products quickly and inexpensively. The newspaper accepted this view, relating how one large American firm doubted that it could have produced any one of the three in the same time frame for the same money. As for meeting RCAF requirements, Avro acknowledged that there were bugs in the engine but claimed that these would be fixed without undue difficulties. And although Avro was having problems with some of its 400 subcontractors, "it is making Canada independent of foreign sources of supply. (A difficult burden in the last war.)" Finally, said the paper, "unlike Canadair, AVRO cannot draw on parts already being duplicated in production in the US and on design and development know-how already done and paid for in the US by the government there."[43]

In a series of articles running from 8 to 10 October 1951, the *Globe and Mail* was less friendly and was critical of both the government's rearmament plans and the RCAF's accomplishments. Billions of dollars had been committed, but everywhere, the reporter claimed, work was behind schedule. Howe, in an interview with reporter James Hornick, had confirmed that there were problems: "In some cases, he conceded, production was far behind schedule. Corrective measures were being applied. 'All one can do is his best,' the Minister said."[44] The second article concentrated on the F-86 program, specifically on the lack of engines. Having apparently visited the factory in the previous month, Hornick described how the plant was working smoothly and how it could easily expand from twenty to fifty aircraft per month. The problem, he said, was that only twenty engines per month were arriving from the US. Engineless aircraft were sitting waiting outside the plant. Plans to put the Orenda in the Sabre were at least one year from fruition; that fact was "indisputable."[45] The third article looked at the Avro situation. After describing the paper air force that had been created in Ottawa since 1946, Hornick contrasted it with the reality of Avro's attempts to design a world-class fighter without any previous experience in the field. The company had achieved miraculous results but not without difficulties. Now the RCAF requirement had gone from five aircraft per month to twenty-five, and engine needs from twenty to a hundred. Hornick concluded that Avro was "totally unprepared for the assignment. It lacked forewarning, tooling and space ... Far from being the air arsenal it has been painted, Avro is still in the throes of production planning. The gap between development and production has not been bridged. Months of plant rearrangement still lie ahead." The RCAF's equipment plans, he concluded, would end up running late. In sum, "the propaganda balloon has exploded. Canada's air defence was a plan not an accomplishment ... Five years of chest thumping was a fraud."[46]

The *Globe and Mail* followed these articles with an editorial attack on 15 October. Agreeing that the development of a Canadian capability was laudable, the paper blamed Claxton and, to a lesser degree, Howe for the apparent fiasco: "So far as jet planes are concerned, we have neither the bird in the hand nor the bird in the bush. Without the jets, it is ridiculous for ministers to go on prating about jet power."[47] Howe's response was reported by the paper five days later. He had spoken at some length, but the essence of his message was positive:

> Furthermore it should be recognized that design, experimentation, and tooling up for production of the latest types of jet engines and aircraft cannot be accomplished overnight. Moreover, when compared to similar projects in the United Kingdom and the United States, the record of the CF100 has been an enviable one. It has taken us less time to get this aircraft and its Canadian designed Orenda engines from the drawing board into production than the case with the Canberra in England and the Scorpion in the US.[48]

One might reasonably conclude that Howe was happy with things at Avro, but politicians can often speak from both sides of their mouth.

ALTHOUGH CAUGHT UNPREPARED, the RCAF was still able to develop a solid model for the fighter forces intended to defend both North America and Europe. The process was at times confusing and compressed, but the ultimate logic of putting F-86s in Europe alongside similar American aircraft, and of operating the purpose-built North American air defence CF-100s over Canada, was sound. This represented a definitive turning away from the desire to equip the Air Force with only one type of fighter, designed and built in Canada. The realities of the day – the pressing defence situation, the ability to buy more F-86s for the same money, and the lagging production of the CF-100 – all contributed to the Air Staff's change in policy. The original goal of an air force equipped with one domestically designed and built world-class all-weather interceptor that was also operated by our major allies could not and would not be realized, especially not with the difficulties faced by Avro, which simply would not go away.

8

Putting Rubber on the Ramp

BY THE END OF 1951, there was a degree of stability with regard to force structure and aircraft needs. Chief of the Air Staff Air Marshal Wilfred Curtis could be satisfied that the Royal Canadian Air Force would be in Europe with a very credible presence, flying the best jet in the NATO arsenal. Cabinet knew that Canada was providing the best forces available within a relatively generous budget and that the nation was doing its bit and more. All had reason to be proud that the fighters being used by Canada were being built from the ground up in Canada and turning heads in the US and Britain.[1]

Perception and reality are two different things, however. In truth, not all was well in the workplace, and stability, even with respect to threat assessments and defence budgets, was a relative thing. Instead of seeing a smooth movement from policy to capability through a strong and capable aviation industry, the years from 1952 through 1954 would be fraught with delays and frustrations, and by the time Avro had worked the bugs out of its planes and their production, the threat of war with the Soviet Union had receded. The return to a sort of stability and the onset of the Cold War meant that governments could once again look at defence spending with an eye to reductions.

By the first week of November 1951, Minister of Defence Production C.D. Howe had had enough of the delays and confusion at Avro. The day after Remembrance Day, in a short, blunt letter to Crawford Gordon, whom he had chosen to head Avro, he told the firm to stop development work until production had been sorted out: "All work in connection with new development is to be suspended, at least until the problems involved in the production of airframes and engines now on order have been resolved and deliveries are being made at a satisfactory rate."[2]

Minister of National Defence Brooke Claxton got wind of this letter and wrote to Howe expressing general agreement but at the same time some reservations. He gave his letter a secret security classification:

> I am sure that you agree that while production is and must be pre-eminent, we must not lose sight of the need for continuous engineering work to ensure that our aircraft is as good as it can be.

> We have, as you know, been seriously disappointed at delays in the production of this aircraft and engine. On the other hand, those failures should not, I believe, at this stage lead us to drop all development work either in respect of the aircraft and engine as they are now or in respect of future development.

Claxton believed that the aircraft and engine were ahead of the competition and felt that "work must be done to ensure that they stay up with the field."[3]

On 19 November, Howe replied to Claxton, explaining his reservations. This letter, too, was classified secret:

> I am greatly concerned about the delay in getting the A.V. Roe production programme under way. I find that development work on the Orenda engine and the CF-100 airframe is far from completed to a point that will permit mass production. I am convinced that all the talent presently involved in development work at the plant is needed to complete development work necessary to put these projects in production. That was the purpose of my letter to Mr. Crawford Gordon ... My experience tells me that it is most difficult to change over a plant engaged in development work to a production plant. If you visit a few of the aircraft plants in the United Kingdom [where Claxton was travelling at the time] you will find that they are all development-minded, not production-minded. The position of A.V. Roe is much the same. I doubt if you have any idea how far away from production the A.V. Roe plant is, particularly in the matter of engines, and also in the matter of the CF-100. It seems to me that, for the time being, every resource must be devoted to production.[4]

Given a few months to get production in gear, Howe concluded, it would be acceptable to resume development work.

Apparently, he was not prepared to wait even that long, however, and in January 1952 he sent Gordon another ultimatum and laid out his final strategy: "If there is no satisfactory solution of the present difficulties in sight in the next two or three weeks, we will have to consider abandoning the project. I am determined that if we can't get production as planned, we will get some other producer." Avro supervisor Fred Smye later commented, "if we had told Howe [how bad the situation was] he would have scrapped the CF-100 and the engine for sure."[5]

As a result of the Hornick articles and other stories in the press (see Chapter 7), the difficulties at Avro had been known for some time, but it was not until February 1952 that the Opposition took the Government to task in the House of Commons. Conservative Douglas Harkness summed it up: "We are not getting these aircraft and engines which we were led to expect two years ago, that we would be getting them in quantity, in fact, we were told that our squadrons would be equipped with them now. I do not think that there is any doubt that the government made a bad miscalculation in connection with these aircraft."[6]

Just what had happened or, more accurately, not happened was explained to some degree in the Avro Aircraft and Gas Turbine Divisions reports that were dispatched to Howe on 20 February.[7] The Orenda report indicated that the first development contract had been issued in April 1947 and that twenty development engines had been produced and tested. By the date of the report, there had been 8,443 test hours, plus an additional 310 hours of flight testing on Lancaster, F-86, and CF-100 aircraft. Engine development (to the first test run) had taken about thirty months, and this met the international standards of the day. Production of fifty engines had been authorized in June 1949, with the production facility to be established with a capacity of twenty engines per month. The engines themselves were needed for the first pre-production aircraft. "Production facilities could not be prepared in sufficient time, therefore 12 of the 50 engines were produced from development facilities by experimental methods. The production rate had since shot up to 100 engines per month and work had been underway to establish the necessary facilities."[8]

The aircraft report indicated that the company had been given the go-ahead for design and manufacture of two prototypes in October 1946 and that the time from start of work to first flight, about forty months, was typical for the industry and the type of aircraft. A technical review section admitted that there had been problems with the centre section spar and that other problems had been found while the former was being analyzed: "Insufficient test flying had been accomplished on the Prototypes, due to the loss of the second aircraft, to allow these deficiencies to be determined at an earlier date. However, the technical aspects of this whole matter have now been thoroughly reviewed with the R.C.A.F. and a reasonable basis of proceeding has now been agreed." Regarding production, the report said that the Mark 4, which would be the first large-scale production model, was being slowed not only by the normal production start-up problems but also by a myriad of changes to production rates and to major aircraft systems and armaments. Despite these problems, a comparison between the CF-100 and other aircraft in its category suggested that the Canuck was clearly the best of the group.[9]

An accompanying letter from Gordon explained some existing problems and the corrective action being taken. He admitted that "the company is blameworthy for not insisting on more prototype aircraft" in order that it might have discovered the centre spar problems more quickly. He confirmed, however, that the problem was in hand and that considerable effort was being spent on correcting the deficiency. He went on to say that the large order for the rocket-equipped Mark 4, which was 70 percent different from the gun-carrying Mark 3, was also causing delays and would result in further slippage. By comparison, North American Aviation had been working on a rocket-firing version of the F-86 for some eighteen months. Had the Air Force wanted large-scale production of a gun-equipped fighter, it would have been possible to offer a better delivery schedule, although there were engine availability problems at present.[10]

The operators had mixed views of the aircraft. Test pilots and those in a position to compare the various jets suitable for the operational task still found the CF-100 to be as good as any. Air Vice-Marshal (A/V/M) Roy Slemon reported to a special Air Members session on 29 May 1952 that during his recent visit to Britain, he had been told by Bill Waterton, now back at Gloster Aircraft, that the CF-100 was still about two years ahead of contemporary British designs.[11] Nevertheless, these remarks did not match the experiences of the RCAF after the ten repaired Mark 2 pre-production aircraft were redelivered in the summer. Problems continued and the Canucks did not gain a good reputation among ground or air crews. There were difficulties with the undercarriage, radios, and fuel management systems. These difficulties arguably had as much to do with an Air Force inexperienced with jet aircraft as with the aircraft itself. This was not a single-engine day fighter but a much larger and more complex two-seat twin-engine all-weather aircraft. By the time the repairs were completed, some eight months after the work began, there had been 4,300 modifications to the aircraft, according to Fred Smye. Jim Floyd, another Avro manager, claimed that the number was closer to 34,000.[12]

Good aircraft or mediocre, the glaring problem was the lack of aircraft. R.D. Macdonald, back from Washington and now assistant director of the Department of Defence Production's Aircraft Division, commented on Avro's delivery difficulties in an internal memo dated 16 September 1952. He felt that the situation had no simple explanation and that there were layers of responsibility:

> In the case of the A.V. Roe company, undoubtedly they are directly responsible for the slippage in the airframe production but there are other contributing causes involving design changes and development work found necessary only after the first airplanes were flown. In addition, it is possible that the R.C.A.F., having been influenced by the British emphasis on research and development, have required A.V. Roe to make additional design changes and to engage in the development of new types at a time when the company was trying to hit its production stride. I am not questioning that it was desirable or necessary, but I am merely saying that it may be true.[13]

In other words, Avro was ultimately responsible for production delays, but perhaps the RCAF, in its desire to ensure that the fighter was the best possible, had distracted the firm from its overriding focus on delivery. The constantly changing nature of both operational requirements and aircraft roles and equipment discussed thus far would seem to confirm this assessment.

Clearly, however, Defence Production was not happy with Avro's performance. The day after Macdonald's attempt to explain the problem, another internal memo, this time from J.P. Donnelly, Chief of the Aircraft Production Section, to G.M. Grant, Acting Director Aircraft Division, was particularly critical of the company. It pointed to the lack of adequate tooling for the production of wing panels, there being only one set, and of horizontal stabilizers, which could be manufactured at a rate of just four sets per month. Donnelly blamed structural failures and management's inability to come to grips with the problem: "The continued setback of this programme has been due to extensive design changes to wings, centre section and tail services [sic] due to structural failures on #18103 [the third prototype]." Management's excuses were simply not acceptable: "Every person in the RCAF and industry knew that if the model was to continue, there would have to be an extensive modification to the design ... [Management's] excuse seemed very weak and indicated to me that there was a lack of co-ordination and liaison between engineering, tooling and production."[14]

If the participants could not sort things out themselves, an oversight body might be needed. At the end of September, Howe and Claxton agreed to form a special panel to both oversee Avro activities and set out specific direction. Howe was "most disturbed with both the present and prospective performance of A.V. Roe ... and attaches great importance to getting it set aright ... The panel will examine, coordinate and expedite Department of Defence Production projects placed with A.V. Roe Limited, but will not relieve either the Departments of Defence Production and National Defence or A.V. Roe Limited of any of their individual responsibilities."[15]

The Interdepartmental Panel on Administration of Defence Contracts with A.V. Roe Canada Limited (IPAV) met at Avro on 31 October to look at the issues surrounding deliveries. After a review of the purpose of the panel, the first item on the agenda was an 18 October DND memo in which Bud Drury had said that the delays were causing the RCAF to rethink its total requirements. The longer it took to get the aircraft in the air, the fewer would be lost to accidents. The corresponding reductions in attrition meant that the Air Force would need fewer aircraft overall to meet its requirements. There was also the question of freezing the Mark 3 design and development and getting on with building the planes.[16]

The nature of design-change difficulties for Avro had been illustrated by a DDP document dated 2 October. The author noted that Mark 3 production was being severely hampered by design changes relating to modifications that were not really necessary for that variant of the aircraft. The Mark 3 "was to go out of production in mid 1953, and it seems obvious that many of the developments proposed will never reach any use in this aircraft." There were problems with the new twenty-channel radio, whereas the existing ten-channel system for the Mark 3 was acceptable. The armament options for the Mark 4 (rockets and bombs) were being reverse-designed into the Mark 3. And was it also necessary to retro-design a target-towing capability, or could this not be done later? The list also covered areas such as canopy design and de-icing, all of which the staff thought more bother than they were worth.[17] Now, at the first IPAV session, Smye indicated that any modifications that had been approved would be incorporated. Finally, the meeting heard of confirmation that by the end of the following month, there would be a firm contract for 400 production aircraft: 59 Mark 3s, 11 Mark 3Ts (trainers), and 225 Mark 4s, with the balance consisting of either Mark 4s, 5s, or 6s.[18]

The decision to build the Mark 3 was reviewed at the second IPAV meeting on 13 November. Crawford Gordon suggested that Avro would have had fewer production difficulties had the RCAF agreed to take more than seventy Mark 3s. A/V/M D.M. Smith countered that the Air Force had never wanted the Mark 3 to go into production and, had the weapons and other configurations been finalized, would have preferred immediate production of the Mark 4; the RCAF had elected to take the Mark 3 in order to get some variant of the Canuck into service as quickly as possible. According to Smith, the company had then stated that the minimum viable order, one that would allow smooth transition to the Mark 4, was for seventy aircraft.[19] It seemed like a circular argument, with each party trying to shift blame to the other.

Just ten days earlier, Claxton had suggested to Howe that limiting modifications might help speed deliveries: "It occurs to me that one way to regulate this would be to lay it down that no modification will be entered upon which would delay production unless the modifications are expressly agreed to by the Deputy Ministers of Defence Production and National Defence." Howe quickly agreed, writing on 7 November that Claxton's suggestion was "timely" and that he had directed the necessary actions to implement this control.[20] The matter was presented at the third IPAV meeting on 3 January 1953, and it was decided that DDP would instruct its office at Avro to curtail all unnecessary work.[21]

While these discussions among politicians, aviators, bureaucrats, and Avro executives went on in private, the press continued to cover those aspects of the story that were known. There was a desire to praise the new aircraft, but reporters were more than ready to point out its problems. A *Toronto Star* editorial on 30 September praised Howe for his determination in seeing through the Avro program.[22] Admitting that there had been problems but stating that these had now been overcome, the column pointed out that both the US and Britain considered the aircraft and engine to be first class. It made reference to a statement by Howe that the US government might consider "Canada as an alternate source of supply in war." Royal Air Force chief Sir John Slessor was also quoted: "I was tremendously impressed with the CF-100 and with Canadian aircraft production in general. The potential of Canada as an aircraft building nation is very great." Howe, the piece concluded, "deserves commendation for his courage in authorizing Avro Canada to develop a powerful jet engine and a versatile jet fighter. These all-Canadian products ought to be the pride of this country. They certainly are the envy of all other countries."

Some weeks later, a *Globe and Mail* article made reference to the design problems at Avro.[23] The reporter, George Bain, had found two ironically juxtaposed articles in the October issue of *Roundel*, the RCAF's internal newsmagazine. One, by Wing Commander (W/C) Bert Houle, the CO of the Central Experimental and Proving Establishment and an experienced fighter pilot, suggested that the best fighter designs were straightforward and uncomplicated. Immediately following Houle's article, one by W/C H.R. Footit described the activities at Avro: costs were up, design hours were up, weight was up. Bain provided extracts from Footit's article:

> The modern all-weather fighter is a maze of radar scopes and scanners, intricate radio and navigation aids, precise instruments and armament sights, air conditioning and cockpit pressurization equipment, ejection seats and other safety features.
>
> At the present pre-production stage, when design changes and service modifications are pouring in, drawing alterations are streaming through the blue print room at the rate of 300 per week. This is normal for any aircraft of comparable complexity at an equivalent stage of production.[24]

If CF-100 production was in disarray, so was engine work. A new engine plant was to open on 29 September, and Gordon believed that it would solve many problems. Howe remained unconvinced.[25]

Availability of engines was no better at Canadair. In January of that year, Curtis had found out that the US Navy intended to use Armstrong Siddeley Sapphires (the British version of the GE J-47 engine)[26] in its F-86s and asked for an update on the Orenda delays.[27] On 27 February, the Air Member for Technical Services (AMTS) gave the other Air Members a comprehensive briefing. The American-built J-47-GE-13 (called in common parlance the "Dash 13"), which was currently going into F-86s, was considered to be underpowered, and the follow-on J-47-GE-27 was only marginally better. The GE-27, which would not be available any sooner than the Orenda, generated just 6,050 pounds of thrust, compared with the Orenda's current 6,300 and projected 6,500 to 6,700 pounds. The Avro engine was clearly better, but there was still concern over whether Avro could make good on its delivery schedule and whether using the Orenda for both the F-86 and the CF-100 would affect the latter's replacement engine stocks and availability to foreign buyers. Since alternative engines were available for the CF-100, it was decided that Orendas would be placed in the F-86. To minimize the impact of delivery problems, it was further decided that Orendas would be installed only on aircraft 353 onward and that all subsequent aircraft would be capable of taking either the GE-13 or the Orenda.[28] It was like playing a shell game, only with very big shells that might or, more likely, might not have an engine under them.

Amid the confusion, a plan to provide Orendas to Canadair had been worked out by the first week of March 1952. Gordon reported to Howe that "on the basis of reducing the spares rate for the CF-100 to 50 percent, and with a boost in production, we have promised to deliver 821 Orendas to Canadair by March, 1954. This, of course, again is predicated on bottlenecked items clearing." The plan would be good for Canada and for Avro, thought Gordon, and Howe agreed.[29] By the end of the year, after opening its new facility, Avro was confident enough to suggest that it could go beyond the mandated delivery of 100 engines per month.[30] The fact that Howe was not completely supportive did not deter Gordon. On 27 February, he wrote Howe to propose an initiative to market the Orenda in the US. The Americans had nothing close to the Orenda and were not likely to meet the Canadian engine's performance for another two years: "Thus I cannot help but conclude that an excellent chance exists if we went after the matter aggressively." Howe's reply the following day was brief: "Regarding the sale of this engine to the United States, my understanding is that your full capacity is required for Canada's aircraft programme and that therefore you have nothing to sell." He did not completely slam the door, however. Licensed manufacture was another option and was open to consideration.[31]

Gordon's optimism and Howe's pessimism continued until the end of 1954. Gordon's writing campaign over the winter of 1952-53 included a letter on 7 November 1952 saying that Avro's problems were waning. Management felt that it could hit its "minimum schedule" for aircraft deliveries by the end of the year, including the ten repaired pre-production machines and the first ten Mark 3s. Engine production was actually a bit better than the monthly quota for October, and Avro had "every anticipation of meeting and possibly exceeding the schedule given by [DDP]."[32] Howe was nowhere nearly as confident and was, in his own words, "frightened." He explained his worries to Claxton in a letter on 19 December 1952. That he would put his views in writing is an indication of how seriously he viewed the problem. Referring to plans for a new fighter, he wrote,

> before authorizing these items, I think you should appreciate what has already been spent on the Orenda engine and on the CF-100 to date. I must say that I am frightened for the first time in my defence production experience. I would urge that at least a year be allowed to pass before any further development work at Avro is undertaken, so that they can work out some sort of amortization ... I must tell you that the design staff at Avro is far from competent to undertake work of this importance. Their designing record to date is very bad indeed, measured by any standard.
>
> I hope you will give serious consideration to the dangers inherent in our worsening financial position at A.V. Roe.[33]

Perhaps foreseeing the troubled future of what would eventually become the Avro Arrow, he concluded by suggesting that the work be given to a British firm that could do a better job at a lower cost.

Howe's doubts may have been based on problems like the one reported a few weeks later. A 19 January 1953 DDP document stated that the RCAF and Avro were not communicating well. The writer referred to one instance in which the Air Force had asked for a three-point mount for the 20 mm cannon; but then even after it had supplied the company with the drawing, Avro had designed a two-point system. Moreover, discussions on whether to use guns or rockets had been going on for two years, although the specification clearly called for both. Avro had apparently "thought fit to almost ignore [the dual requirement] on the basis of 'conversations held prior to the publication of the specification.'" With respect to DDP and Avro, the writer had the definite impression that the company "just 'shrugs' off any reference to D.D.P."[34]

Avro's performance was the subject of another letter from Gordon to Howe in November 1953, in which he emphasized that ongoing criticism of the firm was no longer appropriate: "Whereas some criticism may have been justifiable in the past, it is felt that our actual performance, and particularly over the past year, has been such as to warrant the complete confidence of your Department, and the Department of National Defence." Using a summary report of the

Mark 3 contract as evidence, he showed how the company had met and surpassed deadlines. Gordon wanted the rumours stopped and the achievements of the company recognized. He pointed to the on-time delivery of the Mark 4 (the first aircraft was begun on 8 July and completed on 30 September 1953) to show what the company would do in the future. Howe's reply came the following week. He noted that there had been "an improvement in your operations" but reminded Gordon that his mandate included both producing aircraft *and* finding ways to reduce costs. Howe was "looking forward to hearing that you have succeeded in lowering unit costs."[35]

It took Gordon another year to make good on Howe's wishes. On 6 October 1954, Howe wrote to him and made reference to a recent visit to Toronto. At last he appeared happy with the firm's performance: "I was tremendously impressed with the operating improvements since I last saw them. I congratulate you on having assembled a very efficient organization, and on having achieved your production objectives."[36] The DDP review of production and deliveries in Appendix B shows the firm's slow but steady turnaround in performance. Also significant, positive reviews by the objective British aviation journal *The Aeroplane*, discussed in Chapter 9, suggest that Avro had finally put its house in order.

For the moment though, if everything seemed to be going wrong at Avro, the opposite appeared to be true for Canadair. After initial hard work to figure out how to manufacture the F-86 and to produce the necessary tooling, the firm had never looked back. By the end of 1951, enough F-86s had been manufactured to provide the USAF with sixty fighters for use in Korea and to begin deploying units to Europe. As discussed in Chapter 7, reports from Korea were very positive. A Canadair modification to the flight control hydraulics made the Canadian product much smoother to fly, and the American pilots were impressed.[37]

Canadair was finally able to get its hands on an Orenda engine by June 1952, not by the end of 1951 as Avro had planned, and immediately installed it in the two-hundredth production aircraft – which became the sole instance of the Sabre Mark 3. At the end of the year, the RCAF loaned the jet to American aviatrix Jacqueline Cochrane, who took it to Edwards Air Force Base in California to set a number of speed records. While there, the aircraft was also flown by the famed test pilot Chuck Yeager.[38]

Canadair had intended to switch to the Orenda in the summer of 1952, at the same time that the Mark 3 was built, but Avro's problems delayed this development for a full year, and Canadair had to continue using the GE engine. The Orenda-powered Mark 5 began arriving in Europe in the spring of 1954, and on 20 April Claxton was invited to a ceremony in Montreal celebrating completion of the one-thousandth F-86.[39] A thousand aircraft in less than four years: viewed simply in terms of deliveries, this was a stunning achievement compared with Avro's ninety fighters during the same period.

There is no doubt that there was rubber on the ramp during the period, but going from plans to production was not as easy or efficient as many would have wanted. Happily for the nation and the RCAF, the Sabres that were delivered by Canadair were better than anything that the NATO partners could muster. Sadly for Avro, however, despite the fact that its engine was equally a winning product, the Canadian-designed and built CF-100 fighter did not fare as well.

9
Growing Needs, Growing Concerns

Despite the problems of Avro Canada discussed in the previous chapter, the Royal Canadian Air Force appeared to have a steady appetite for the CF-100, and some dreams for the future. As the Air Force and Avro worked out their disagreements over CF-100 production, and Sabres continued to roll out of the Canadair facility, however, there was growing recognition that the threat of global conflict had been overstated and increasing concern that the level and rate of build-up were similarly inflated. Fundamental reviews and correctives would be necessary.

A summary of actual and projected deliveries prepared by the RCAF at the end of 1951 indicated that orders had been placed for 790 F-86s and 728 CF-100s. These would be needed at an optimal rate of 50 and 25 aircraft per month, respectively. Orenda engines would be required at a rate of 100 per month. The report reiterated that the CF-100 was to be used to equip nine Regular and twelve Auxiliary squadrons in Canada, with the F-86 filling the much more visible NATO commitment.[1] On 17 January 1952, Cabinet discussed the various factors related to force structure and size, including a report from the NATO Screening and Costing Staff as well as public and Opposition views. The ministers agreed that the formal reply to the Screening and Costing Staff must point out that the government would continue to provide an air contribution of 300 aircraft to the Integrated Force, but that initially these squadrons would have 16 rather than 25 aircraft each.[2] The desire to weigh financial obligations continued to play a strong role in government thinking.

In contrast, Minister of National Defence Brooke Claxton was not reserved when describing the overall program to the Canadian public. His remarks on procurement, made on CBC Radio, were reported in the *Ottawa Citizen* on 30 January 1952. About $1.5 billion would be spent to acquire a total of 3,000 new aircraft. Once the CF-100 production was coupled with that of the F-86, the Air Force was planning to field a formed fighter squadron, in Claxton's words, "every two months ... That is quite an undertaking and sometimes we will not always meet the target but we shall do our best." The article reported that "the air force represented the biggest and toughest part of the whole defence effort. The aircraft program alone would eat up one-third of the total equipment program of all three forces."[3]

Several weeks later, Claxton briefed Parliament on the status of the Canadian military. He made a point of quoting General Dwight D. Eisenhower, who, as Supreme Allied Commander Europe (SACEUR), NATO's senior military commander, saw air power as "the dominant factor in war today." Thus, Canada had focused its efforts on its Air Force:

> There has been an increase to twenty-four squadrons of the regular and auxiliary air force. One squadron has had a tour of duty in the United Kingdom and has returned to Canada, and two more are in the United Kingdom. We have provided the manning and training machinery, and the aircraft, for the build-up at a rate of approximately one squadron every two months, equipped and manned with aircrew and ground crew, until the total of forty squadrons for NATO and the defence of Canada is reached.[4]

Although it appeared that the nation had embarked on a full-speed-ahead policy, there were voices of concern. The Air Members had met on 9 January to conduct a very preliminary examination of the budget for the 1953-54 fiscal year, still some fifteen months away. Looking directly at fighter strength, the Vice Chief of the Air Staff (VCAS) felt that too many F-86s were being held in war reserve – that the number was "unrealistic." This comment precipitated a great deal of discussion as to whether the number could or should be decreased, but in the end it was decided that "no further reduction should be contemplated in the F86 war reserve figures. It was the consensus of opinion that these aircraft would be required in the event of a war."[5]

By the end of 1952, the budget situation was more concrete, and when the Air Members met in special session on 20 December, they were able to review several related issues. First, there was the projected decrease in funding for the following fiscal year: it appeared that the Department of National Defence (DND) would have to shave some $180 million from its budget and that the RCAF's share of this would be about $70 million. Although this did not appear to be a serious reduction, the government intended to ensure that the $325 million earmarked for Mutual Aid was in fact spent for that purpose. If the services did not use the money, it would be given to the Department of Defence Production (DDP) for the letting of contracts to satisfy NATO requirements. This apparent all-or-nothing approach was not good news for the RCAF. The air marshals would have preferred that production be turned over to Mutual Aid only after immediate domestic needs had been met. A sort of shared production and delivery schedule would mean that completing RCAF requirements would take longer, but it would also mean that the production lines of aircraft and materiel needed by the Air Force would stay open longer, so long as the government did not cut RCAF requirements. A split procurement strategy for the CF-100 was a case in point for flexible delivery schedules. The existing project called for deliveries of twenty-five aircraft per month so that the nine Regular squadrons would be fully equipped with eighteen aircraft each by the end of 1954. But there was now an option to equip them with just twelve aircraft initially. And another option called for a shift in deliveries: instead of taking all twenty-five aircraft per month, the RCAF could take twenty per month until the Regular squadrons were equipped, and then just fifteen per month for the Auxiliary units, which would slow down the equipping programs by just two and six months, respectively. The uncommitted aircraft could then be offered to Mutual Aid by mid-1954, with the added benefit, as long as there were no security problems, of placing the CF-100 in the hands of other nations.[6]

It was the F-86 that remained the government's showpiece well into the new year. On 15 May 1953, Claxton reviewed with the Cabinet Defence Committee (CDC) the F-86 component of the 1953-54 Mutual Aid program. A staff review in February had proposed that an additional 54 aircraft and associated spares be offered to NATO; the $24 million price tag would be included in the 1953-54 Mutual Aid package. There was still a serious shortage of first-line fighters in Europe, and these 54 aircraft would be well used. Moreover, Claxton continued, offering up what were now scheduled to be RCAF aircraft would enable the Air Force to acquire an additional 54 Orenda-engined Sabres later on. Of particular concern had been the availability of these engines, and Claxton was able to confirm that supply no longer posed a difficulty. In sum, of the 790 aircraft to be produced with General Electric engines, 370 would go to the Royal Air Force, 120 would be sold to the US Air Force, and now an additional 54 would be for NATO; only about 250 would end up being used by the RCAF. Although these shifts in plans would cause some delays in delivery, it would still be possible to meet the NATO commitment of 219 RCAF aircraft by the end of 1953. The proposal was approved without much discussion.[7]

At the next CDC meeting, on 6 October, Claxton proposed a further transfer of GE-engined F-86s to NATO.[8] The briefing note described the situation:

> Based on a production rate of 20 Orenda equipped F-86s a month during 1954-55, which is the scheduled production rate, the RCAF could transfer an additional 110 F-86s with General Electric J-47 Engines at an estimated value of $55,000,000 (including one year's aircraft spares, spare engines and training equipment) as Mutual Aid and at the same time meet the target of 300 unit establishment aircraft for the Air Division at December, 1954.

In addition, GE engines, which were now considered surplus (due to better-than-anticipated engine life), could be offered for another $24 million. This meant that of the original equipment plan for 790 GE-engined aircraft, the RCAF would now be keeping only 136 and as a result would have 650 of the better Orenda-powered models.

There had been some question at first about splitting Mutual Aid efforts, but the results now appeared very much to the benefit of the Air Force. This was a successful stratagem for Canada, and the RCAF must surely have been happy to have the more capable Orenda Sabres. Unfortunately, however, this cascading strategy had done nothing to promote the cause of the CF-100. In fact, the very initiatives that had been proposed to make the CF-100 more available to NATO had, if anything, helped its competitor.

More daunting still for Avro proponents must have been the blunt comment made by the Deputy Chief of the Air Staff (CAS) of the RAF, Air Marshal Sir Ronald Ivelaw-Chapman, on 24 February 1953, during a visit to Canada. At a special meeting of the Air Members, he stated that the RAF was positively not interested in acquiring the CF-100 as there were several British aircraft of like performance capable of the all-weather role.[9] This may have been more a declaration of national procurement policy than a statement of fact, because two years later the British aviation journal *The Aeroplane* reported that Britain had yet to produce an aircraft that could match the CF-100.[10]

Weeks before Ivelaw-Chapman's visit, the Air Members had reviewed the equipment policy for 1 Air Division yet again. Of the many issues considered, the most intriguing was the notion of replacing the F-86 with the CF-100. This would give the Allied Air Forces in Central Europe (AAFCE) an all-weather capability and give the RCAF much more flexibility. These were not new arguments and why they were put on the table again is not clear, particularly in light of the earlier decision not to station CF-100s in Europe.

NATO was interested in having Canada send CF-100s to Europe, however. In 1953, it was proposed that Canada deploy a complete wing of the jets by 1955. At the Chiefs of Staff Committee (CSC) meeting of 29 September 1953, Curtis's successor, Air Marshal Roy Slemon, said that it could be done but admitted that it would cause problems and would cost in the order of $200 million. CSC chairman General Charles Foulkes thought it impossible to supply aircraft to NATO until North American air defence had been addressed. Although Claxton referred to the proposal as "preposterous," he did admit that the request simply reflected the lack of all-weather resources and the good reputation of the Canadian aircraft.[11]

Just weeks later, in November, the Air Members learned that production of the CF-100 was now down to 15 aircraft per month since the Reserve squadrons could not absorb them more quickly.[12] Surplus CF-100 manufacturing capacity was also looked at by DDP in February 1954. No major NATO equipping could be undertaken until 1955-56 for a number of economic reasons. There were the issues of stable workforce and financing, which had been predicated on the current production rate of one aircraft per working day (240 per year). This rate was deemed appropriate in order to maintain a reasonable long-term production capability, as desired by NATO, and to keep the plant in production until the new CF-105 came onto the assembly line in 1958. Due to this and to RCAF needs, there was no surplus capacity other than for potential small orders for Spain or South America before the 1955 date, at which time there would be a surplus of fifty aircraft. These could then be used as part of Canada's Mutual Aid contribution, which, perhaps not coincidentally, was about the same size as the actual transfer of aircraft to Belgium. Similar transfers would also be possible in 1956 and 1957 as the numbers required by the RCAF decreased.[13]

The DDP review was probably the result of efforts by Curtis, who had reached the end of his term as CAS in 1953 and was now in the employ of Avro, to find new markets for the aircraft. The possible sale of CF-100s to Colombia was a topic of considerable discussion in the early part of February 1954. Correspondence between External Affairs, T.N. Beaupré, now an Associate Deputy Minister at DDP, and Deputy Minister of National Defence C.M. "Bud" Drury reveals that the company had been in touch with the Colombians, who were interested in the current version of the aircraft (probably the Mark 3). More to the point, Curtis apparently had been told by C.D. Howe and Lester Pearson that the government would not be averse to such sales.[14] Two questions were posed by the former CAS: (1) Could Avro make more CF-100s? and (2) Could the current version be released to another country?[15] The first question was relatively easy. The plant would soon reach a rate of one aircraft per day using just one shift. It should be possible to increase the rate to fifty aircraft per month by adding a second shift and without having to spend much more on capital equipment (tooling, etc.).[16] If this was the case, however, should the RCAF (and NATO) not have a call on these additional aircraft?[17] The second question was problematic. The Americans had been and would probably remain quite picky regarding who would have access to the Hughes fire control systems, and it was unlikely that the Colombians could be offered anything other than the Mark I, which was not a production variant in any case.[18] No Third World export version was available then or ever.

In June, a related discussion took place between Avro and the government concerning sales and Mutual Aid for NATO nations. It was confirmed that the US would not allow the fire control system, the Hughes MG-2, to be operated by nations other than Canada and Britain.[19] Even if there had been a possibility of direct sales, DDP pointed out to Avro, the European nations were not generally, given their dollar situations, capable of purchasing the aircraft.[20]

There seemed little chance of selling the CF-100 to anyone at this point, but Howe would not even permit the aircraft to be put on show. In fact, there had also been a plan, until early June 1954, to send two CF-100s to Britain for a September appearance at the Farnborough International Airshow. Howe was against the idea, not only because the costs would exceed $100,000 but also because the show was intended to display advanced pre-production types that, compared with the CF-100's old design, would cast the Canadian jet in an unfavourable light.[21]

If the CF-100 was considered old by 1954, surely a replacement was needed. Indeed, such thoughts had been circulating since 1948, when both the RCAF and Avro had begun thinking about a follow-on interceptor. The Air Force was interested in an ultra-modern tailless aircraft, whereas the Avro design office was concentrating on modifying the CF-100 design. Even so, it was not until two years later that Avro was ready with a proposal for what amounted to a swept-wing CF-100.[22]

By January 1952, the RCAF had established an All-Weather Interceptor Requirements Team to "study the Air Defence problem and make recommendations on the performance requirements of an aircraft to fit into the present Air Defence System."[23] The team's final report, published on 20 March 1952, concluded generally that a conventional jet-powered fighter carrying air-to-air missiles and rockets would be capable of meeting the threat. It came to no conclusion on whether Canada would develop such an aircraft itself or cooperate with or buy from the US. It was thought that regardless of the manufacturing arrangement, there would be a sharing of technologies.[24] Several months later, in November, the Air Staff issued the operational requirement "ORI 1-63 Supersonic All Weather Interceptor Aircraft."[25]

Early in 1953, Air Marshal Slemon took the issue of a follow-on aircraft to the CSC. There was no doubt that it would be an expensive undertaking, but no more expensive than similar projects in the US.[26] By the fall of 1953, the questions, left unanswered by the All-Weather Interceptor Requirements Team, had moved to the forefront of force structure and procurement discussions. On 6 October, Slemon again brought the question of a replacement fighter before the CSC. He began by asking for additional funds to keep the Avro design team employed, but the discussion soon focused on the merits of a Canadian-designed and built advanced interceptor. The new CAS pointed to the success of the CF-100, which was at last taking to the field and which was considered to be some two years ahead of its contemporaries. General Foulkes wondered whether it might not be possible to look into a combined project with another nation, or perhaps at having just one type of fighter; might not this sort of arrangement simplify the personnel and unit rotation problems related to having two different types of aircraft and roles on opposite sides of the Atlantic?[27] How soon people seemed to have forgotten that the RCAF had planned the initial CF-100 program in such a fashion! It was too bad that the CF-100 had been slow coming off the production line, and that circumstances had been so pressing that the RCAF could not wait for its optimal force structure.

The specialization and standardization questions were re-examined about six weeks later. On 17 November, while the CSC was considering future aircraft requirements, the point was made that NATO's interest in all-weather fighters appeared to indicate that Canada might be able to specialize in one type of aircraft.[28] The CAS brought this to the attention of the Air Members the following day, and it was generally agreed that although the unit cost of all-weather aircraft would be higher than for a replacement day fighter, there would be fewer aircraft per squadron and a lower loss rate.[29]

Some staff felt that the F-86 should be replaced with a new day fighter, but the VCAS saw the situation differently. Replying to a memo from the Chief of Air Operations that suggested it was time to consider a replacement for the Sabre on the basis of the stated Plan H role of air superiority, he penned an illuminating comment: "So far as I am aware the role of our o'seas force has never been defined by the Operational Commander in the NATO Org. *We had day fighters available and sent them o'seas* [emphasis added]."[30]

Overall, there seemed to be a general desire to move ahead with the design of a Canadian all-weather replacement for both the CF-100 and the F-86. It had been the original intent to support and operate just one type of fighter, and the next-generation aircraft would permit this vision to be realized. But perhaps the problems at Avro had already sown permanent doubts in the minds of Cabinet. Back from a visit to the United States, Slemon announced at the 7 April 1954 Air Members meeting that he was surprised to learn that the USAF was looking at an operational requirement similar to that for the proposed CF-105. An RCAF liaison team had just been to the US and had not uncovered this information. Slemon reviewed his understanding of the situation:

> It was subsequent to the return of this team that the decision was made to proceed with the C105 project as it was assured no other country was planning on building an aircraft to meet the RCAF operational requirement. When governmental approval was granted for the C105, *the CAS assured the Minister that if there was a possibility of procuring a new type to fill the RCAF requirements from other sources, the project would be curtailed* [emphasis added].[31]

There is no corresponding record of this item in Cabinet papers, but it leaves little doubt that there was a conscious retreat from large-scale defence spending – or at least support for domestic aircraft production – as early as 1954. Furthermore, it was the Chief of the Air Staff himself who had made the statement.

While discussions about the future were underway, the short-term NATO desire for an all-weather capability led the RCAF towards the force structure model that it had originally wanted for Europe and that it still hoped to achieve with the contemplated introduction of the CF-105. In October, Slemon agreed to the recommendation from NATO's Supreme Headquarters (SHAPE) that Canada provide all-weather units for the Continent. These would come in the form of one squadron equipped with eighteen CF-100s in 1956 and an additional three units in 1957. The squadrons would be an integral part of 1 Air Division, based in France, and the surplus F-86 units repatriated to Canada would be incorporated in Air Defence Command.[32] The Avro fighter was well received in the press, as shown by an extract from an article in *The Aeroplane,* which stated, "one of the best current two-seat all-weather fighters, in terms of handling, equipment and firepower ... is the CF-100."[33] The last act in the CF-100 implementation would not take place until 1957, when the Belgian Air Force received fifty-three aircraft through Mutual Aid.[34] Though a bit passé by this point, they made a good interceptor when provided free of charge. The greatly reduced nature of the threat also did much to make the CF-100 an acceptable option.

The force structure and acquisition activities that played out in the 1952-54 period were predicated on the threat analyses of the previous years, which, as we have seen, concluded that the Soviet menace and the West's response would send Air Force acquisitions escalating upward. Thus, with NATO building up frantically to face the predicted attacks in the mid-1950s, there must have been some surprise and even consternation when the threat assessments began to paint a much less ominous and more stable picture for the short term. Two examples will illustrate this.

Having been asked to comment on several questions by the Canadian representative to the North Atlantic Council, the CSC considered a number of issues at its 15 October 1952 meeting. Chief among them was the nature of the threat – the Department of External Affairs' assessment was that the risk was diminishing, but the service chiefs did not share this view. External Affairs felt that if the Soviets had not attacked in the previous two years, when NATO had no forces to speak of and before the US had built up its nuclear arsenal, they were less likely to do so in 1952. The CSC finally adopted the position that although it was unlikely that the Soviet Union would deliberately attack, the Soviets had considerable military power that they could bring to bear in the event of an accidental conflict.[35]

About a year later, Eisenhower, now President of the United States, visited Canada and met with Cabinet on 14 November 1953:

> On balance, in the light of the great power possessed by the free world, he did not believe that the Soviet authorities would provoke a war but they would endeavour by every means possible to weaken us ... It was not too difficult to deal with the military threat. Divisions could be raised and the free world geared to war production. The real problem was to counter the gradual subversion of democratic ideas.[36]

Did this signal to the politicians in Ottawa that they had spent enough on defence? It was through the prism of the public's beliefs about Soviet intentions that Canada's defence policy and aircraft program were scrutinized in the press. As in the past, there were views both for and against the government's decisions. A *Vancouver Province* article on 8 January 1952 criticized the aircraft program. Was it not realized that this was a very expensive proposition? Costs were extremely high, with F-86s costing $500,000 each and CF-100s $1 million. Now Ottawa was thinking of a supersonic fighter, but could not Canada have used, or, in the future, use, other nations' aircraft? True, the current crisis had led to the decision in favour of domestic production, but there was still the question of just how far the nation should carry this domestic capability.[37] Opposing arguments, notably those in support of the F-86 program, were equally represented. An 18 February *Montreal Star* editorial pointed to the obvious jobs and money that would flow into Montreal, as well as the evidence of improved economic cooperation between Canada and the US.[38] Similar remarks were found in a *Saskatoon Star Phoenix* editorial the following day, the writer believing that sales and the associated production under Mutual Aid were good for Canada since they would help correct the balance-of-payments situation and demonstrate Canada's solidarity with NATO.[39] The writer of a column in the 28 February *Victoria British Colonist* concluded "that Canadian-American defence co-operation is of a high order; that standardization on common weapons and equipment pays big dividends, and that Canada's young aircraft industry is becoming an important factor in Western defence plans."[40]

The *Montreal Star* turned its attention to Avro's performance in an editorial on 27 February, asking whether the $500 million used in designing the CF-100 and Orenda and in getting them into production had been well spent. Had Parliament done its duty in questioning the government's decisions? Just how much had Avro contributed? The whole issue demanded a review.[41] These and other criticisms brought Sir Roy Dobson back to Canada in early April, partly at Howe's request, to set the record straight. He gave the *Globe and Mail* a full interview in which he stated, "we are a private enterprise organization. But we are very useful to the government because of the planes and techniques we have developed." He countered the perception that the government had spent $100 million on Avro, placing the figure at closer to $10 million. The criticism was not too strong for the government to weather, but another eighteen months passed before it decided to go ahead with the development of the CF-105. In January 1954, Howe announced the awarding of the design contract. The decision had been "delayed by the Cabinet in order to consider the implications of supporting a vigorous domestic aircraft industry."[42]

There seems little doubt that Cabinet's deliberations in 1952 had centred to a large degree on the nation's finances. Even Claxton was concerned by the implications of what he called a "crash buildup" as early as November 1951. He perceived that the rapid build-up begun in the summer of 1950 could become a bottomless drain in which the nations, once they had funded and fielded the medium-term forces, would be constantly pouring money in to keep equipment up to date and personnel trained to use the kit.[43] Claxton made significant mention of the crash plan and its impact in his own papers. Recording his remarks to the eighth session of the NATO Council held from 24 to 28 November 1951 in Rome, he reported that he had forcefully made his concerns known by pointing to the projected need for Canada to spend some $500 million each year until 1958 just to keep the Air Force technically up to date. He spoke about how the "hardware" of war was becoming "obsolete before the first numbers were coming off the line. This was true in the sense that there was already somewhere on the drawing board work which would be so greatly superior that the next one back would cease to be competitive." He continued: "After anxious study I had reached the conclusion that to carry on our contributions to NATO at its present high level of efficiency and do what was necessary in the continental defence would take more money than we were spending today – not less. And our people would not support increased defence expenditures." The solution was to develop a "new look" for the "long pull."[44]

Cabinet discussed the draft report of the Temporary Council Committee (TCC) of the North Atlantic Council on 14 December and felt that it "would not be possible to accept ... that Canada provide additional assistance to European N.A.T.O. countries in the form of economic aid." Indeed, it was thought appropriate that "the costs of services performed by civilian departments as a direct contribution to the defence programme be included in the appropriations of the Department of National Defence."[45] Here was another sign that the government was nearing its limit in terms of the cost of its participation in NATO and defence generally.

This in no way resolved the matter of money. The TCC draft report and defence spending in general were again the subjects of two long discussions at the 5 February 1952 Cabinet meeting. There was definite consensus that defence spending for fiscal year 1952-53 should not exceed $2.4 billion, out of a total budget of $4.4 billion. Prime Minister Louis St-Laurent wanted to hold to the $2.4 billion figure since alliance members would be concerned if Canada appeared to be backing away from its commitments. It was recognized, however, that Canada had said that there could be a flexible approach to spending the money and that if the TCC wanted more Mutual Aid, this could be done – but at the expense of direct Canadian defence spending. Turning to specifics, Claxton reported that of the $2.251 billion that DND had estimated, DDP would be using $1.39 billion for acquisition. DND would also spend $611 million, presumably on personnel and day-to-day operations. The remaining $250 million would go towards paying for the activities that other departments were carrying out in support of DND. Howe then reminded his colleagues that the public was becoming more optimistic about avoiding a war and was questioning the large defence budget. Pearson countered that if the situation seemed to have improved, it was because the Soviets were less inclined to be bellicose when facing a well-equipped NATO. Ultimately, Cabinet decided to spend $2.1 billion on defence.[46]

Attempting to satisfy the NATO requirements for statements of commitment had become a truly unpleasant task but one that simply would not go away. In July 1952, Cabinet was asked to approve the contents of the draft NATO Annual Review. The document presented figures for the year, but as the period after 1 April 1953 would be Canadian fiscal year 1953-54, and the budget had not yet been finalized, the ministers were very reluctant to make any information available. Other nations were inclined to state high values for their contributions since the moneys were coming from US-funded Mutual Aid, but such was not the case for Canada. Although withholding figures would leave Canada segregated from the other member nations, it was thought that the most realistic response would be to simply state that Canada could not at this early stage define precisely what it intended to spend, but that it did intend to "carry out and pay for the planned physical programme already announced."[47] Here was a stratagem that Mackenzie King would have been proud of!

Canada, however, was not the only alliance member that had doubts about its level of financial commitment. By late 1952, opinion across NATO, particularly from the political oppositions, on the need for a massive military build-up – ninety-seven army divisions, 10,000 aircraft (larger than the expeditionary force sent against Hitler a decade earlier) – was turning towards frugality, since the situation in Korea had calmed and the Soviets had not invaded the West. In Ottawa, Claxton remained opposed to increases in the Canadian contribution, saying that the costs that Canada had taken on were already too high.[48] The same issues were topical south of the border, where during the 1952 presidential election Eisenhower was concerned over the fact that defence was costing the US huge sums. In addition, his future Secretary of State, John Foster Dulles, suggested that the existing policy of containment would not work – it would eventually lead to the exhaustion of the West. What Eisenhower wanted was "more bang for the buck" and "security with solvency."[49]

In the normal fashion, the main estimates for fiscal year 1953-54 were reviewed and discussed in early 1953, with Cabinet meeting to approve the budget on 22 January. The total, excluding old age security, sat at $4.405 billion, compared with $4.376 billion for the current year, an increase of just $29 million. There had been only negligible adjustments to defence activities: Defence Production was down $50 million, whereas National Defence was essentially unchanged.[50] This was true Canadian compromise: defence spending had been neither cut, which would have attracted criticism from NATO, nor, just as important, increased on the eve of an election.

The general election of 1953 focused, among other things, on the defence question and the matter of public expenditures. The Currie investigation of 1952 into allegations of misuse of public funds to create a fishing pond for officers at Petawawa had revealed flawed ethics up the Army chain of command. Although the Conservatives could not disagree with the Liberals' defence policy, they could now attack the latter's ability to spend money carefully, since at this point defence amounted to about 40 percent of federal spending.[51] The Liberals won the election, but the issue of defence spending remained close to the surface. On 23 September, Claxton advised St-Laurent of spending shifts in the United States:

> The only substantial reduction so far made was effected through arbitrarily slicing five billion dollars off the appropriations for the U.S.A.F., effected not through economies but through a sharp decrease in the planned effective strength of the US Air Force. A good part of the saving has been made through the cancellation of aircraft building programmes, e.g., Canadair Limited, where a good many millions of dollars spent on [pre-production work] will be completely lost without any remaining benefit.[52]

Claxton's words signalled a stabilization and subsequent retrenchment in defence activities and the end of a tumultuous decade. At the same time, they highlighted the very direct link between government policy, Air Force needs, and aircraft production.

In the two years preceding Claxton's telling letter to St-Laurent, the RCAF and industry had achieved unparalleled results. Canada had provided a contribution to NATO that was remarkable considering the nation's relative size. By the spring of 1954, more than a thousand F-86s had been completed for NATO air forces, CF-100 production was finally showing signs of success, and plans were in place for a follow-on interceptor with remarkable potential. The defence budget did not grow in 1954, however. In the end, Canada fielded only enough CF-100s for its own needs, and even Canadair's success could not escape the reality of shrinking requirements. The great adventure had reached its climax.

10
Fact and Fancy

The typical Canadian – or, more particularly, the typical Canadian who has a passing knowledge of the aviation history of this country – is likely to look on the accomplishments of the late 1940s and early 1950s with pride. These were the spectacular and halcyon days of achievements far and away beyond the greatest dreams of air power promoters, were they not? Such hyperbole is representative, if only to stretch the point for the sake of argument, of the broad lines of the popular history of our Air Force and aviation industry in the decade centred on 1950. Yet this study has shown that there is much that is wrong with such a perception. There was glory and success but failure too. What, then, should we make of the facts that we have just examined? How do we interpret the real story? So far, this book has concentrated on bridging the gap between strategic studies and popular accounts of the Royal Canadian Air Force during this period of history. This chapter will attempt to weave the common strands of earlier histories with the new threads found here.

There was a complex dynamic between a desire to build up and maintain a Canadian capability to design and manufacture fighters and a desire to cooperate for the good of the Atlantic Alliance, all within the constraints imposed by the need to minimize the impact on the country's finances and economic health. Throughout this period, the relative importance of these factors seesawed back and forth, with the RCAF sometimes reacting to external pressures but as often as not making or influencing key decisions. A number of conclusions emerge from this. They point to the important, often central, place of the RCAF in helping set the course for national air power policy; at the same time, they clarify the overarching factors that were beyond the control of air marshals and politicians alike.

The size, organization, and function of the RCAF underwent dramatic changes between 1945 and 1954. Although reactive at times, the Air Staff largely made logical, cogent recommendations and conscious decisions. On those occasions when they were caught unprepared, the air marshals were in good company with their British and American counterparts.

Air Force leaders initially proposed a small but balanced force but soon found themselves obliged to adjust to many conflicting factors. We have seen that in terms of identifying the threat and making appropriate defence plans, the Air

Staff was usually well attuned to the developing situation. There was what might be deemed a false start in the peace of 1945, when Wilfred Curtis's predecessor as Chief of the Air Staff, Robert Leckie, admitted that he had not forced the issue adequately and was thus responsible for the initial unpreparedness of the air service. After that, however, the RCAF was in a constant state of focused, if at times harried, rearticulation and realignment as the Soviet threat and the nation's response to it changed. Leckie said that neither he nor the government could have expected the world situation to develop as it had and that he had implemented the reductions to the RCAF in good faith.[1] Although this may have been his view in retrospect, one may recall that at the time his correspondence with his Royal Air Force counterpart showed significant doubt about the viability of such a small Air Force. There seems, therefore, little question that in 1945 the Chief of the Air Staff saw the situation for what it really was and felt that the Plan B structure was far too slim.

A good part of Leckie's concern was due to the American threat assessment, which he often called alarmist. He was sure that what the Americans were concerned about – a Soviet incursion into Canada's North – would amount to only a diversionary action. This did not stop the RCAF from cooperating with the US, however, or from preparing contingency plans for bilateral action. So earnest were the air planners that the politicians were more than once forced to slow them down and limit their actions, but there was no doubt that a bilateral air defence initiative was effectively in place soon after the end of the Second World War. As Charles Foulkes later wrote, "air defence was to be a joint effort from the start," and the decision was made in 1946, not when the North American Aerospace Defence Command (NORAD) was established in 1958.[2]

It will be remembered that during the immediate postwar period, the RCAF worked closely with the RAF, maintaining the links that had been in place for many years, particularly during the Second World War. Regardless of the decisions that the RCAF made to align itself with the US Air Force, there was never any doubt that it would continue to offer its support and ultimately its aircraft to the RAF. That said, the RCAF did elect to forge operational ties with the Americans. In the context of North American operations, there was no other viable option, but even with regard to NATO, the Air Force took the lead in proposing that it work with the Americans, with logistics being the great selling point. It was a deft solution to the problem of maintaining connections with both of Canada's major allies while ensuring that the RCAF had the most effective operation possible.

One of the most critical areas of cooperation with the allies was the field of equipment standardization, and here the RCAF played both sides of the game. On the one hand, the Air Staff made conscious decisions to ensure commonality and efficiencies when working with other air arms. Conversely, it pushed constantly for a domestic aircraft industry, guaranteeing a source of domestic supply regardless of the possibility of selling the product overseas.

A number of examples of cooperation come to mind. Work with the British began during the closing days of the war, with constant correspondence between the two Chiefs of the Air Staff. Canada was happy to purchase the Vampire jet from Britain. It was the first operational jet fighter to be put in service in North America, and although it did not meet the Canadian requirement for long-range and autonomous action, it was touted as an excellent aircraft for the transition to the CF-100. Curtis was keen to help the RAF in any way that he could. Although he clearly would have preferred to sell the British the CF-100, he was not in the least reluctant to help them acquire Canadian-made F-86s. He and his deputies were deeply involved in setting up the mechanisms that would enable the British to acquire the best available fighter as quickly as possible.

The notion of a domestic design and production capability went back to the early 1920s. In the context of this book, the Air Staff convinced the politicians of the need for a Canadian-based capability to design and manufacture combat aircraft for the RCAF as early as 1942. The government made the final decisions, but it was the RCAF that brought the issue to the ministers' attention and supported the concept through the following decade.

As suggested above, support for the F-86 did not mean that the RCAF was not interested in selling the CF-100 to the RAF, which had expressed a definite though fleeting interest, or even to the Americans. The air marshals had no doubt that the Canadian product was world-class; indeed, they had been told as much by British and American fliers and senior leaders alike. Selling the CF-100 to the allies would have ensured its viability, with the full potential of economies of scale. Foreign sales could only make Canada's aviation industry stronger, and from its earliest days the Air Force had been a keen proponent of a sustainable aviation industrial base, particularly after its difficulties during the Second World War. The best way to maintain the health of Canadian defence production was to seek sales within the allied camp. Sadly, however, these were simply not forthcoming in the numbers that were needed, particularly not in the case of the CF-100.[3]

The air marshals wanted two things of the aircraft industry at the end of the war: ongoing production to "keep the fires lit," as it were, and with those fires a source of operational aircraft to meet national needs first and foremost. The Air Force's Long Range Plan of 1948 said as much:

> The success of the long range plan for the RCAF depends to a large extent on the ability of Canadian industry to produce the weapons. Industry must be nourished

> in peacetime so that it will be ready to play its part in war. If the RCAF is to be a potent force in war, Canadian industry must produce a large percentage of the required aircraft. As the air force is the first line of defence and the only effective means of striking early at the enemy heartland, it must have priority from industry.[4]

The wisdom of this approach was extrapolated beyond the basic issue of self-sufficiency in materiel, making the air marshals' premise all the more remarkable:

> When Canada spends money in Canada to design, develop, and manufacture high technology products like aircraft, the unit cost of such items is not of overriding importance. The money is spent in Canada to provide jobs for Canadian workers who in turn pay Canadian taxes and buy goods and services, helping to strengthen other Canadian companies and the economy as a whole. Design, research, and development are investments in the future, raising the level of Canadian technology and lowering our reliance on foreign technology and expertise.[5]

Wanting a solid industrial base was one thing; making a profitable go of it was another. As we have seen, Canada deliberately embarked on a program of domestic production for domestic military needs and had to accept the probable inefficiencies of a small production run. This issue was noted in a Cabinet Defence Committee (CDC) meeting in the summer of 1949 when the problem of surplus capacity was discussed:

> This characteristic – a great capacity and a small requirement – makes it impossible for us to be self contained in our planning. We cannot base our planning, as most countries do, on the requirements of the Services, because our Services need so little in most lines in relation to our capacity that we would not be justified in setting up production.[6]

This realization, made sixty years ago, provides firm evidence that Canada has and continues to use a combination of military procurement options but has not been able to employ a fully domestic design and production strategy due to limited demand.[7]

There was no doubt that both the CF-100 and the F-86 were world-class aircraft with considerable potential. Development and manufacture of Canada's intended star, the CF-100, did not go well, however. Recall that Minister of Defence Production C.D. Howe forbade its showing at the Farnborough

International Airshow because, in his view, the aircraft was becoming passé even before going into full-scale production; recall also the exchange of terse letters between Howe and Avro Canada's Crawford Gordon and the disappointing rate of aircraft deliveries. The CF-100 was the aircraft that the RCAF wanted to succeed; sadly, however, Avro's production capabilities proved to be too immature to respond quickly to the changes in priorities and design requirements and the demands of the crash programs sparked by the events of 1950.

Although the air marshals wanted a successful Canadian fighter, they also recognized that money was quite simply the major issue. There have been a number of references to this, but a simple statement from the minutes of the 8 March 1946 meeting of the Air Council bears repeating: "The meeting agreed that there was no question as to the advisability of having facilities for production of aircraft and engines in Canada. The dominant factor in any such decision must be economy of production."[8] Perhaps unknowingly, the air marshals were acknowledging a basic truth underscored by Canadian defence economist John Treddenick. When a product is designed and built at home but not as economically as it could be purchased elsewhere, a double-edged sword presents itself: "On the one hand it contributes to the goal of full employment, yet on the other, it reduces the military capability which could be achieved from a limited defence budget. In the absence of a higher order criterion, such tradeoffs are difficult to disentangle and economic significance difficult to assess."[9]

Some researchers feel that economy and jobs tend to win out over maximization of the defence purse, that over the last fifty years there has been a "predominance of economic over military considerations in shaping the defence industrial base."[10] During the period covered in this book, however, this was not necessarily the case: the seesaw between defence and economy was there, to be sure, but it remained relatively balanced. Writing to Wilfred Curtis on the occasion of his retirement as Chief of the Air Staff, Finance Minister Douglas Abbott said,

> it has not always been possible to arrive at complete agreement [with Finance]. The build up of the Armed Forces and particularly the Air Force in the past three years has been a major national task but I feel now that the build-up is largely over and that we have, by this programme, strengthened to a remarkable degree the defences of Canada and our position abroad as a member of [NATO]. This strengthening has been both in the military and the industrial field and in this age those fields are so interdependent that it is essential that they be treated together in any defence consideration.[11]

One does not have to read too far between the lines to find Treddenick's "higher order criterion." Simply stated, the government wanted to reduce defence spending, particularly in view of a stabilizing world security situation. Indeed, we might look to a more recent essay by Treddenick in which he says that the events of the immediate postwar period "created expectations about a Canadian military stature in international affairs whose fulfilment could not survive the fleeting and fortuitous circumstances in which they were forged."[12]

We have seen that Brooke Claxton, too, was aware of this conundrum. He perceived that the rapid build-up that began in the summer of 1950 could become a bottomless drain into which the NATO nations, Canada included, once they had funded and fielded the forces needed for the Integrated Force, would be constantly pouring money to keep equipment up to date and personnel properly trained to use the weaponry.[13]

Serendipity might be the easy way to describe the convergence of sympathetic factors that led to the rapid build-up of the RCAF and to the acquisition of so many Canadian-built aircraft for its fighting elements. Certainly, the combination of a significant threat and the relative strength and prosperity of the nation, particularly compared with its European allies, meant that Canada was bound to play an important role financially, industrially, and militarily. These factors alone, however, do not take into account the nation's ability to field aircraft as good as any, and indeed better than most. To explain this, we need to look to and acknowledge the RCAF's desire to create a capable force equipped with Canadian-built fighters and the air marshals' persistence in pursuing this goal. These were not the plans of dreamers but of visionaries, whose definition of air power for Canada was founded on a technologically capable and economically viable aircraft industry. It was neither this concept nor any lack of willingness to get on with the job that thwarted success. Rather, when the visions proved too technically demanding to succeed and too expensive to endure, they turned, one might conclude, into passing flights of fancy.

Appendix A

Royal Canadian Air Force Headquarters Organization Chart, c. 1947

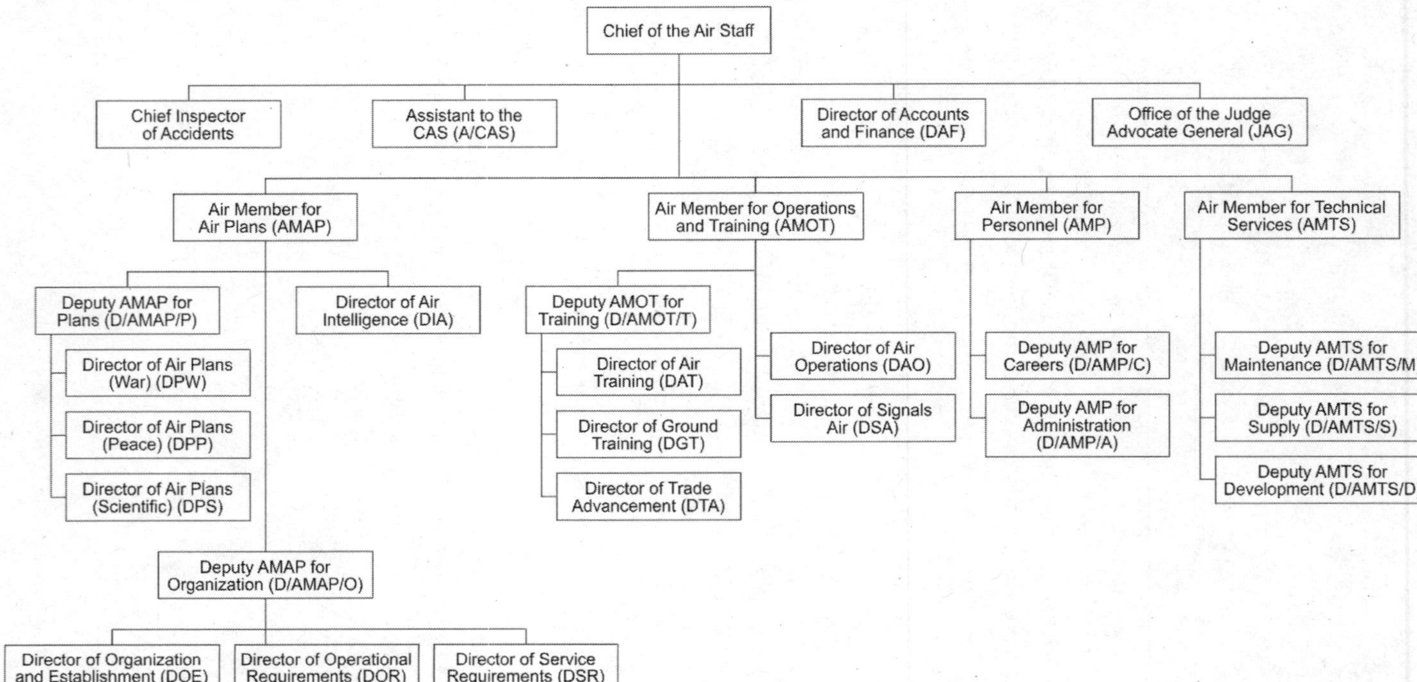

A.1 Organization and Functions – Royal Canadian Air Force Headquarters, c. 1947. Drawn by Michael Bechthold

Source: DHH 181.005 (D1971) "Organization and Functions – Royal Canadian Air Force Headquarters," signed by A/M W.A. Curtis, undated.

Appendix B
Department of Defence Production Aircraft Delivery Statistics, 1951-54

Two different measures of the production successes of Avro Canada and Canadair can be found in primary sources. One gets a good feel for the winner and the loser just by comparing the files kept by the Air Force, the Department of Defence Production (DDP), and Minister of Defence Production C.D. Howe. There is almost no material on Canadair, but the Avro dossiers are thick and contain case after case of problems that needed extensive efforts by the company, the departments, and the politicians to straighten out.

The other, and certainly more precise, analysis tool is the record of monthly aircraft production maintained by the Aircraft Division of DDP.[1] The production figures shown in Tables B.1 to B.4 provide conclusive evidence that, whereas Avro almost never met its monthly quotas, Canadair almost never missed its. A quick comparison of total deliveries each year is also possible and again shows that Canadair was by far the better performer. The wisdom of the Air Force's reversal of its equipping policies during the winter of 1951 was confirmed by the deliveries in subsequent years.

Table B.1

Production figures for 1951

Type	Status	Jan	Feb	Mar	Apr	May	Jun	Jul	Aug	Sep	Oct	Nov	Dec
F-86	Due					16	9	19	18	23	27	23	20
	Delivered					4	9	17	8	22	21	13	28
	Total					8	17	34	42	64	85	98	126
CF-100	Due								1	1	0	0	1
	Delivered								1	1	0	0	1
	Total								1	2	2	2	2
Orenda	Due								4	4	8	0	4
	Delivered								0	0	0	0	0
	Total								6	6	6	6	6

Note: In two cases there appear to be arithmetic errors in the data; however, in the case of Orenda totals for June and July 1952, the source notes that this period was a switchover point between pre-production and production engines – the result is a large (8-engine) anomaly that is not explained.

Source: Adapted from LAC, RG 49, vol. 458, file 200-3-2-1, Aircraft Branch Monthly Progress Report for 1951.

Table B.2

Production figures for 1952

Type	Status	Jan	Feb	Mar	Apr	May	Jun	Jul	Aug	Sep	Oct	Nov	Dec
F-86	Due	24	24	24	20	20	20	20	16	23	26	29	33
	Delivered	24	29	21	18	26	21	21	20	19	13	26	27
	Total	150	179	200	218	244	265	286	306	325	338	364	391
CF-100 pre-production	Due	0	0	1	0	1	1	1	0	0	0	0	0
	Delivered	0	0	0	1	0	0	2	2	2	1		
	Total				3	3	3	5	7	9	10		
CF-100 production	Due										1	2	3
	Delivered										0	2	3
	Total										0	2	5
Orenda	Due	3	4	5	4	6	10	14	18	24	35	40	42
	Delivered	4	0	1	11	8	11	4	4	5	21	22	8
	Total	13	13	14	25	33	44	36	40	45	66	88	96

Source: Adapted from LAC, RG 49, vol. 458, file 200-3-2-1, Aircraft Branch Monthly Progress Report for 1952.

TABLE B.3

Production figures for 1953

Type	Status	Jan	Feb	Mar	Apr	May	Jun	Jul	Aug	Sep	Oct	Nov	Dec
F-86	Due	31	35	38	41	42	42	44	22	42	42	42	0
	Delivered	33	58	18	41	59	47	40	18	35	35	15	
	Total	424	482	500	541	600	647	687	705	740	775	790	
F-86 Sabre Mark 5	Due									1	3	25	44
	Delivered									0	0	7	38
	Total									0	0	7	45
CF-100*	Due	3	3	5	6	9	9	13	12	4	0	0	0
	Delivered	4	5	4	4	3	13	19	0	5	5	1	1
	Total	9	14	18	22	25	38	57	57	62	67	68	69
Orenda	Due	40	45	50	55	60	65	70	68	80	85	85	85
	Delivered	39	45	47	52	110	54	83	0	94	103	88	107
	Total	135	180	227	279	389	443	526	526	620	723	811	918

* This is largely Mark 3 production. Mark 4 production began in November, and two of the three aircraft due by year's end were delivered.

Source: Adapted from LAC, RG 49, vol. 458, file 200-3-2-1, Aircraft Branch Monhtly Progress Report for 1953.

Table B.4

Production figures for 1954

Type	Status	Jan	Feb	Mar	Apr	May	Jun	Jul	Aug	Sep	Oct	Nov	Dec
F-86 Sabre Mark 5	Due	40	40	34	21	20	21	21	12	21	20	22	23
	Delivered	19	64	64	23	29	21	15	26	21	20	17	5
	Total	64	128	192	215	244	265	280	306	327	347	364	369
CF-100 Mark 4	Due	3	5	7	10	12	15	17	11	21	20	22	22
	Delivered	3	4	1	0	9	15	8	2	4	8	24	15
	Total	5	9	10	10	19	34	42	44	48	56	80	95
Orenda	Due	95	95	95	90	85	90	85	45	80	80	90	110
	Delivered	102	86	117	95	93	82	102	49	83	74	83	44
	Total	1,020	1,106	1,223	1,318	1,411	1,493	1,595	1,644	1,727	1,801	1,884	1,928

Source: Adapted from LAC, RG 49, vol. 458, file 200-3-2-1, Aircraft Branch Monthly Progress Report for 1954.

Notes

Abbreviations Used in the Notes

A/DM	Assistant Deputy Minister
AMAE	Air Member for Aeronautical Engineering
AMAP	Air Member for Air Plans
AMAS	Air Member for Air Staff
AMOT	Air Member for Operations and Training
AMRD	Air Member for Research and Development
AMSO	Air Member for Supply and Organization
AMTS	Air Member for Technical Services
AOC	Air Officer Commanding
CAS	Chief of the Air Staff
CDRB	Chief of the Defence Research Board
CGS	Chief of the General Staff
CJS(W)	Canadian Joint Staff (Washington)
CNS	Chief of the Naval Staff
CSC	Chiefs of Staff Committee
CWC	Cabinet War Committee
D/AMAP/O	Deputy Air Member for Air Plans (Organization)
D/AMAP/P	Deputy Air Member for Air Plans (Plans)
D/AMTS/D	Deputy Air Member for Technical Services, Development
DAO	Director of Air Operations
DAP	Director of Air Plans
DAPP	Director of Air Plans – Peace
DARD	Director Air Research and Development
DGR	Director General Research
DHH	Directorate of History and Heritage, Department of National Defence
DM	Deputy Minister
DMDDP	Deputy Minister of Defence Production
DOR	Director of Operational Requirements
DPR	Director of Public Relations
DRB	Defence Research Board
F/L	Flight Lieutenant
G/C	Group Captain
LAC	Library and Archives Canada
MG	Manuscript Group
MND	Minister of National Defence
MND(A)	Minister of National Defence for Air
PARC	Public Archives Record Collection
PCO	Privy Council Office
PSOC	Permanent Supply Officers' Committee

RG	Record Group
S/L	Squadron Leader
USSEA	Under-Secretary of State for External Affairs
VCAS	Vice Chief of the Air Staff
WAC	Western Air Command

Preface

1 A.V. Roe Canada was created when the British firm Hawker Siddeley purchased the Canadian wartime manufacturer Victory Aircraft in 1945. In July 1954, the firm reorganized, setting up its aircraft division as Avro Aircraft Limited and its engine division as Orenda Engines Limited. Greig Stewart, *Shutting Down the National Dream: A.V. Roe and the Tragedy of the AVRO Arrow* (Toronto: McGraw-Hill, 1988), 190.

Chapter 1: An Air-Minded Middle Power

1 The Silver Dart was designed and built by Sir Alexander Graham Bell at Baddeck, Nova Scotia. It was the first aircraft to fly in Canada and accomplished its maiden flight on 23 February 1909. H.A. Halliday, *Chronology of Canadian Military Aviation,* Canadian War Museum Paper No. 6, National Museum of Canada Mercury Series (Ottawa: National Museums of Canada, 1975), 1.

2 At this point, it is appropriate to distinguish between airframes (the body of the aircraft) and a complete aircraft, which includes an engine or engines, either piston or jet. Canada had manufactured no engines during the Second World War.

3 Norman Hillmer and J.L. Granatstein, *Empire to Umpire: Canada and the World to the 1990s* (Toronto: Copp Clark Pittman, 1994), 181-82.

4 See, for example, C.P. Stacey, *Canada and the Age of Conflict,* vol. 2 (Toronto: University of Toronto Press, 1981); James Eayrs, *In Defence of Canada,* vol. 3, *Peacemaking and Deterrence* (Toronto: University of Toronto Press, 1972), and *In Defence of Canada,* vol. 4, *Growing Up Allied* (Toronto: University of Toronto Press, 1980); Hillmer and Granatstein *Empire to Umpire.*

5 R.D. Cuff and J.L. Granatstein, *American Dollars – Canadian Prosperity: Canadian-American Economic Relations 1945-50* (Toronto: Samuel-Stevens, 1978), 2.

6 Ibid., 180-90.

7 Eayrs, *Growing Up Allied,* 14-15.

8 Quoted in Cuff and Granatstein, *American Dollars,* 180.

9 David Dewitt and David Leyton-Brown, eds., *Canada's International Security Policy* (Scarborough, ON: Prentice Hall Canada, 1995), 6.

10 Hillmer and Granatstein, *Empire to Umpire,* 182-83.

11 Eayrs, *Peacemaking and Deterrence,* 137-67; King to Leighton McCarthy, 1 March 1943, King papers, quoted in ibid., 152. See also Cuff and Granatstein, *American Dollars,* 17.

12 Stacey, *Canada and the Age of Conflict,* 363-70.

13 Cuff and Granatstein, *American Dollars,* 19.

14 Hillmer and Granatstein, *Empire to Umpire,* 184-85.

15 Ibid., 185-90.

16 Kim Nossal, "A European Nation? The Life and Times of Atlanticism in Canada," in *Making a Difference – Canada's Foreign Policy in a Changing World Order,* ed. John English and Norman Hillmer (Toronto: Lester Publishing 1992), 83-84.

17 Donald Creighton, *Canada's First Century, 1867-1967* (Toronto: Macmillan of Canada, 1970), 269-70.

18 Nossal, "A European Nation?" 80-81.
19 Lawrence Aronsen, "From World War to Cold War: Cooperation and Competition in the North Atlantic Triangle, 1945-1949," in *The North Atlantic Triangle in a Changing World: North American Relations 1902-1956*, ed. Brian McKercher and Lawrence Aronsen (Toronto: University of Toronto Press, 1996), 201-2.
20 Ibid., 203-4.
21 Creighton, *Canada's First Century*, 274-78.
22 Hillmer and Granatstein, *Empire to Umpire*, 193-96.
23 Aronsen, "From World War to Cold War," 191.
24 Ibid., 192.
25 Cuff and Granatstein, *American Dollars*, 21-23.
26 Dexter to Sifton, 3 June 1947, quoted in Cuff and Granatstein, *American Dollars*, 29.
27 Ibid., 28-30.
28 Ibid., 30.
29 Hillmer and Granatstein, *Empire to Umpire*, 193-96.
30 Cuff and Granatstein, *American Dollars*, 37-63.
31 Ibid., 84-90.
32 Ibid., 110-39.
33 Ibid., 162-70.
34 Michael Slack and John Skynner, "Defence Production and the Defence Industrial Base," in *Canada's International Security Policy*, ed. David Dewitt and David Leyton-Brown (Scarborough, ON: Prentice Hall Canada, 1995), 370.
35 Ibid., 371. See also Cuff and Granatstein, *American Dollars*, 162-70.
36 US State Department memorandum, 20 May 1949, quoted in Cuff and Granatstein, ibid., 173.
37 Ibid., 170-75.
38 Eayrs, *Peacemaking and Deterrence*, 75-77.
39 Ibid., 89-91.
40 Aronsen, "From World War to Cold War," 205-9.
41 Hillmer and Granatstein, *Empire to Umpire*, 200-3.
42 Halliday, *Chronology of Canadian Military Aviation*, 2-3.
43 Larry Milberry, *Aviation in Canada* (Toronto: McGraw-Hill Ryerson, 1979), 103-5.
44 W.A.B. Douglas, *The Creation of a National Air Force: The Official History of the Royal Canadian Air Force*, vol. 2 (Toronto: University of Toronto Press; Supply and Services Canada, 1986), 46-48.
45 Ibid., 43.
46 Milberry, *Aviation in Canada*, 105-10.
47 Stacey, *Canada and the Age of Conflict*, 198-202.
48 Ibid., 219-20.
49 H. Duncan Hall, *North American Supply* (London: Longmans, 1955), 28-31.
50 E.W. Stedman, *From Boxkite to Jet: The Memoirs of an Aeronautical Engineer*, Canadian War Museum Paper No. 1 (Ottawa: National Museums of Canada, 1972), 171.
51 C.P. Stacey, *Arms, Men and Governments: The War Policies of Canada 1939-1945* (Ottawa: Information Canada, 1970), 17.
52 Hall, *North American Supply*, 31-35.
53 Stacey, *Arms, Men and Governments*, 105-6.
54 Eayrs, *Appeasement and Rearmament*, 123-25.
55 J.W. Pickersgill, *The Mackenzie King Record*, vol. 1, *1939-1944* (Toronto: University of Toronto Press, 1960), 159.

56 David J. Bercuson and J.L. Granatstein, *Dictionary of Canadian Military History* (Toronto: Oxford University Press, 1992), 97.

57 Hall, *North American Supply,* 23.

58 Fred Gaffen, "Canada's Military Aircraft Industry: Its Birth, Growth and Fortunes," *Canadian Defence Quarterly* 15, 2 (Fall 1985): 51.

Chapter 2: Planning for Peace

1 LAC, RG 24, vol. 6179, RCAF file 60-1-59, Aircraft Manufacture and Development in Canada, folder 1, DGR to AMAE, "The Canadian Aircraft Industry," 6 November 1942; Minute 2, AMAE to CAS, n.d.; Minute 3, CAS to AMAS, 10 December 1942; Minute 4, AMAS to CAS, 18 December 1942; Minute 5, AMAE to CAS, 23 December 1942. Although no explanation for this change is offered in the material reviewed, the approach is consistent with the RCAF's equipment and operations during the 1920s and much of the 1930s, when the airmen had been heavily involved in supporting other branches of the government. This work was largely paramilitary or non-military in nature, and combat aircraft had not been required. Moreover, as we shall see, the Air Force was, quite reasonably, counting on using the combat aircraft that would be in production and use at the end of the fighting for at least three years.

2 LAC, ibid., Ralph Bell to S.L. de Carteret, DM for Air, no subject, 12 February 1943, covering memo dated 12 February 1943, "Mr. Howe is in."

3 Ibid., AMAS to AMAE, "Construction of Transport Aircraft in Canada," covering "Draft Specification Operational Requirements for High-Speed Military Transport Aeroplane," 15 April 1943. This file contains considerable correspondence between C.D. Howe, the Minister of Munitions and Supply, and C.G. Power, the Minister of National Defence for Air.

4 Ibid., DGR to CAS, "Post-War Type Aircraft to Be Built in Canada," 20 May 1943.

5 Ibid., "Draft Minutes of First Meeting of Committee on Post-War Manufacture of Aircraft," 7 June 1943.

6 DHH, PARC, RCAF file 840-108, vol. 7, "Supporting Data for Item No. 8, Précis the Post-War Aircraft Industry," 6 March 1944; Minutes of Air Council Meeting 5/1944, 7 March 1944, 4. Public Archives Record Collection (hereafter PARC) files are part of the Library and Archives Canada collection held on long-term loan by DHH.

7 Ibid., Minutes of Air Council Meeting 7/1944, 18 April 1944, describes the twin trainer concept.

8 DHH, PARC, RCAF file 840-108, vol. 7.

9 LAC, RG 2, 7C, reel C4876, vol. 16, Minutes of Cabinet War Committee, 27 September 1944, 2; Cabinet War Committee Document 868, "Memorandum to Cabinet War Committee re: Aircraft Industry in Canada," prepared by PCO, n.d.

10 Robert Bothwell and William Kilbourn, *C.D. Howe: A Biography* (Toronto: McClelland and Stewart, 1979), 191-95. The authors indicate that Howe was more interested in the aviation industry than in the needs of the Air Force. Aviation "would expand and it would be an important feature of his reconstruction program, a splendid example of 'intensive action' under his direction."

11 LAC, RG 2, 7C, reel C4876, vol. 15, Minutes of Cabinet War Committee, 3 May 1944, 2; Cabinet War Committee Document 765, "The Post-War Aircraft Industry," n.d.

12 K.H. Sullivan and Larry Milberry, *Power: The Pratt and Whitney Canada Story* (Toronto: CANAV Books, 1989), 43; J.W. Pickersgill, *The Mackenzie King Record,* vol. 1, *1939-1944* (Toronto: University of Toronto Press, 1960), 86-87.

13 DHH, PARC, RCAF file 840-108, vol. 7, Minutes of Air Council Meeting 18/1943, 10 November 1943, 2.
14 LAC, RG 24, vol. 6179, RCAF file 60-1-59, Aircraft Manufacture and Development in Canada, folder 1, Bell to Stedman, no subject, 26 January 1944.
15 LAC, MG 27 III B 20, vol. 209, folder 26, *Globe and Mail* article, 14 June 1944.
16 Greig Stewart, *Shutting Down the National Dream: A.V. Roe and the Tragedy of the AVRO Arrow* (Toronto: McGraw-Hill, 1988), 74-80.
17 James Eayrs, *In Defence of Canada*, vol. 3, *Peacemaking and Deterrence* (Toronto: University of Toronto Press, 1972), 102-5.
18 DHH, PARC, RCAF file 840-108, vol. 7, Minutes of Air Council Meeting 11/1944, 6 September 1944, 1-2.
19 LAC, RG 2, 7C, reel C4876, vol. 16, Minutes of Cabinet War Committee, 13 December 1944, 2; Cabinet War Committee Document 899, Memorandum to CWC from MND(A), no subject, 15 November 1944.
20 LAC, RG 24, vol. 5404, RCAF file 60-5-26, Turbo Research Ltd., Stedman to Brigadier F.C. Wallace, General Manager Turbo Research Ltd., no subject, 14 March 1945.
21 F.W. Hotson, *The de Havilland Canada Story* (Toronto: CANAV Books, 1983), 73.
22 Eayrs, *Peacemaking and Deterrence*, 79-80.
23 In the initial postwar period, the part of the Air Force that was active on a part-time basis was known as the Auxiliary, whereas those personnel and units that would respond only in time of crisis or war were called the Reserve. Slowly the terms became mixed in their usage until by about 1950 it was common to refer to the Regular and the Reserve, although, as with all lexicons, the term "Auxiliary" did not cease to be used on any one date. The terms "Regular" and "Reserve" continued to be used to the end of the century with little change in significance.
24 LAC, RG 24, vol. 5224, RCAF file 19-71-1, RCAF Post War Establishment, folder 1, "Organization Order No. 196, Post War Organization Committee – R.C.A.F.," n.d., 2; Beardmore to G/C E.C. Luke WAC HQ, "Organization – R.C.A.F.," 21 July 1944; Rabnett to AOC WAC, "Organization RCAF," 28 July 1944; Secretary Post War Organization Committee to AMAP, "Post War Organization Committee," 9 August 1944; folder 2, MND(A) to CWC, no subject, n.d.
25 Ibid., folder 2, Assistant CAS to AMSO, "Post-War RCAF – Aircraft Requirements," 16 January 1945.
26 Ibid., folder 3, Curtis (Acting CAS) to Chair of Advisory Committee on Post Hostilities Problems, "Armed Forces Post-War Requirements," 29 March 1945. In this document, Curtis asks the chair to direct the commencement of the associated studies without delay as "this is a matter of considerable urgency."
27 Eayrs, *Peacemaking and Deterrence*, 84-86.
28 LAC, RG 2, vol. 2748, Minutes of Cabinet Committee on Defence Questions, 13 August 1945, 2.
29 Ibid., 14 August 1945, 1.
30 Ibid., 17 and 23 August, 21 and 24 September 1945.
31 LAC, RG 2, A5a, vol. 2637, Minutes of Cabinet Meeting, 28 September 1945; Eayrs, *Peacemaking and Deterrence*, 88-90.
32 Eayrs, ibid., 86-87.
33 Stewart, *Shutting Down the National Dream*, 36.
34 LAC, RG 24, vol. 6179, RCAF file 60-1-59, Aircraft Manufacture and Development in Canada, folder 1, Howe to Bell, no subject, 12 February 1944. Bell provided a "private and confidential" copy to Ferrier (Bell to Ferrier, no subject, 18 February 1944), which no doubt sparked the latter's memo to the CAS.

35 Bothwell and Kilbourn, *C.D. Howe*, 187-88.
36 LAC, RG 24, vol. 6179, RCAF file 60-1-59, Aircraft Manufacture and Development in Canada, folder 1, AMAE to CAS, "The Post War Aircraft Industry," 28 February 1944.
37 LAC, RG 2, 7C, reel C4876, vol. 15, Minutes of Cabinet War Committee, 24 May 1944, 5; Cabinet War Committee Document 788, "Memorandum to Cabinet War Committee re: Aircraft Manufacturing Industry in Canada," prepared by PCO, n.d.
38 LAC, RG 2, vol. 2748, Minutes of Cabinet Defence Committee, Meeting 7, 24 September 1945, 2.
39 Eayrs, *Peacemaking and Deterrence*, 319-23.
40 LAC, RG 24, vol. 5224, RCAF file 19-71-7, RCAF Post War Establishment, folder 4, "Strategic Factors Affecting Canada's Post-War Military Requirements," 30 June 1945, 4-5.
41 David J. Bercuson and J.L. Granatstein, *Dictionary of Canadian Military History* (Toronto: Oxford University Press, 1992), 58, 115.
42 LAC, RG 24, vol. 5224, RCAF file 19-71-7, RCAF Post War Establishment, folder 6, AMAS to CAS, "Submission to Cabinet Defence Committee," 29 November 1945.
43 LAC, RG 24, vol. 5224, RCAF file 19-71-7, RCAF Post War Establishment, folder 1A, "Report of the Post War Planning Committee: Proposed Post-War Plan for the Royal Canadian Air Force," revised 1 December 1945, 1-3.
44 Ibid., 16.
45 DHH, PARC, RCAF file 840-108, vol. 8, "Report of the Post War Planning Committee: Proposed Post-War Plan for the Royal Canadian Air Force," revised 31 October 1945, 2.
46 LAC, RG 2, A5a, vol. 2637, Minutes of Cabinet Meeting, 19 December 1945.
47 DHH, PARC, RCAF file 840-108, vol. 8, Minutes of Air Council Meeting 1946/2, 29 January 1946, 5-6.
48 LAC, RG 2, A5a, vol. 2637, Minutes of Cabinet Meeting, 6 February 1946.
49 Text of "An Address by Col. the Hon. Colin Gibson, M.C., M.P., Minister of National Defence for Air to the Empire Club of Toronto February 28th, 1946," 8. A copy of this speech is held in the collection of the Information Resource Centre, Canadian Forces College Toronto.
50 DHH, CH3/8, Leckie to Sir Arthur Tedder, "Bomber Mail," no subject, 12 February 1946.
51 DHH, CH3/9, Curtis to Col. F.J. Graling, no subject, 28 February 1946.
52 DHH, file 181.004(D44), "Plan B – Post War Plan for the Royal Canadian Air Force," April 1946, ch. 1, paras. 1.01–.04.
53 Ibid., para. 2.01.
54 Ibid., para. 7.01
55 LAC, RG 24, vol. 5225, RCAF file 19-9-71, folder 9, Extract dated 14 November 1946 of Air Members Meeting 6-7 November 1946, para. 164, "Preliminary Proposed Plan of Operation of RCAF Fiscal Year 1947-48"; DHH, PARC, RCAF file 840-108, vol. 9, Minutes of Air Council Meeting 23/1946, 31 October 1946, 3.

Chapter 3: International and Industrial Alliances

1 DHH, PARC, RCAF file 840-108, vol. 8, Minutes of Air Council Meeting 1/1946, 3 January 1946, 2-3.
2 James Eayrs, *In Defence of Canada*, vol. 3, *Peacemaking and Deterrence* (Toronto: University of Toronto Press, 1972), 96-97. Eayrs states that though Canada would not get the Vampire in any appreciable strength before 1948, it still had jet fighters in operation months before the US Air Force.
3 DHH, PARC, RCAF file 840-108, vol. 9, Minutes of Air Members Meeting 17/1946, 11 September 1946, 1-3.
4 Ibid., Minutes of Air Members Meeting 18/1946, 23 September 1946, 5.

5 Eayrs, *Peacemaking and Deterrence,* 101-2. Eayrs suggests that Canada would develop its own aircraft not only because of problems of supply during the Second World War but also because its operational requirements differed from those of its allies. To operate in the north, Canadians would face long distances and so would need aircraft with long-range capability and autonomous target detection capacity.
6 DHH, PARC, RCAF file 840-108, vol. 9, Minutes of Air Council Meeting 16/1946, 25 September 1946, 1-3.
7 Eayrs, *Peacemaking and Deterrence,* 336-38.
8 LAC, RG 2, A5a, vol. 2637, Minutes of Cabinet Meeting, 19 December 1945.
9 Ibid., vol. 2639, Minutes of Cabinet Meeting, 14 November 1946. For King's earlier comments, see ibid., vol. 2638, Minutes of Cabinet Meeting, 9 May 1946.
10 Brian Cuthbertson, *Canadian Military Independence in the Age of the Superpowers* (Toronto: Fitzhenry and Whiteside, 1977). In a view that opposes the primary material cited here, Cuthbertson contends that there was really no impetus to develop an air defence system in North America until the 1948 May Day Parade, when the Soviets first displayed their long-range bombing capability (31). If he was suggesting that no significant moneys were spent, his thesis would make more sense; clearly, however, planners, leaders, and politicians were aware of the problem and were taking action.
11 Eayrs, *Peacemaking and Deterrence,* 339-45.
12 LAC, RG 2, A5a, vol. 2639, Minutes of Cabinet Meeting, 14 November 1946. Like the Air Force, the Army and Navy had developed plans based on the approved establishments from the previous year.
13 Ibid.
14 DHH, 73/1223/1301, Minutes of the 372nd meeting of CSC, 1 December 1946, paras. 2-4.
15 Ibid., Minutes of the 373rd meeting of CSC, 9 December 1946, paras. 1-4.
16 Eayrs, *Peacemaking and Deterrence,* 343; David Bercuson, *True Patriot: The Life of Brooke Claxton, 1898-1960* (Toronto: University of Toronto Press, 1993), 156.
17 LAC, RG 24, vol. 6179, RCAF file 60-1-59, Aircraft Manufacture and Development in Canada, folder 1. Five personal letters were exchanged between the two CAS: Portal to Leckie, 25 April 1945; Leckie to Portal, 23 May 1945; Portal to Leckie, 17 June 1945; Leckie to Portal, 26 June 1945; and Portal to Leckie, 26 September 1945.
18 DHH, 73/1223/1301, Minutes of the 362nd meeting of CSC, 5 September 1946, paras. 4-5; Minutes of the 364th meeting of CSC, 24 September 1946, paras. 4-5.
19 Greig Stewart, *Shutting Down the National Dream: A.V. Roe and the Tragedy of the AVRO Arrow* (Toronto: McGraw-Hill, 1988), 45.
20 Ibid., 50-51.
21 Ibid., 59-61. More detail is provided in a 1979 article by Stewart. In "Canada and the Development of the Aircraft Jet Engine," *Canadian Defence Quarterly* 9, 1 (Summer 1979): 52, he cites Avro employee Winnett Boyd, who attended the meeting.
22 Stewart, *Shutting Down the National Dream,* 63-64.
23 Ibid., 69.
24 LAC, MG 27 III B20, vol. 48, file 9-85-30, folder 5, A.V. Roe Canada Ltd. 1949-1951. Extract from a *Globe and Mail* article, "Flashbacks on the AVRO Story of Engines and Airframes," James Hornick, 10 October 1951.
25 DHH, PARC, RCAF file 840-108, vol. 8, Minutes of Air Council Meeting 5/1946, 8 March 1946, 1-2.
26 Stewart, "Canada and the Development of the Aircraft Jet Engine," 52.
27 LAC, RG 24, vol. 5404, RCAF file 60-5-19, Aircraft Engines Chinook (T.R. 4), K.F. Tupper, Chief Engineer, Turbo Research Ltd., to A/V/M A.L. James, AMTS, "Present Position of R.C.A.F. Jet Engine," 13 April 1946.

28 Ibid., S/L D.L. Holman, Resident Engineer Officer, A.V. Roe Canada Ltd., to Secretary DND (Air) attn.: AMRD/DARD, "Gas Turbine Specifications," 30 December 1946; F.T. Smye, AGM Sales and Contracts, A.V. Roe, to G/C J.A. Easton, no subject, 27 January 1947.
29 Ron Pickler and Larry Milberry, *Canadair: The First Fifty Years* (Toronto: CANAV Books, 1995), 31-37.
30 Kenneth Sullivan and L. Milberry, *Power: The Pratt and Whitney Canada Story* (Toronto: CANAV Books, 1989), 61.
31 Pickler and Milberry, *Canadair,* 36-51.

Chapter 4: Caught Flat-Footed

1 LAC, RG 2, vol. 2748, Minutes of Cabinet Defence Committee, Meeting 25, 9 January 1947; RG 2, vol. 2750, folder 3, Cabinet Document D-97, Memorandum to Cabinet, "Joint Defence Program for the Fiscal Year 1947-48," 11 December 1946; this document includes "Joint Appreciation and Plan Canadian Armed Services," December 1946.
2 LAC, RG 2, vol. 2750, folder 3, Cabinet Document D-97, 11 December 1946; and "Joint Appreciation and Plan Canadian Armed Services," December 1946.
3 DHH, 73/1223/1302, Minutes of 378th Meeting of CSC, 4 February 1947, para. 8.
4 LAC, RG 2, A5a, vol. 2639, Minutes of Cabinet Meeting, 14 January 1947.
5 LAC, RG 2, vol. 2748, Minutes of Cabinet Defence Committee, 14 January 1947, 3-4. Plan E included four Regular fighter squadrons and seven Auxiliary squadrons, but the latter were limited to four aircraft each, thus a total of sixty operational fighters. Plan B had included two Regular fighter squadrons and thirteen Auxiliary squadrons, with a total fighter strength of 120. Details of Plan E are presented later in this chapter.
6 David Bercuson and J.L. Granatstein, *Dictionary of Canadian Military History* (Toronto: Oxford University Press, 1992), 48, 238.
7 James Eayrs, *In Defence of Canada,* vol. 3, *Peacemaking and Deterrence* (Toronto: University of Toronto Press, 1972), 91-92; David Bercuson, *True Patriot: The Life of Brooke Claxton, 1898-1960* (Toronto: University of Toronto Press, 1993), 165.
8 LAC, RG 2, vol. 2748, Minutes of Cabinet Defence Committee, 11 February 1947, 3-4.
9 DHH, 73/1223/1302, Minutes of 383rd Meeting of CSC, 17 March 1947.
10 Ibid.
11 LAC, RG 2, vol. 2748, Minutes of Cabinet Defence Committee, 1 April 1947; RG 2, vol. 2750, folder 3, Cabinet Document D-113, Memorandum to Cabinet Defence Committee, "Review of Joint Appreciation and Plan – Canadian Armed Services," 24 March 1947.
12 LAC, RG 2, vol. 2748, Minutes of Cabinet Defence Committee, 1 April 1947.
13 LAC, RG 2, vol. 2750, folder 3, Cabinet Document D-113, Memorandum to Cabinet Defence Committee, "Review of Joint Appreciation and Plan – Canadian Armed Services," 24 March 1947, Appendix B, "Principal Effects of Recent Reductions of Service Activities," 4.
14 Eayrs, *Peacemaking and Deterrence,* 95; Bercuson, *True Patriot,* 173-74.
15 LAC, RG 24, vol. 5193, RCAF file 15-9-124, folder 1, Minutes of the Second Meeting of the Current Plans and Estimates Committee, 12 May 1947, Item 5, Working Plan for the Committee, 2-3; Minutes of the First Meeting of the AMAP Current Plans Committee, 30 June 1947, Item 1, Preparation of Current Plans, 1-2; Minutes of the Third Meeting of the AMAP Current Plans Committee, 14 July 1947, Item 1, Revision of Plan B, 1-2.
16 DHH, 73/1223/1302, Minutes of 392nd Meeting of CSC, 3 June 1947.
17 Joseph Jockel, *No Boundaries Upstairs* (Vancouver: UBC Press, 1987), 20.
18 DHH, 73/1223/1302, Minutes of 392nd Meeting of CSC, 3 June 1947; Bercuson, *True Patriot,* 180, reports that Claxton had a major influence in the role of the Defence Research Board. Apparently, it was he who made Solandt a member of both the CSC and the CDC.

19 DHH, 73/1223/1302, Minutes of 394th Meeting of CSC, 26 June 1947.
20 Ibid., Minutes of 400th Meeting of CSC, 4 September 1947, para. 10.
21 LAC, RG 24, vol. 6174, RCAF file 19-7-92, Short Range Plan, folder 1, Memorandum, Joint Planning Committee to CSC, "Roles and Relative Sizes of the Canadian Armed Services," 2 September 1947, 6.
22 DHH, 73/1223/1302, Minutes of 400th Meeting of CSC, 4 September 1947.
23 LAC, RG 2, vol. 2748, Minutes of Cabinet Defence Committee, 28 October 1947.
24 Ibid.
25 Ibid.; RG 2, vol. 2750, folder 4, Cabinet Document D-150, Memorandum to Cabinet Defence Committee, "Armed Forces Programme for 1948-49," 20 October 1947, Appendix C, "RCAF Requirements," Part 2, 2.
26 LAC, RG 2, vol. 2748, Minutes of Cabinet Defence Committee, 28 October 1947, 6.
27 Ibid., 4 November 1947, 2-3.
28 LAC, RG 24, vol. 5179, RCAF file 15-1-516, Industrial Mobilization, folder 1, Secretary CSC to CGS, CAS, CNS, CDRB, "Aircraft Industry in Canada," 28 January 1948, covering "Memorandum by the Joint Air Policy Committee: Aircraft Industry in Canada," 30 December 1947.
29 DHH, 73/1223/1303, Minutes of 413th Meeting of CSC, 3 February 1948, para. 23.
30 Ibid., para. 25.
31 LAC, RG 2, A5a, vol. 2642, Minutes of Cabinet Meeting, 19 April 1948.
32 R.D. Cuff and J.L. Granatstein, *Ties That Bind: Canadian-American Relations in Wartime from the Great War to the Cold War,* 2nd ed. (Toronto: Samuel Stevens, 1977), 165-68.
33 Bercuson, *True Patriot,* 164-68.
34 LAC, RG 2, A5a, vol. 2641, Minutes of Cabinet Meeting, 19 February 1948.
35 Ibid., 20 February 1948.
36 Ibid., 23 February 1948.
37 Ibid., vol. 2642, Minutes of Cabinet Meeting, 21 April 1948.
38 LAC, RG 24, vol. 5179, RCAF file 15-1-516, Industrial Mobilization, folder 1, F/L T.L. Scovill, Secretary PSOC to Chairman IDB, "Industrial Mobilization," 4 May 1948.
39 LAC, RG 24, vol. 6174, RCAF file 19-7-92, Short Range Plan, folder 1, D/AMAP/P to AMAP, "Air Force Policy Air Requirements," 4 May 1948; AMAP to CAS, "Aide Memoire for Cabinet Defence Committee Meeting," 2 June 1948.
40 LAC, RG 2, A5a, vol. 2642, Minutes of Cabinet Meeting, 18 June 1948.
41 LAC, RG 24, vol. 6174, RCAF file 19-7-92, Short Range Plan, folder 1, D/AMAP/P to AMAP, no subject, 29 June 1948. Despite these words about a new plan, Plan F was not ready until the later part of 1948 and was quickly overtaken by circumstances. These questions are examined in the following chapter.
42 DHH, 181.004(D45), "Royal Canadian Air Force Plan 'E' (Plan E 1948-49 with Amendments to 11 August 1949)," n.d.
43 LAC, RG 24, vol. 3195, RCAF file 601-38-1, Equipment and Supplies, folder 8, AMAP to CAS, "RCAF Aircraft Holdings," 7 July 1948; Minute 2, CAS to AMAP, n.d.
44 LAC, RG 2, vol. 2750, folder 5, Cabinet Document D-184, "Memorandum for Cabinet Defence Committee Procurement of Vampire Aircraft," 9 June 1948.
45 LAC, RG 2, vol. 2748, Minutes of Cabinet Defence Committee, Meeting 43, 29 July 1948, 3-4.
46 LAC, RG 24, vol. 6174, RCAF file 19-7-92, Short Range Plan, folder 1, Acting AMAP to D/AMAP/P, "Defence Planning – Emergency Plans," 18 September 1948; D/AMAP/O to Acting AMAP, "Aircraft Requirements – Implementation of the 1953 Plan," 20 September 1948.
47 Ibid., Acting AMAP to CAS, no subject, 30 September 1948.

48 DHH, 73/1223/1303, Minutes of 431st Meeting of CSC, 28 September 1948; including JPC document on joint capabilities, 28 September 1948, 5.
49 Ibid., Minutes of 432nd Meeting of CSC, 29 September 1948.
50 LAC, RG 2, A5a, vol. 2640, Minutes of Cabinet Meeting, 27 March 1947.
51 LAC, MG 32 B5, vol. 100, unnumbered folder "Claxton – Statements on Defence," including loose collection of Hansard extracts under cover "Statements by Honourable B. Claxton Minister of National Defence Indicating Flexibility on Defence Policy or Anticipation of Difficulties," Extract from Hansard re Canadian Commercial Corporation Act, 4975, 2 July 1947.
52 Michael Slack and John Skynner, "Defence Production and the Defence Industrial Base," in *Canada's International Security Policy,* ed. David B. Dewitt and David Leyton-Brown (Scarborough, ON: Prentice Hall Canada, 1995), 370; R.F. Swanson, "An Analytical Study of the United States/Canadian Defence Relationship as a Problem of Structure, Response and Process: Problems and Potentialities" (PhD thesis, American University, 1969), 54-55.
53 LAC, RG 24, vol. 6179, RCAF file 60-1-59, Manufacture and Development in Canada, folder 1, "Minutes of Extraordinary CAS Staff Conference," 4 June 1948.
54 LAC, RG 24, vol. 5352, RCAF file 44-1-1, Equipment Procurement from USA – Procedure, folder 2, AMTS to CAS, no subject, 14 February 1948.
55 LAC, RG 24, vol. 5394, RCAF file 60-1-76, Aircraft Operational Requirements – Future Aircraft, Acting AMAP to AMOT, "Operational Requirements Future Aircraft," 23 June 1948. The document introduces the following ORs: OR/1, Day Interceptor Aeroplane; OR/2, Night Fighter Aeroplane; OR/3, Ground Attack Fighter Aircraft; OR/4, All Weather Interceptor Aeroplane; OR/5, Long Range Transport; OR/6, Medium Range Transport.
56 Ibid.; also Minute 2, AMOT to file, 14 July 1948.
57 Ibid., Acting AMAP to AMOT, "Operational Requirements Future Aircraft," 23 June 1948; Operational Requirement No. OR/2 Night Fighter Aeroplane, para. 1.
58 Stewart, *Shutting Down the National Dream,* 90-93.
59 Ibid., 93-97.
60 Ibid., 102-4.
61 LAC, RG2, A5a, vol. 2640, Minutes of Cabinet Meeting, 23 April 1947.
62 LAC, RG 24, vol. 5404, RCAF file 60-5-19, Aircraft Engines Chinook (T.R. 4), Smye to AMTS, no subject, 1 March 1948.
63 Stewart, *Shutting Down the National Dream,* 105-8.
64 LAC, RG 2, A5a, vol. 2641, Minutes of Cabinet Meeting, 30 October 1947.
65 LAC, MG 27 III B20, vol. 49, file 9-85-30, A.V. Roe Canada Ltd., folder 6, Curtis to Claxton, "Acceleration of Development at A.V. Roe," 5 April 1948; Minute 2, Claxton to Howe, 5 April 1948; Howe to Claxton, no subject, 12 April 1948.
66 LAC, RG 2, vol. 2748, Minutes of Cabinet Defence Committee, 15 April 1948.
67 Ron Pickler and Larry Milberry, *Canadair: The First Fifty Years* (Toronto: CANAV Books, 1995), 66-74, 82-83.

Chapter 5: Facing the Threat in Earnest

1 LAC, RG 2, vol. 2748, Minutes of Cabinet Defence Committee, Meeting 48, 8 October 1948; vol. 2750, folder 6, Cabinet Document CD D-196, "Canadian Armed Forces Programme for Fiscal Year 1949-50," 5 October 1948.
2 Ibid., A5a, vol. 2642, Minutes of Cabinet Meeting, 6 October 1948.
3 Ibid., vol. 2750, folder 6, Cabinet Document CD D-196, "Canadian Armed Forces Programme for Fiscal Year 1949-50," 5 October 1948, Tab F, 2.

4 Ibid., vol. 2748, Minutes of Cabinet Defence Committee, Meeting 47, 8 October 1948, 9.
5 Ron Pickler and Larry Milberry, *Canadair: The First Fifty Years* (Toronto: CANAV Books, 1995), 88-90.
6 LAC, RG 2, vol. 2748, Minutes of Cabinet Defence Committee, Meeting 49, 26 October 1948, 2, and Meeting 50, 28 October 1948.
7 Ibid., Minutes of Cabinet Defence Committee, 26 October 1948, 2; LAC, RG 24, vol. 6174, RCAF file 19-7-79, Joint Services Program 1947-48, 1948-49, 1949-50, folder 1, Secretary to CAS to AMAP, AMTS, DAP, "Introductory Speech by CAS to Cabinet Defence Committee, 30 October 1948," 8 November 1948.
8 LAC, RG 2, vol. 2748, Minutes of Cabinet Defence Committee, Meeting 51, 30 October 1948, 5-6.
9 DHH, file R A/C 72 (Canadair Sabre).
10 James Eayrs, *In Defence of Canada*, vol. 3, *Peacemaking and Deterrence* (Toronto: University of Toronto Press, 1972), 104.
11 LAC, MG 27 III B 20, vol. 209, folder 25, *Toronto Daily Star*, 18 November 1948.
12 LAC, RG 49, vol. 1, Organization of Defence Production, folder 1, Order-in-Council PC 5700, 8 December 1948, 1-2.
13 Robert Bothwell and William Kilbourn, *C.D. Howe: A Biography* (Toronto: McClelland and Stewart, 1979), 255. The legislation creating the Department of Defence Production was enacted on 9 March 1951.
14 LAC, RG 49, vol. 1, Organization of Defence Production, folder 1, Order-in-Council PC 1483, 22 March 1951.
15 Ibid., "The Business of Canada's Defence Spending," by G.F. Wevill, 1956.
16 LAC, RG 24, vol. 5352, RCAF file 44-1-1, Equipment Procurement from U.S.A. – Procedure, folder 2, Chairman Canadian Joint Staff Washington to Secretary CSC, "Procurement of U.S. Army, Navy and Air Force Equipment from U.S. Government Sources," 16 July 1948.
17 Ibid., AMTS to CAS, "Procurement of Equipment and Supplies from US by RCAF," 11 August 1948, 2.
18 Ibid., A/V/M Dunlap, Air Member PJBD, to Mr. David Johnson, Canadian Secretary PJBD, no subject, 28 October 1948.
19 R.D. Cuff and J.L. Granatstein, *American Dollars – Canadian Prosperity: Canadian-American Economic Relations 1945-50* (Toronto: Samuel-Stevens, 1978), 6-7; Dan Middlemiss, "The Road from Hyde Park: Canada-US Defence Economic Cooperation," in *Fifty Years of Canada–United States Defence Cooperation*, ed. J.J. Sokolsky and J.T. Jockel (Lewiston, NY: Edwin Mellen Press, 1992), 178; David Bercuson, *True Patriot: The Life of Brooke Claxton, 1898-1960* (Toronto: University of Toronto Press, 1993), 179.
20 LAC, RG 24, vol. 5352, RCAF file 44-1-1, Equipment Procurement from U.S.A. – Procedure, folder 2, Canadian Ambassador to the United States to SSEA, Teletype no. WA210, 26 January 1949.
21 Ibid., AMAP to Mr. C.C. Eberts, Secretary, Canadian Section PJBD, no subject, 2 February 1949.
22 LAC, RG 2, A5a, vol. 2643, Minutes of Cabinet Meeting, 4 February 1949.
23 Ibid., 8 February 1949.
24 DHH, 73/1223/1324, DM to CAS, "Purchase of U.S. Fighter Aircraft," 2 March 1949.
25 LAC, RG 24, vol. 5352, RCAF file 44-1-1, Equipment Procurement from U.S.A. – Procedure, folder 2, AMAP to CAS, AMTS, "Procurement of Equipment from the US," 21 March 1949.
26 Cuff and Granatstein, *American Dollars*, 172-75; Bercuson, *True Patriot*, 180; Desmond Morton, *A Military History of Canada* (Edmonton: Hurtig, 1985), 233.
27 Morton, *A Military History*, 232; Bercuson, *True Patriot*, 204-5.

28 David J. Bercuson and J.L. Granatstein, *Dictionary of Canadian Military History* (Toronto: Oxford University Press, 1992), 146.
29 James Eayrs, *In Defence of Canada,* vol. 4, *Growing Up Allied* (Toronto: University of Toronto Press, 1980), 198.
30 Bercuson, *True Patriot,* 204.
31 LAC, RG 2, vol. 2748, Minutes of Cabinet Defence Committee, 23 November 1949; vol. 2751, folder 8, Cabinet Document CD D-234, "National Defence Programmes," 23 November 1949, Statement 1 – Approved Programme, 1.
32 LAC, RG 2, A5a, vol. 2644, Minutes of Cabinet Meeting, 21 December 1949.
33 Ibid., vol. 2645, Minutes of Cabinet Meeting, 18 January 1950.
34 LAC, RG 2, vol. 2751, folder 8, Cabinet Document CD D-241, "Defence Estimates 1950-51," 16 February 1950, Appendix C – Royal Canadian Air Force Fighter Aircraft Requirements, 1-2.
35 Eayrs, *Growing Up Allied,* 190-92. Eayrs draws different conclusions. He feels that there was significant opposition to the obligations of the treaty. He notes that the 1949-50 Department of National Defence Annual Report described the treaty as a "pact for peace." He indicates that Claxton thought that by pooling the resources of the alliance a creditable force could be fielded without significant expenditures. See also 276.
36 DHH, 73/1223/1305, Minutes of CSC Special Meeting, 30-31 January 1950, 2.
37 LAC, RG 24, vol. 6174, RCAF file 19-7-79, Joint Services Program 1947-48, 1948-49, 1949-50, folder 1, Introductory Speech by CAS to Cabinet Defence Committee, 30 October 1948, 1, and "Aide Memoire on RCAF Aircraft Procurement and Production Programme," apps. A-C.
38 Ibid., RCAF file 19-7-92, RCAF Short Range Plan, folder 1, AMAP to D/AMAP/P, no subject, 7 December 1948.
39 Ibid., DAPP document "Supporting Data ... Air Defence Units, Plan F," 1 March 1949, app. F.
40 Ibid., D/AMAP/P to AMAP, Air Defence Units, Plan F, 1 March 1949; AMAP to D/AMAP/P, "Air Defence Units Plan F," 3 March 1949; D/AMAP/P to AMAP, "Air Defence Units Plan F," 11 March 1949.
41 Ibid., DOR to D/AMAP/O, "Plan F – Financial Aspects," 14 March 1949.
42 DHH, 73/1223, Minutes of 70th Meeting of Air Members, 14 March 1949. See also LAC, RG 24, vol. 6174, RCAF file 19-7-92, RCAF Short Range Plan, folder 1, Extract from Minutes of 70th Meeting of Air Members, 14 March 1949.
43 LAC, RG 24, vol. 6175, RCAF file 19-7-92, Short Range Plan, folder 2, D/AMAP/P to AMAP, "Plan F," 5 April 1949.
44 DHH, 73/1223, Minutes of 77th Meeting of Air Members, 25 May 1949, 3-4.
45 LAC, RG 2, A5a, vol. 2644, Minutes of Cabinet Meeting, 10 August 1949.
46 DHH, 73/1223, Minutes of 83rd Meeting of Air Members, 3 August 1949; Minutes of 84th Meeting of Air Members, 5 August 1949.
47 DHH, 181.004(D46), "A Summary of Plans and Estimates for Plan F," November 1949.
48 LAC, RG 24, vol. 6174, RCAF file 19-7-79, Joint Services Program 1947-48, 1948-49, 1949-50, folder 1, Secretary to CAS to AMAP, AMTS, DAP, "Introductory Speech by CAS to Cabinet Defence Committee, 30 October 1948," 8 November 1948.
49 DHH, 181.004(D46), "A Summary of Plans and Estimates for Plan F," November 1949, sec. D, tab 5.
50 DHH, 73/1223, Minutes of 63rd Meeting of Air Members, 7 January 1949, 1-2. The bulk of the report was presented in detail in the Minutes of the 67th Meeting of Air Members, 14 February 1949, 3-9.

51 LAC, RG 24, vol. 17884, RCAF file 900-25, Public Relations – Publicity Re Aircraft, folder 1, R.V. Dodds, DPR, RCAF, to Des Allard, *The Citizen,* no subject, 5 March 1949.
52 LAC, RG 24, vol. 17885, RCAF file 900-25, Public Relations – Publicity Re Aircraft, folder 2, DPR (RCAF) to DPR (DND), "Publicity – RCAF Aircraft Procurement Policy" (covering draft article "The RCAF's Aircraft Procurement Policy"), 3 November 1949.
53 LAC, RG 24, vol. 5403, RCAF file 60-3-63A, CF100 Operational Requirements, folder 1, G/C C.L. Annis, DAO, to AMAP/DOR, "XC 100 Aircraft Use in Tactical Support Roles," 24 November 1948. Minutes 4 (DAO to AMAP/DOR, 18 January 1948) and 5 (D/AMAP/O to D/AMTS/D, 11 February 1949) develop the issue, bringing forward performance considerations as well as the F-86 alternative.
54 Ibid., D/AMAP/O to D/AMAP/P, "Fighter Bomber Tactical Aircraft," 17 November 1949.
55 Ibid., AMAP to AMTS, "Operational Requirement ORI/1-27 All Weather Fighter CF100," 19 September 1949, covering "Operational Requirement No. ORI/1-27 All Weather Fighter – CF-100 *First* Issue Dated 22 June 1949."
56 Ibid., AMAP to AMTS, "Operational Requirement ORI/1-27 All Weather Fighter CF100," 10 February 1950, covering "ORI/1-27(2) *Second* Issue Dated 10 February 1950."
57 Ibid., folder 2, G/C Davis, Secretary Aircraft Fitment Committee, to D/AMAP/O, "Operational Requirement No. ORI/1-27 CF-100 Autopilot," 8 June 1950. This particular document underscored the original concept and need for an autopilot. Acting AMAP to AMTS, "Operational Requirement No. OR.I/1-27 CF-100 – Amendment," 12 July 1950. This memo stated that "it is necessary to include [an autopilot] in the Operational Requirement."
58 Ibid., folder 1, G/C Davis, Secretary Aircraft Fitment Committee, to D/AMAP/O, "Operational Requirement No. ORI/1-27 CF-100 Long Range Tanks," 19 June 1950.
59 Ibid., folder 2, DOR to DDA, "CF100 – Tactical Version," 30 April 1954.
60 Ibid., AMAP to AMTS, 3 February 1949, covering "Operational Requirement No. OR/1-28 Dual Control Trainer XC-100."
61 Ibid., Acting AMAP to AMTS, "Operational Requirement No. ORI/1-31 Photographic Reconnaissance Aircraft – CF100P," 5 October 1949, covering "Operational Requirement No. ORI/1-31 Photographic Reconnaissance Aircraft – CF100P, *First* Issue Dated 8 July 1949."
62 Ibid., DAO to DOR, "Op Requirement No. OR1/1-31 [sic] Photo Recce Aircraft XC-100," 17 October 1949.
63 Ibid., folder 1, Curtis to Smye, no subject, 5 July 1950.
64 LAC, RG 24, vol. 18141, RCAF file 981-101-23, F86 Operational Requirement, folder 1, "Operational Requirement No. ORI/1-23 ... Dated 6 June 1950."
65 DHH, 73/1223, Minutes of the 82nd Meeting of the Air Members, 14 July 1949.
66 Ibid., Minutes of the 83rd Meeting of the Air Members, 3 August 1949.
67 Ibid., Minutes of the 84th Meeting of the Air Members, 5 August 1949.
68 DHH, 181.004(D46), "A Summary of Plans and Estimates for Plan F," November 1949, sec. D, para. 3 and tab 5.
69 DHH, 73/1223, Minutes of the 79th Meeting of the Air Members, 10 June 1949.
70 LAC, RG 24, vol. 6174, RCAF file 19-7-79, Joint Services Program 1947-48, 1948-49, 1949-50, folder 2, CAS to MND, no subject, 25 October 1949.
71 Eayrs, *Peacemaking and Deterrence,* 105.
72 Pickler and Milberry, *Canadair,* 88-95.
73 LAC, RG 24, vol. 6174, RCAF file 19-7-79, Joint Services Program 1947-48, 1948-49, 1949-50, folder 2, CAS to MND, no subject, 25 October 1949.
74 Greig Stewart, *Shutting Down the National Dream: A.V. Roe and the Tragedy of the AVRO Arrow* (Toronto: McGraw-Hill, 1988), 127-29.

Chapter 6: And So to War

1 LAC, RG 2, A5a, vol. 2645, Minutes of Cabinet Meeting, 20 June 1950.
2 Ibid., vol. 2646, Minutes of Cabinet Meeting, 2 August 1950; James Eayrs, *In Defence of Canada,* vol. 4, *Growing Up Allied* (Toronto: University of Toronto Press, 1980), 201.
3 Eayrs, ibid., 203.
4 D.W. Middlemiss, "A Pattern of Cooperation: The Case of the Canadian-American Defence Production and Development Sharing Arrangements, 1958-1963" (PhD diss., University of Toronto, 1975), 129-30.
5 Eayrs, *Growing Up Allied,* 202-3.
6 Ibid., 204-5.
7 David Bercuson, *True Patriot: The Life of Brooke Claxton, 1898-1960* (Toronto: University of Toronto Press, 1993), 226-27.
8 Eayrs, *Growing Up Allied,* 275-76.
9 Ibid., 200. Eayrs quotes Claxton further: "The momentum we gained in the Korean war carried us through to the buildup of our collective strength in Europe. In Canada we did everything possible to bring it home to the people that Korea and NATO were just two aspects of the same operation; two places where we met the communist challenge in precisely the same way, by building up our strength."
10 LAC, RG 2, vol. 2748, Minutes of Cabinet Defence Committee, Meeting 67, 12 October 1950, 5.
11 Bercuson, *True Patriot,* 222-23.
12 LAC, RG 2, vol. 2748, Minutes of Cabinet Defence Committee, Meeting 69, 28 December 1950.
13 Eayrs, *Growing Up Allied,* 204-5; Document 4 (Memorandum by Pearson and Claxton to Cabinet, "The International Situation," 28 December 1950, Department of External Affairs files, 50069-D-40), 376-78.
14 LAC, RG 2, vol. 2748, Minutes of Cabinet Defence Committee, Meeting 69, 28 December 1950, 2.
15 Ibid.
16 Eayrs, *Growing Up Allied,* 218-20.
17 LAC, RG 2, vol. 2748, Minutes of Cabinet Defence Committee, Meeting 69, 28 December 1950, 10-11.
18 Bercuson, *True Patriot,* 215.
19 DHH, 73/1223/1306, Minutes of 480th Meeting of CSC, 9 January 1951, 2.
20 LAC, MG 32 B5, vol. 100, file "Statements on Defence," folder "Research," "House of Commons Debates Official Report on the Defence Program, February 5, 1951."
21 Eayrs, *Growing Up Allied,* 285-95.
22 LAC, RG 2, vol. 2748, Minutes of Cabinet Defence Committee, Meeting 73, 17 April 1951.
23 DHH, 73/1223/1306, Minutes of 493rd Meeting of CSC, 10 May 1951, 2-4.
24 Ibid., Minutes of 496th Meeting of CSC, 23 May 1951.
25 LAC, RG 2, vol. 2748, Minutes of Cabinet Defence Committee, Meeting 74, 29 May 1951.
26 LAC, RG 2, A5a, vol. 2648, Minutes of Cabinet Meeting, 6 June 1951.
27 LAC, RG 2, vol. 2748, Minutes of Cabinet Defence Committee, Meeting 76, 29 June 1951.
28 Ibid.
29 DHH, 73/1223/1305, Minutes of a Special Meeting of CSC, 3 July 1950, 2-3.
30 LAC, RG 24, vol. 6179, RCAF file 60-1-59, Aircraft Manufacture and Development in Canada, folder 2, Extract, dated 2 July 1950, of Minutes of Air Members Meeting 108, 21 June 1950.
31 LAC, RG 24, vol. 5404, RCAF file 60-5-20-3, Aircraft Engines Orenda TR5, folder 1, Curtis to Claxton, no subject, 19 October 1950.

32 DHH, 73/1223, Minutes of Special Air Members Meeting with Sir John Slessor, Chief of the Air Staff, RAF, 11 October 1950, 2.
33 LAC, RG 24, vol. 6180, RCAF file S.60-9-12, F86A Aircraft Procurement of, by United Kingdom, folder 1, Slessor to Curtis, no subject, 7 November 1950.
34 Ibid., Slessor to Curtis (by signal A2618), no subject, 20 November 1950; A/V/M James, Acting CAS, to A/V/M Campbell, Chairman CJS(W) (by signal Ops117), no subject, 22 November 1950.
35 LAC, RG 2, A5a, vol. 2646, Minutes of Cabinet Meeting, 8 December 1950.
36 LAC, RG 2, vol. 2748, Minutes of Cabinet Defence Committee, Meeting 71, 20 February 1951.
37 Ibid., Meeting 78, 12 September 1951.
38 Ibid., Meeting 79, 2 October 1951.
39 LAC, RG 24, vol. 6180, RCAF file S.60-9-12, F86A Aircraft Procurement of, by United Kingdom, folder 1, CAS to Chairman CSC, "Canadian Mutual Aid to Other Countries: Contribution of Combat Aircraft," 9 December 1950.

Chapter 7: Juggling Numbers

1 DHH, 73/1223/2000, "Minutes of a Conference of Air Officers Commanding ... 20-21 March 1950," 5-6.
2 DHH, 181.004 D(48), Plan H – Post War Plan for the RCAF, 1 April 1951, sec. A, Green Tab 1, 1-2. Perhaps the best, and certainly the most succinct, version of events is found in the preamble to Plan H, which is titled, not by chance, "Information." That the April 1951 plan would have to lay out the key events of the previous twelve months for those very officers working with the problem is testimony to the instability of the situation and the unavoidable complexity of the Air Force's response to it.
3 LAC, RG 24, vol. 6175, RCAF file 19-9-72, Short Range Plan, folder 4, CAS to Air Members, no subject, 12 July 1950.
4 DHH, 73/1223/1305, Minutes of Special Meeting of CSC, 17 July 1950, 4.
5 Ibid., 18 July 1950, 4.
6 LAC, RG 24, vol. 6175, RCAF file 19-9-72, Short Range Plan, folder 4, DAPP (Director of Air Plans – Peace) to AMAP, "Planning Korea Situation," 17 July 1950.
7 LAC, RG 49, vol. 136, file 13:11:5, Procurement of Mustang Aircraft from USA for RCAF, Heeney to Canadian Ambassador to the United States (signal EX-1140), no subject, 19 July 1950; Charge d'affaires Washington to SSEA (signal WA-2009), no subject, 1 September 1950.
8 DHH, 181.004(D47), Plan G – Post War Plan for the RCAF, September 1950.
9 Ibid.
10 Ibid.
11 LAC, RG 24, vol. 6175, RCAF file 19-9-72, Short Range Plan, folder 5, D/AMAP/P to AMAP, "Plan G – 1 Sep 50 Revision Increase to 42 Squadrons," 23 August 1950, 1.
12 Ibid., app. A.
13 Ibid., para. 14.
14 LAC, RG 24, vol. 5394, RCAF file 60-1-76, Aircraft Operational Requirements – Future Aircraft, DOR to D/AMAP/O, "Aircraft Requirements," 7 September 1950, with table "Aircraft Requirements Accelerated Plan G," 6 September 1950.
15 LAC, RG 24, vol. 6179, RCAF file 60-1-59, Aircraft Manufacture and Development in Canada, folder 2, Acting D/AMAP/O to AMAP, "Proportion of All-Weather and Day Interceptor Fighters Required by the RCAF" covering staff study "The Proportion of All-Weather and Day Interceptor Fighters Required by the RCAF," 13 October 1950; Minute

by AMAP/P, 25 October 1950, to ibid.; Acting AMAP to AMOT, "Proportion of All Weather and Day Interceptor Fighters Required in the RCAF," 31 October 1950.

16 LAC, RG 24, vol. 6177, RCAF file 19-81-3, Medium Term War Plan, folder 1, G/C E.C. Luke, CLP, to D/AMAP/P, "RCAF Medium Term War Plan," 18 December 1950.

17 DHH, 73/1223/1305, Minutes of 478th Meeting of CSC, 27 December 1950, 1-3.

18 DHH, 73/1223/1306, Minutes of 482nd Meeting of CSC, 16 January 1951, 4.

19 LAC, RG 2, A5a, vol. 2647, Minutes of Cabinet Meeting, 24 January 1951.

20 LAC, MG 27 III B 20, vol. 48, file 9-85-30, A.V. Roe Canada Ltd., folder 5, Dobson to Howe, no subject, 14 August 1950.

21 Ibid., Howe to Dobson, no subject, 25 August 1950.

22 LAC, RG 49, vol. 136, file 13:11:6, United States Armed Forces Procurement Military Equipment from Canada, folder 1, Beaupré to Mackenzie, no subject, 18 November 1950.

23 LAC, MG 27 III B20, vol. 49, file 9-85-30, A.V. Roe Canada Ltd. 1949-1951, folder 6, Smye to Douglas Owen, Private Secretary to Minister of Trade and Commerce, no subject, 20 November 1950.

24 LAC, RG 49, vol. 136, file 13:11:6, United States Armed Forces Procurement Military Equipment from Canada, folder 1, Macdonald to Beaupré, 11 December 1950. "Memorandum of Meetings Held at the U.S.A.F. Materiel Command Wright-Patterson Fields, Dayton, Ohio, November 20-23, 1950."

25 LAC, RG 24, vol. 6167, RCAF file 15-6-6, North Atlantic Treaty Organization – RCAF Participation SHAPE, folder 1, Study for AMAP, "RCAF Short Range Planning – Study of the Employment of RCAF Forces in Europe," 8 March 1951, 2.

26 Ibid., D/AMAP/P to AMAP, "Composition of Canadian Offer to NATO (SHAPE)," 20 March 1951; Minute 2, AMAP to D/AMAP/P, 21 March 1951.

27 Ibid., CAS to Secretary CSC, "RCAF Contribution to SHAPE Desired Affiliation with USAF," 22 May 1951.

28 DHH, 73/1223, Minutes of Air Members Meeting 130, 14 May 1951, 2. A detailed report of the visit, dated 12 May 1951, is contained in RG 24, vol. 6167, RCAF file 15-6-6, folder 1.

29 DHH, 181.004 D(48), Plan H – Post War Plan for the RCAF, 1 April 1951.

30 Ibid.

31 The F-86, like all other aircraft operated by the RCAF, was given a name, in this case the "Sabre." This was in keeping with the RAF custom that had produced the Mosquito, Spitfire, and Lancaster, to name only a few of the better-known aircraft. Different versions of a specific type were assigned different Mark numbers. The Spitfire, for example, having passed through twenty-four different variants, could be found from Mark I through Mark 24 (even the British would carry Roman numerals only so far). There were eventually six different Marks of the Sabre. The Americans, from whom the aircraft was initially imported, preferred a system of numerical designators, adding a letter suffix for each variant; hence, F86A, F86E, etc. Even with this official and certainly popular name, the bulk of the primary material refers to the Canadair aircraft under the general heading of F-86, so this identifier is used for the most part in this book. Similarly, even after the name "Canuck" was assigned to the CF-100, it was still most often referred to by its numerical designation. It also knew worse labels, including "Clunk" and "Lead Sled."

32 Ron Pickler and Larry Milberry, *Canadair: The First Fifty Years* (Toronto: CANAV Books, 1995), 92-95.

33 LAC, RG 24, vol. 5404, RCAF file 60-5-20-3, Aircraft Engines Orenda TR5, CAS to MND, "Production of Orenda Engine," 23 September 1950.

34 Greig Stewart, *Shutting Down the National Dream: A.V. Roe and the Tragedy of the AVRO Arrow* (Toronto: McGraw-Hill, 1988), 109-10. The variant eventually became known as the F-86EO; "O" stood for Orenda.

35 LAC, RG 24, vol. 5404, RCAF file 60-5-20-3, Aircraft Engines Orenda TR5, CAS to MND, no subject, 19 October 1950; Minute 2, 19 October 1950.
36 DHH, 73/1223, Minutes of Air Members Meeting 122, 20 January 1951.
37 Ibid., Minutes of Air Members Meeting 129, 9 May 1951.
38 LAC, RG 24, vol. 5404, RCAF file 60-5-20-3, Aircraft Engines Orenda TR5, Paul Dilworth, Chief Engineer, Gas Turbine, to W.K. Ebel, VP Engineering, Canadair Ltd., "Orenda Engine for F86EO," 22 June 1951.
39 Stewart, *Shutting Down the National Dream*, 126-41.
40 Ibid., 142-43.
41 Ibid., 144.
42 Ibid., 148.
43 LAC, MG 27 III B 20, vol. 48, file 9-85-30, AVRO Canada Ltd., folder 5, *Financial Post*, "AVRO Fights Trouble," 6 October 1951.
44 Ibid., *Globe and Mail*, "Defence Plans Stalled, Weapons Undelivered," by James Hornick, 8 October 1951.
45 Ibid., "Canada's Jet Engine Ration, 20 a Month, Brakes Output of Airframes," by James Hornick, 9 October 1951.
46 Ibid., "Avro Achievements in Jet Field Bring Prestige Aplenty, but Few Tangible Accomplishments Yet," by James Hornick, 10 October 1951.
47 Ibid., editorial, 15 October 1951.
48 Ibid., "$1,500,000,000 Seen Year's Cost for Defense Items," by Warren Baldwin, 20 October 1951.

Chapter 8: Putting Rubber on the Ramp

1 "Putting the rubber on the ramp" is a common air force term for towing aircraft from the hangar onto the apron or "ramp" in preparation for flying operations.
2 LAC, MG 27 III B 20, vol. 48, file 9-85-30, folder 5, A.V. Roe Canada Ltd. 1949-1951, Howe to Gordon, no subject, 12 November 1951.
3 Ibid., Claxton to Howe, no subject, 16 November 1951.
4 Ibid., Howe to Claxton, no subject, 19 November 1951.
5 Greig Stewart, *Shutting Down the National Dream: A.V. Roe and the Tragedy of the AVRO Arrow* (Toronto: McGraw-Hill, 1988), 146.
6 Ibid., 144.
7 Copies of the actual reports are found in Howe's papers, LAC, MG 27 III B20, vol. 48, file 9-85-30, folder 4, A.V. Roe Canada Ltd. 1949-1951, "A.V. Roe Canada Limited Gas Turbine Division: Report of Development – Production 1947-51, 20 February 1952"; "A.V. Roe Canada Limited Aircraft Division: Report of Development – Production 1947-51, 20 February 1952."
8 Ibid., "A.V. Roe Canada Limited Gas Turbine Division: Report of Development – Production 1947-51, 20 February 1952."
9 Ibid., "A.V. Roe Canada Limited Aircraft Division: Report of Development – Production 1947-51, 20 February 1952."
10 LAC, RG 49, vol. 5, file 159-RA-1, folder 1, Avro Aircraft Ltd., General, Letter, Gordon to Howe, no subject, 20 February 1952.
11 DHH, 73/1223, Minutes of Special Air Members Meeting, 29 May 1952, 2.
12 Stewart, *Shutting Down the National Dream*, 150-70.
13 LAC, RG 49, vol. 432, file 159-RA-8, folder 1, Avro Aircraft Ltd. – CF100 Coordinating Committee, Memorandum, R.D. Macdonald to G.M. Grant, no subject, 16 September 1952.
14 LAC, RG 49, vol. 434, file 159-R1-8, A.V. Roe Canada Ltd. – Visits to and from A.V. Roe Plants, Memorandum, J.P. Donnelley to G.M. Grant, no subject, 17 September 1952.

15 LAC, RG 49, vol. 432, file 159-RA-8, folder 1, Avro Aircraft Ltd. – CF100 Coordinating Committee, 19 September 1952, Unsigned memorandum (and attachment) to: Brigadier Chelsey; AMTS; Chairman DRB, no subject, 19 September 1952.
16 Ibid., Minutes of First IPAV Meeting, 31 October 1952.
17 LAC, RG 49, vol. 5, file 159-RA-1, folder 1, AVRO Aircraft Limited, General, Stephenson to G.M. Grant, Acting Director, Aircraft Division, "Panel on A.V. Roe Operations – Discussions on CF-100 Mk. 3, Orenda 2-1," 2 October 1952.
18 LAC, RG 49, vol. 432, file 159-RA-8, folder 1, Avro Aircraft Ltd. – CF100 Coordinating Committee, Minutes of First IPAV Meeting, 31 October 1952, 3; IPAV Document No. 4, Drury to DM DDP, "CF100 Production Contract Demand," 30 October 1952.
19 Ibid., Minutes of Second IPAV Meeting, 13 November 1952, 3.
20 Ibid., Claxton to Howe, no subject, 3 November 1952; Howe to Claxton, no subject, 7 November 1952.
21 Ibid., Minutes of Third IPAV Meeting, 3 January 1953, 6.
22 LAC, MG 27 III B 20, vol. 210, folder 27, Clippings, Statements, Speeches, *Toronto Star,* "Canada Made Safer," 30 September 1952.
23 LAC, MG 32 B5, vol. 94, Aircraft Clippings folder, *Globe and Mail,* "Too Many Gadgets? Don't Overload Fighter Air Engineer Advises," by George Bain, 22 October 1952.
24 W/C H.R. Footit, "The Party Line. File Analysis AFHQ S60-3-63: The AVRO CF-100," *Roundel* 4, 9 (October 1952): 16.
25 Stewart, *Shutting Down the National Dream,* 172.
26 Leonard Bridgeman, ed., *Jane's All the World's Aircraft 1951-1952* (New York: McGraw-Hill, 1951), 3d.
27 DHH, 73/1223, Minutes of Air Members Meeting 146, 25 January 1952, 1.
28 Ibid.
29 LAC, MG 27 III B20, vol. 48, file 9-85-30, A.V. Roe Canada Ltd., folder 3, Gordon to Howe, no subject, 5 March 1952; Howe to Gordon, no subject, 6 March 1952.
30 Ibid., folder 4, Howe to Gordon, no subject, 14 November 1952. Howe talked about this Avro initiative in the letter. He indicated that he had heard of the proposal through his staff.
31 LAC, MG 27 III B20, vol. 47, file 9-85-30, A.V. Roe Canada Ltd., folder 2, Gordon to Howe, no subject, 27 February 1953; Howe to Gordon, no subject, 28 February 1953.
32 Ibid., vol. 48, file 9-85-30, A.V. Roe Canada Ltd., folder 4, Gordon to Howe, no subject, 7 November 1952.
33 Ibid., Howe to Claxton, "Re – Estimates for 1953-54," 19 December 1952.
34 LAC, RG 49, vol. 5, file 159-RA-1, Avro Aircraft Ltd., General, folder 1, S.S. Payne, Technical Officer, Aircraft Division, to G.M. Grant, Acting Director, Aircraft Division, 19 January 1953, amplifying "Report on Meeting Held at R.C.A.F. H.Q., 14 January 1953."
35 LAC, MG 27 III B20, vol. 47, file 9-85-30, A.V. Roe Canada Ltd., folder 1, Gordon to Howe, no subject, 6 November 1953; Howe to Gordon, no subject, 12 November 1953.
36 Ibid., Howe to Gordon, no subject, 6 October 1954.
37 Ron Pickler and Larry Milberry, *Canadair: The First Fifty Years* (Toronto: CANAV Books, 1995), 94-95.
38 Ibid., 96-102.
39 Ibid., 102-3.

Chapter 9: Growing Needs, Growing Concerns

1 LAC, RG 24, vol. 6179, RCAF file 60-1-59, Aircraft Manufacture and Development in Canada, folder 2, A/V/M Smith to Mr. R.G. MacNeil, "RCAF Aircraft Programs," 21 December 1951; Aircraft Programs, covering "RCAF Development Programs," 21 December 1951, and "RCAF Aircraft Programs," 21 December 1951.

2 LAC, RG 2, A5a, vol. 2649, Minutes of Cabinet Meeting, 17 January 1952.
3 LAC, MG 32 B5, vol. 94, Aircraft Clippings folder, *Ottawa Citizen,* 30 January 1952, "RCAF Aims to Build Up Jet Force."
4 James Eayrs, *In Defence of Canada,* vol. 4, *Growing Up Allied* (Toronto: University of Toronto Press, 1980), 225.
5 DHH, 73/1223, Minutes of Air Members Meeting 145, 9 January 1952, 2.
6 Ibid., Minutes of Special Air Members Meeting, 20 December 1952.
7 LAC, RG 2, vol. 2749, Cabinet Defence Committee Meeting 94, 15 May 1953, 5-6; Cabinet Document D28-53, Memorandum to CDC, from MND, "Inclusion of Additional F86 Aircraft in the 1953-54 Mutual Aid Programme," 14 May 1953.
8 Ibid., Cabinet Defence Committee Meeting 95, 6 October 1953; Cabinet Document D34-53, Memorandum to CDC, from MND, "Canadian Mutual Aid Programme – Inclusion of Additional F86 Aircraft," 1 October 1953.
9 DHH, 73/1223, Minutes of Special Meeting of Air Members, 24 February 1953.
10 James Stevens, "Farnborough Newcomer," *The Aeroplane* 89, 2300 (19 August 1955): 268-73.
11 Eayrs, *Growing Up Allied,* 223-30.
12 DHH, 73/1223, Minutes of Air Members Meeting 189, 18 November 1953.
13 LAC, MG 27 III B20, vol. 47, file 9-85-30, A.V. Roe Canada Ltd., folder 1, "Notes on A.V. Roe Production," filed 26 February 1954.
14 LAC, RG 49, vol. 432, file 159-RA-12, AVRO Aircraft Limited – Sale of Aircraft to Other Countries, Pearson to Canadian Ambassador Bogota (telex), "Jet Planes for Colombia," 10 February 1954.
15 Ibid., C.S.A. Ritchie, Acting USSEA, to DM DDP, "Production Capabilities for CF100 Aircraft," 2 February 1954.
16 Ibid., T.N. Beaupré to Ritchie, no subject, 9 February 1954; ADM, DDP to Drury, no subject, 3 February 1954.
17 Ibid., C.S.A. Ritchie, Acting USSEA, to DM DDP, "Production Capabilities for CF100 Aircraft," 2 February 1954.
18 Ibid., Pearson to Canadian Ambassador Bogota (telex), "Jet Planes for Colombia," 10 February 1954.
19 Ibid., T.E. Stephenson, Director Aircraft Branch, to G.W. Hunter, ADM, DDP, "Sale or Mutual Aid of CF100 Aircraft," 7 June 1954.
20 Ibid., T.E. Stephenson to Gordon, no subject, 7 June 1954.
21 LAC, MG 27 III B20, vol. 47, file 9-85-30, A.V. Roe Canada Ltd., folder 1, Howe to R.O. Campney, Associate MND, no subject, 23 April 1954; Howe to R.O. Campney, Associate MND, no subject, 12 May 1954.
22 Greig Stewart, *Shutting Down the National Dream: A.V. Roe and the Tragedy of the AVRO Arrow* (Toronto: McGraw-Hill, 1988), 175-77.
23 LAC, RG 24, vol. 6180, RCAF file 60-3-94, Aircraft All Weather Requirements Study, folder 1, "Minutes of a Meeting on the Air Defence Problem Held in the Director of Requirements Office, Headquarters, United States Air Force on 3 January 1952."
24 Ibid., "Final Report of the All-Weather Interceptor Requirements Team," 20 March 1952.
25 Stewart, *Shutting Down the National Dream,* 178.
26 Ibid., 179.
27 DHH, 73/1223/1307, Minutes of CSC Meeting 545, 6 October 1953.
28 Ibid., Minutes of CSC Meeting 549, 17 November 1953.
29 DHH, 73/1223, Minutes of Air Members Meeting 189, 18 November 1953.

30 LAC, RG 24, Acc 83-84/049, vol. 112, RCAF file 96-106-11, Plan H – Air Defence of Europe, VCAS to CAOps, minute, no date, to CAOps to VCAS, "Plan 'H' – Aircraft Establishment RCAF Air Division," 1 March 1954.
31 DHH, 73/1223, Minutes of Air Members Meeting 194, 7 April 1954.
32 Ibid., Minutes of Air Members Meeting 200, 7 October 1954.
33 "Canadian All-Weather Fighters for NATO," *The Aeroplane* (12 April 1957).
34 Larry Milberry, *The AVRO CF-100* (Toronto: CANAV Books, 1981), 152.
35 DHH, 73/1223/1307A, Minutes of CSC Meeting 530, 15 October 1952, 4.
36 LAC, RG 2, A5a, vol. 2653, Minutes of Cabinet Meeting, 14 November 1953.
37 LAC, MG 32 B5, vol. 94, Aircraft Clippings folder, *Vancouver Province*, 8 January 1952, "Why Millions for Super Planes?" by Ross Munro.
38 Ibid., *Montreal Star*, 18 February 1952, "Expanding Production," editorial.
39 Ibid., *Saskatoon Star Phoenix*, 19 February 1952, "Jet Production," editorial.
40 Ibid., *Victoria British Colonist*, 28 February 1952, "Reports from Ottawa," by Gerald Waring.
41 Ibid., *Montreal Star*, 27 February 1952, "The CF100 Present and Future," editorial.
42 Stewart, *Shutting Down the National Dream*, 174-78.
43 Eayrs, *Growing Up Allied*, 208-9.
44 LAC, MG 32 B5, vol. 222-223, file B.C. 1946-1954 Defence, folios 1291-3.
45 LAC, RG 2, A5a, vol. 2649, Minutes of Cabinet Meeting, 14 December 1951.
46 Ibid., Minutes of Cabinet Meeting, 5 February 1952.
47 Ibid., vol. 2651, Minutes of Cabinet Meeting, 15 July 1952.
48 David Bercuson, *True Patriot: The Life of Brooke Claxton, 1898-1960* (Toronto: University of Toronto Press, 1993), 242-43.
49 Douglas Murray, "NORAD and U.S. Nuclear Operations," in *Fifty Years of Canada–United States Defence Cooperation*, ed. J.J. Sokolsky and J.T. Jockel (Lewiston, NY: Edwin Mellen Press, 1992), 211-14.
50 LAC, RG 2, A5a, vol. 2652, Minutes of Cabinet Meeting, 22 January 1953.
51 Bercuson, *True Patriot*, 258-59.
52 DHH, 73/1223/89, Claxton to PM, no subject, 23 September 1953, 4.

Chapter 10: Fact and Fancy

1 LAC, MG 30 E251, Undated article, "RCAF 'Pitifully Small'; Wartime Chief Takes Unpreparedness Blame."
2 Charles Foulkes, *Canadian Defence Policy in a Nuclear Age* (Toronto: Canadian Institute for International Affairs, 1961), 2.
3 Robert Bothwell, "Defense and Industry in Canada 1935-1970," in *War, Business and World Military-Industrial Complexes*, ed. Benjamin Cooling (Port Washington, NY: Kennikat Press, 1981), 113.
4 LAC, RG 24, vol. 6175, RCAF file 19-7-93, Long Range Plan, folder 1, AMAP to CAS, "RCAF Long Range Plans," 27 February 1948, 3.
5 Greig Stewart, *Shutting Down the National Dream: A.V. Roe and the Tragedy of the AVRO Arrow* (Toronto: McGraw-Hill, 1988), 3-4.
6 Laurence Aronsen, "From World War to Limited War: Canadian-American Industrial Mobilization for Defence," *Revue Internationale d'Histoire Militaire* 51 (1982): 291. Aronsen quotes "Smith to CDC 5 August 1949; DEA records file 10763-40."
7 D.W. Middlemiss, "A Pattern of Cooperation: The Case of the Canadian-American Defence Production and Development Sharing Arrangements, 1958-1963" (PhD diss., University of Toronto, 1975), 63-85; Melvin Conant, *The Long Polar Watch: Canada and the Defence*

of North America, 2nd ed. (Westport, CT: Greenwood Press, 1974), 56-57; C.F.W. Pound, *The Defence Program and National Industrial Development*, Defence Research Analysis Establishment Report No. 34 (Ottawa: Department of National Defence, 1973), 29.

8 DHH, PARC, RCAF file 840-108, folder 8, Minutes of Air Council Meeting 5, 8 March 1946.

9 John Treddenick, *The Economic Significance of the Canadian Defence Industrial Base*, Centre for Studies in Defence Resource Management, Report No. 15 (Kingston, ON: Royal Military College of Canada, 1987), 1.

10 Dan Middlemiss, "Canada and Defence Industrial Preparedness: A Return to Basics," in *Canada's Defence Perspectives on Policy in the Twentieth Century*, ed. B.D. Hunt and R.G. Haycock (Toronto: Copp Clark Pitman, 1993), 244.

11 LAC, MG 31, G9, vol. 1, folder 5, Douglas Abbott to Curtis, no subject, 31 January 1953.

12 John Treddenick, "The Defence Budget," in *Canada's International Security Policy*, ed. David Dewitt and David Leyton-Brown (Scarborough, ON: Prentice Hall Canada, 1995), 427.

13 James Eayrs, *In Defence of Canada*, vol. 3, *Peacemaking and Deterrence* (Toronto: University of Toronto Press, 1972), 208-9.

Appendix B: Department of Defence Production Aircraft Delivery Statistics, 1951-54

1 LAC, RG 49, vol. 458, file 200-3-2-1, Aircraft Branch Monthly Progress Reports. The tables in the appendix are a compilation of monthly reports for the years 1951-54.

Bibliography

Primary Sources

Library and Archives Canada

Record Group 2	Cabinet Conclusions
	Defence Committee
Record Group 24	Department of National Defence
Record Group 49	Department of Munitions and Supply
	Department of Defence Production
Manuscript Group 27 III B20	Hon. C.D. Howe, Minister of Defence Production
Manuscript Group 30 E251	Air Marshal Robert Leckie
Manuscript Group 31 G9	Air Marshal W.A. Curtis
Manuscript Group 32 B5	Hon. Brooke Claxton, Minister of National Defence

Department of National Defence, Directorate of History and Heritage

Records 73/1223, the "Raymont Papers," including minutes of the following organizations during the period 1945-55: Cabinet Defence Committee, Defence Council, Chiefs of Staff Committee, and Air Council/Air Members Committees.

Official Histories, Memoirs, and Other Primary Materials

Douglas, W.A.B. *The Creation of a National Air Force: The Official History of the Royal Canadian Air Force.* Vol. 2. Toronto: University of Toronto Press, 1986.

Gibson, Colin. An Address by Col. the Hon. Colin Gibson, M.C., M.P., Minister of National Defence for Air to the Empire Club of Toronto, 28 February 1946.

Pickersgill, J.W. *The Mackenzie King Record.* Vol. 1, *1939-1944.* Toronto: University of Toronto Press, 1960.

Stedman, E.W. *From Boxkite to Jet: The Memoirs of an Aeronautical Engineer.* Canadian War Museum Paper No. 1. Ottawa: National Museums of Canada, 1972.

Wise, S.F. *Canadian Airmen and the First World War: The Official History of the Royal Canadian Air Force.* Vol. 2. Toronto: University of Toronto Press, 1980.

Secondary Sources

Books and Monographs

Baglow, Bob. *Canucks Unlimited: Royal Canadian Air Force CF-100 Squadrons and Aircraft 1952-1963.* Ottawa: Canuck Publications, 1985.

Bercuson, David. *True Patriot: The Life of Brooke Claxton, 1898-1960.* Toronto: University of Toronto Press, 1993.

Bercuson, David, and J.L. Granatstein. *Dictionary of Canadian Military History.* Toronto: Oxford University Press, 1992.

Bothwell, Robert. *Canada and the United States: The Politics of Partnership.* Toronto: University of Toronto Press, 1992.

Bothwell, Robert, and William Kilbourn. *C.D. Howe: A Biography.* Toronto: McClelland and Stewart, 1979.

Bridgeman, Leonard, ed. *Jane's All the World's Aircraft: 1951-1952.* New York: McGraw-Hill, 1951.

Conant, Melvin. *The Long Polar Watch: Canada and the Defence of North America.* 2nd ed. Westport, CT: Greenwood Press, 1974.

Creighton, Donald. *Canada's First Century: 1867-1967.* Toronto: Macmillan of Canada, 1970.

Cuff, R.D., and J.L. Granatstein. *American Dollars – Canadian Prosperity: Canadian-American Economic Relations: 1945-50.* Toronto: Samuel Stevens, 1978.

–. *Ties That Bind: Canadian-American Relations in Wartime from the Great War to the Cold War.* 2nd ed. Toronto: Samuel Stevens, 1977.

Cuthbertson, Brian. *Canadian Military Independence in the Age of the Superpowers.* Toronto: Fitzhenry and Whiteside, 1977.

Dewitt, David, and David Leyton-Brown. *Canada's International Security Policy.* Scarborough, ON: Prentice Hall Canada, 1995.

Eayrs, James. *In Defence of Canada.* Vol. 2, *Appeasement and Rearmament.* Toronto: University of Toronto Press, 1965.

–. *In Defence of Canada.* Vol. 3, *Peacemaking and Deterrence.* Toronto: University of Toronto Press, 1972.

–. *In Defence of Canada.* Vol. 4, *Growing Up Allied.* Toronto: University of Toronto Press, 1980.

Emme, Eugene. *The Impact of Air Power.* New York: Van Nostrand, 1959.

English, John, and Norman Hillmer, eds. *Making a Difference? Canada's Foreign Policy in a Changing World Order.* Toronto: Lester Publishing, 1992.

Fuller, G.A., et al. *125 Years of Canadian Aviation: A Chronology, 1840-1965.* Willowdale, ON: Canadian Aviation Historical Society, 1983.

Granatstein, J.L., ed. *Canadian Foreign Policy: Historical Readings.* Rev. ed. Toronto: Copp Clark Pitman, 1993.

Granatstein, J.L., and Norman Hillmer. *For Better or for Worse: Canada and the United States to the 1990s.* Toronto: Copp Clark Pitman, 1991.

Haglund, David, ed. *Canada's Defence Industrial Base.* Kingston, ON: Ronald P. Frye, 1988.

Haglund, David, and Joel Sokolsky, eds. *The US-Canadian Security Relationship: The Politics, Strategy, and Technology of Defence.* Boulder, CO: Westview Press, 1989.

Hall, H. Duncan. *North American Supply.* London: Longmans, 1955.

Halliday, H.A. *Chronology of Canadian Military Aviation.* Canadian War Museum Paper No. 6, National Museums of Canada Mercury Series. Ottawa: National Museums of Canada, 1975.

Hotson, Fred. *The de Havilland Canada Story.* Toronto: CANAV Books, 1983.

Hunt, B.D., and R.G. Haycock. *Canada's Defence Perspectives on Policy in the Twentieth Century.* Toronto: Copp Clark Pitman, 1993.

Jockel, Joseph. *No Boundaries Upstairs: Canada, the United States and the Origins of North American Air Defence, 1945-1958.* Vancouver: UBC Press, 1987.

MacMillan, Margaret, and David Sorenson, eds. *Canada and NATO: Uneasy Past, Uncertain Future.* Waterloo, ON: University of Waterloo Press, 1990.

McKercher, Brian, and Lawrence Aronsen, eds. *The North Atlantic Triangle in a Changing World: North American Relations, 1902-1956.* Toronto: University of Toronto Press, 1996.

McLin, Jon B. *Canada's Changing Defence Policy, 1957-1963.* Baltimore: Johns Hopkins University Press, 1967.

Milberry, L. *Aviation in Canada.* Toronto: McGraw-Hill Ryerson, 1979.
–. *The AVRO CF-100.* Toronto: CANAV Books, 1981.
–. *The Canadair Sabre.* Toronto: CANAV Books, 1986.
–. *Sixty Years: The RCAF and CF Air Command, 1924-1984.* Toronto: CANAV Books, 1984.
Molson, K.M., and H.A. Taylor. *Canadian Aircraft since 1909.* Stittsville, ON: Canada's Wings, 1982.
Morton, Desmond. *A Military History of Canada.* Edmonton: Hurtig, 1985.
Pickler, Ron, and Larry Milberry. *Canadair: The First Fifty Years.* Toronto: CANAV Books, 1995.
Sokolsky, Joel, and Joseph Jockel. *Fifty Years of Canadian–United States Defense Cooperation.* Lewiston, NY: Edwin Mellen Press, 1992.
Stacey, C.P. *Arms, Men and Government: The War Policies of Canada, 1939-1945.* Ottawa: Information Canada, 1970.
–. *Canada and the Age of Conflict.* Vol. 2, *1921-1948.* Toronto: University of Toronto Press, 1984.
Stairs, Denis. *The Diplomacy of Constraint: Canada, the Korean War and the United States.* Toronto: University of Toronto Press, 1974.
Stewart, Greig. *Shutting Down the National Dream: A.V. Roe and the Tragedy of the Avro Arrow.* Toronto: McGraw-Hill Ryerson, 1988.
Sullivan, Kenneth, and L. Milberry. *Power: The Pratt and Whitney Canada Story.* Toronto: CANAV Books, 1989.
Whitaker, Reg, and Gary Marcuse. *Cold War Canada: The Making of a National Insecurity State, 1945-1957.* Toronto: University of Toronto Press, 1994.
Williams, Geoffrey, et al. *Crisis in Procurement: A Case Study of the TSR-2.* Whitehall: Royal United Service Institution, 1969.

Chapters and Readings

Aronsen, Lawrence. "From World War to Cold War: Cooperation and Competition in the North Atlantic Triangle, 1945-1949." In *The North Atlantic Triangle in a Changing World: North American Relations, 1902-1956,* ed. Brian McKercher and Lawrence Aronsen, 184-219. Toronto: University of Toronto Press, 1996.
Bercuson, David. "The Return of the Canadians to Europe: Britannia Rules the Rhine." In *Canada and NATO: Uneasy Past, Uncertain Future,* ed. Margaret MacMillan and David Sorenson, 15-26. Waterloo, ON: University of Waterloo Press, 1990.
Bothwell, Robert. "Defence and Industry in Canada, 1935-1970." In *War, Business and World Military-Industrial Complexes,* ed. B.F. Cooling, 106-19. Port Washington, NY: Kennikat Press, 1981.
Buteux, Paul. "NATO and the Evolution of Canadian Defence and Foreign Policy." In *Canada's International Security Policy,* ed. David B. Dewitt and David Leyton-Brown, 153-70. Scarborough, ON: Prentice Hall Canada, 1995.
Conliffe, Christopher. "The Permanent Joint Board on Defence, 1940-1988." In *The US-Canada Security Relationship: The Politics, Strategy, and Technology of Defence,* ed. David Haglund and Joel Sokolsky, 145-66. Boulder, CO: Westview Press, 1989.
Granatstein, J.L. "The American Influence on the Canadian Military, 1939-1963." In *Canada's Defence Perspectives on Policy in the Twentieth Century,* ed. B.D. Hunt and R.G. Haycock, 129-40. Toronto: Copp Clark Pitman, 1993.
Halloran, Mary. "Canada and the Origins of the Post-War Commitment." In *Canada and NATO: Uneasy Past, Uncertain Future,* ed. Margaret MacMillan and David Sorenson, 1-14. Waterloo, ON: University of Waterloo Press, 1990.

Jockel, Joseph. "The Military Establishments and the Creation of NORAD." In *Canada's Defence Perspectives on Policy in the Twentieth Century,* ed. B.D. Hunt and R.G. Haycock, 163-78. Toronto: Copp Clark Pitman, 1993.

MacIsaac, David. "Voices from the Central Blue: The Air Power Theorists." In *Makers of Modern Strategy from Machiavelli to the Nuclear Age,* ed. Peter Paret, 624-47. Princeton, NJ: Princeton University Press, 1986.

Middlemiss, Dan. "Canada and Defence Industrial Preparedness: A Return to Basics." In *Canada's Defence Perspectives on Policy in the Twentieth Century,* ed. B.D. Hunt and R.G. Haycock, 142-57. Toronto: Copp Clark Pitman, 1993.

–. "The Road from Hyde Park: Canada-US Defence Economic Cooperation." In *Fifty Years of Canada–United States Defence Cooperation,* ed. J.J. Sokolsky and J.T. Jockel, 175-208. Lewiston, NY: Edwin Mellen Press, 1992.

Murray, Douglas. "NORAD and US Nuclear Operations." In *Fifty Years of Canada–United States Defence Cooperation,* ed. J.J. Sokolsky and J.T. Jockel, 209-38. Lewiston, NY: Edwin Mellen Press, 1992.

Nossal, Kim. "A European Nation? The Life and Times of Atlanticism in Canada." In *Making a Difference? Canada's Foreign Policy in a Changing World Order,* ed. John English and Norman Hillmer, 79-102. Toronto: Lester Publishing, 1992.

Purver, Ron. "The Arctic in Canadian Security Policy, 1945 to the Present." In *Canada's International Security Policy,* ed. David B. Dewitt and David Leyton-Brown, 81-110. Scarborough, ON: Prentice Hall Canada, 1995.

Reid, Escott. "Canada and the Creation of the North Atlantic Alliance, 1948-1949." In *Canadian Foreign Policy Historical Readings,* rev. ed., ed. J.L. Granatstein, 150-57. Toronto: Copp Clark Pitman, 1993.

Slack, Michael, and John Skynner. "Defence Production and the Defence Industrial Base." In *Canada's International Security Policy,* ed. David B. Dewitt and David Leyton-Brown, 365-90. Scarborough, ON: Prentice Hall Canada, 1995.

St-Laurent, Louis. "The Foundation of Canadian Policy in World Affairs" (an address at the University of Toronto, 13 January 1947). In *Canadian Foreign Policy Historical Readings,* rev. ed., ed. J.L. Granatstein, 28-37. Toronto: Copp Clark Pitman, 1993.

Sumida, Jon A., and David A. Rosenberg. "Machines, Men, Manufacturing, Management, and Money: The Study of Navies as Complex Organizations and the Transformation of Twentieth Century Naval History." In *Doing Naval History: Essays towards Improvement,* ed. John B. Hattendorf, 25-39. Newport, RI: Naval War College Press, 1995.

Articles

Aronsen, Laurence. "Canada's Post-War Re-Armament: Another Look at American Theories of the Military Industrial Complex." *Canadian Historical Association Historical Papers* (1981): 175-96.

–. "From World War to Limited War: Canadian-American Industrial Mobilization for Defence." *Revue Internationale d'Histoire Militaire* 54 (1982): 208-45.

"Canadian All-Weather Fighters for NATO." *The Aeroplane* 92, 2380 (12 April 1957): 505-9.

Footit, H.R. "The Party Line. File Analysis AFHQ S60-3-63: The AVRO CF-100." *Roundel* 4, 9 (October 1952): 15-24.

Gaffen, Fred. "Canada's Military Aircraft Industry: Its Birth, Growth and Fortunes." *Canadian Defence Quarterly* 15, 2 (1985): 48-53.

Hacker, Barton C. "Military Institutions, Weapons, and Social Change: Toward a New History of Military Technology." *Technology and Culture* 35, 4 (1994): 768-834.

Johnson, William. "Canadian Defence Industrial Policy and Practice: A History." *Canadian Defence Quarterly* 18, 6 (Special Issue no. 2) (1989): 21-28.

Roland, Alex. "Technology and War: The Historiographical Revolution of the 1980s." *Technology and Culture* 34, 1 (1993): 117-34.

Stevens, James. "Farnborough Newcomer." *The Aeroplane* 89, 2300 (19 August 1955): 268-73.

Stewart, Greig. "Canada and the Development of the Aircraft Jet Engine." *Canadian Defence Quarterly* 9, 2 (1979): 48-56.

Reports

Foulkes, Charles. *Canadian Defence Policy in a Nuclear Age.* Toronto: Canadian Institute for International Affairs, 1961.

Pound, C.F.W. *The Defence Program and National Industrial Development.* Defence Research Analysis Establishment Report 34. Ottawa: Department of National Defence, 1973.

Regher, Ernie. *The Utilization of Resources for Military Purposes in Canada and the Impact on Canadian Industrialization and Defence Procurement.* Waterloo, ON: University of Waterloo, Institute for Peace and Conflict Studies, 1980.

Treddenick, John. *The Economic Significance of the Canadian Defence Industrial Base.* Centre for Studies in Defence Resource Management, Report No. 15. Kingston, ON: Royal Military College of Canada, 1987.

Unpublished Theses

Berg, Glen. "Scrambling for Dollars: Resource Allocation and the Politics of Canadian Fighter Aircraft Procurement 1943-1983." MA thesis, Royal Military College of Canada, 1983.

Gingrich, Stephen K. "Defence Production Sharing and Canada and the United States 1957-1967: National Defence Needs in an Age of Continentalism." MA thesis, University of Western Ontario, 1990.

Middlemiss, D.W. "A Pattern of Cooperation: The Case of the Canadian-American Defence Production and Development Sharing Arrangements, 1958-1963." PhD thesis, University of Toronto, 1975.

Swanson, R.F. "An Analytical Study of the United States/Canadian Defence Relationship as a Problem of Structure, Response and Process: Problems and Potentialities." PhD thesis, American University, 1969.

Index

Note: "(f)" after a page number indicates a figure

Studies in Canadian Military History

Canadian War Museum
Musée canadien de la guerre

John Griffith Armstrong, *The Halifax Explosion and the Royal Canadian Navy: Inquiry and Intrigue*

Andrew Richter, *Avoiding Armageddon: Canadian Military Strategy and Nuclear Weapons, 1950-63*

William Johnston, *A War of Patrols: Canadian Army Operations in Korea*

Julian Gwyn, *Frigates and Foremasts: The North American Squadron in Nova Scotia Waters, 1745-1815*

Jeffrey A. Keshen, *Saints, Sinners, and Soldiers: Canada's Second World War*

Desmond Morton, *Fight or Pay: Soldiers' Families in the Great War*

Douglas E. Delaney, *The Soldiers' General: Bert Hoffmeister at War*

Michael Whitby, ed., *Commanding Canadians: The Second World War Diaries of A.F.C. Layard*

Martin Auger, *Prisoners of the Home Front: German POWs and "Enemy Aliens" in Southern Quebec, 1940-46*

Tim Cook, *Clio's Warriors: Canadian Historians and the Writing of the World Wars*

Serge Marc Durflinger, *Fighting from Home: The Second World War in Verdun, Quebec*

Richard O. Mayne, *Betrayed: Scandal, Politics, and Canadian Naval Leadership*

P. Whitney Lackenbauer, *Battle Grounds: The Canadian Military and Aboriginal Lands*

Cynthia Toman, *An Officer and a Lady: Canadian Military Nursing and the Second World War*

Michael Petrou, *Renegades: Canadians in the Spanish Civil War*

Amy J. Shaw, *Crisis of Conscience: Conscientious Objection in Canada during the First World War*

Serge Marc Durflinger, *Veterans with a Vision: Canada's War Blinded in Peace and War*

James G. Fergusson, *Canada and Ballistic Missile Defence, 1954-2009: Déjà Vu All Over Again*

Benjamin Isitt, *From Victoria to Vladivostok: Canada's Siberian Expedition, 1917-19*

James Wood, *Militia Myths: Ideas of the Canadian Citizen Soldier, 1896-1921*

Timothy Balzer, *The Information Front: The Canadian Army and News Management during the Second World War*

Andrew Godefroy, *Defence and Discovery: Canada's Military Space Program, 1945-74*

Douglas E. Delaney, *Corps Commanders: Five British and Canadian Generals at War, 1939-45*

Timothy Wilford, *Canada's Road to the Pacific War: Intelligence, Strategy, and the Far East Crisis*

Printed and bound in Canada by Friesens

Set in Helvetica Condensed and Minion by Artegraphica Design Co. Ltd.

Copy editor: Frank Chow

Proofreader: Deborah Kerr